Time To Remember

The Journal of Lance Sergeant William Webb
October 1914–January 1916 2nd Battalion Royal
Warwickshire Regiment Seventh Division 1914–1918

Gerald W. Buxton

 Helion & Company Limited

Helion & Company Limited
26 Willow Road
Solihull
West Midlands
B91 1UE
England
Tel. 0121 705 3393
Fax 0121 711 4075
Email: info@helion.co.uk
Website: www.helion.co.uk
Twitter: @helionbooks
Visit our blog http://blog.helion.co.uk/

Published by Helion & Company 2016
Designed and typeset by Mach 3 Solutions Ltd (www.mach3solutions.co.uk)
Cover designed by Paul Hewitt, Battlefield Design (www.battlefield-design.co.uk)
Printed by Short Run Press, Exeter, Devon

Front cover, top image: Consolidating a captured German trench, December 1915;
bottom image: Route to Neuve Chapelle, March 1915 (both *War Illustrated*). Rear
cover reproduces elements of top front cover image.

ISBN 978-1-910777-34-3

British Library Cataloguing-in-Publication Data.
A catalogue record for this book is available from the British Library.

For details of other military history titles published by Helion & Company Limited
contact the above address, or visit our website: http://www.helion.co.uk.

We always welcome receiving book proposals from prospective authors.

Contents

List of Photographs and Illustrations   iv

List of Maps   v

Preface   vi

Acknowledgements   ix

Introduction – William Webb's service history (1894–1914)   x

Part I

First World War (1914–1915)   13

War Diary: Landing in Belgium (October 1914)   15

War Diary: First Battle of Ypres (October–November 1914)   21

War Diary: 'Splendid Hotel' Boulogne Hospital (November–December 1914)   45

War Diary: Christmas in the trenches (December 1914)   52

War Diary: Trench Warfare in winter (January–March 1915)   56

War Diary: Battle of Neuve Chapelle (March 1915)   70

War Diary: Aubers Ridge Trenches and the Second Battle of Ypres (April 1915)   79

War Diary: Aubers Ridge and Festubert (May 1915)   84

War Diary: Battle of Givenchy (June 1915)   92

War Diary: Back in the trenches (July–August 1915)   101

War Diary: Battle of Loos (September–October 1915)   111

War Diary: Recovery after Loos (November 1915–January 1916)   134

Part II

The 2nd Royal Warwickshire Regiment 1916-1918   141

Royal Warwickshire Regiment: The Somme (July–October 1916)   143

Royal Warwickshire Regiment: The Hindenburg Line
(November 1916–July 1917)   159

Royal Warwickshire Regiment: Third Battle of Ypres
(September–November 1917)   168

Royal Warwickshire Regiment: Move to Italy
(November 1917–December 1918)   174

Epilogue

Lance Sergeant William Webb Service Number 4361 2nd Battalion Royal
Warwickshire Regiment William Webb (1880–1953) – 'Memories of war'   181

Bibliography   184

List of Photographs and Illustrations

1	Young William Webb with his mother Millicent Webb and sister Hannah.	vii
2	Lance Sergeant William Webb c. 1918.	xii
3	First wounded of 7th Division, Ypres October 1914.	24
4	7th Division ambulance horse wagon October 1914.	27
5	Wounded soldiers being loaded into an ambulance wagon October 1914.	33
6	The 2nd Battalion Royal Warwickshire Regiment passing through Dickebusch 6 November 1914.	38
7	Princess Mary's Christmas card sent to the British troops.	54
8	Crucifix still standing after bombardment Neuve Chapelle 10 March 1915.	67
9	Battle of Neuve Chapelle – fire trench.	75
10	Neuve Chapelle after capture of the village 15 March 1915.	76
11	Royal Warwickshire Regiment Band William Webb—middle row, second from left.	115
12	Battle of Loos 25 September 1915, British soldiers lying dead near German barbed wire defences.	120
13	Battle Loos 25 September 1915, British soldiers lying dead in front of a captured German trench.	122
14	Poison gas attack 13 October 1915 at Hohenzollern Redoubt.	127
15	The Loos Memorial to the Missing surrounds the graves of Dud Corner Cemetery in France.	132
16	Lance Sergeant William Webb was 'Mentioned in Despatches' for gallant and distinguished service in the field at the Battle of Loos. It was published in *The London Gazette* on Saturday 1 Jan 1916.	133
17/18	Le Havre camp pantomime December 1915.	140
19	Royal Warwickshire Regiment Advancing up a communication trench 1 July 1916.	150
20	Royal Warwickshire Regiment Lying exhausted in the grass after battle.	154
21	British soldiers digging a communication trench in Delville Wood.	157
22	Royal Warwickshire Regiment 20 April 1917 Front line trench near St Quentin.	164
23	Third Battle of Ypres 22 August 1917, British soldier stands over the grave of a comrade.	172
24	Royal Warwickshire Regiment Italian Front 1918 Purchasing hot chestnuts.	176
25	7th Division troops during Battle of Piave River June 1918 King Victor Emmanuel III inspecting the troops.	177
26	The Webb twins: Eric and Joyce.	181
27	William Webb with his wife Edith and Daughters.	182
28	Grandma and Grandad Webb with three of their grandchildren.	182

List of Maps

1   Royal Warwickshire Regiment route from Zeebrugge to Ypres via Ghent
     6–15 October 1914.   19
2   Positions of the Royal Warwickshire Regiment during the First Battle
     of Ypres 15–18 October 1914.   22
3   Positions of the Royal Warwickshire Regiment during the Battle for
     Polygon Wood 21–24 October 1914.   30
4   Position held by the Royal Warwickshire Regiment 27 October 1914.   32
5   Positions of the Royal Warwickshire Regiment 29–30 October 1914.   35
6   Position of the Royal Warwickshire Regiment November 1914–March 1915.   65
7   Position of the Royal Warwickshire Regiment Neuve Chapelle 12–18 March 1915.   73
8   Loos and vicinity.   113
9   Battle of the Somme 1 July–19 November 1916 XV Corps including Royal
     Warwickshire Regiment.   145
10   Mametz 1 July 1916.   146
11   Bazentin Ridge 14 July 1916.   151
12   Positions of the Royal Warwickshire Regiment during the German withdrawal
     to the Hindenburg Line.   162
13   Position of Royal Warwickshire Regiment at the Third Battle of Ypres
     9 October 1917.   170
14   The Italian theatre of war up to October 1918.   175

Preface

I was inspired to write 'Time To Remember' the story of William Webb and the 2nd Battalion Royal Warwickshire Regiment after I read his personal war diaries and became aware of the terrible tragedies and discomforts that soldiers faced during the First World War (1914–1918). The continual acts of bravery that ordinary officers and men like William carried out, in order to perform their duty and support their comrades, has often been overlooked by those who were not involved. Certainly 100 years later, there are very few people living who can appreciate what these brave men tolerated in order that we would be free to live the way we do today.

William was born on 26 May 1880 at 6 Linen Street in the Parish of St Paul's, Warwick, England and died in Plymouth, England on 9 March 1953 at the age of 72 years. His father John William Webb was born in Leamington, Warwickshire (born 1851–died 1902) and his mother Millicent Webb was born in County Limerick, Ireland (born 1853–died 1917). William had five brothers Harry, Charles, Robert, James and John (who died young) and three sisters Florence, Hannah and Adelaide. They later moved to 22 Bowling Green Street, Warwick. William was 4 feet 10 inches (1.5 metres) tall at 14 years old when he enlisted and had a fresh complexion, grey eyes, brown hair and a tattooed pierced heart on his left arm. His religion was Church of England and he was educated in a 'hedge school' the name given to an educational practice in 18th and 19th century Ireland, so called due to its rural nature. While the 'hedge school' label suggests the classes always took place outdoors (next to a hedgerow), classes were sometimes held in a house or barn.

According to British Army Service Records, William Webb, Service Number [S/N] 4361, was 15 years 7 months old when he joined the 2nd Battalion Royal Warwickshire Regiment on 26 September 1894. I have since discovered from family records that his actual age was 14 years 4 months. In October 1894 he was posted with the Royal Warwickshire Regiment to Ceylon, where he served until March 1896. From March 1896 until November 1899 he was stationed at home in England with his regiment.

On 26 November 1899, at 19 years old, William went to fight for his country in the Boer War of South Africa (1899–1902). He was involved in many skirmishes in the Cape Colony and Orange Free State and fought in the Battles of Diamond Hill, Johannesburg and Belfast. For his service he was awarded the Queen's South Africa Medal with three Campaign Clasps and three Battle Clasp. At the end of 1901 he

1 Young William Webb with his mother Millicent Webb and sister Hannah.

was posted with the Royal Warwickshire Regiment to Bermuda to guard POWs from the Boer War and eventually returned to England on 17 November 1902, remaining there until 22 November 1912.

On 20 November 1905, at 25 years old, he married Edith Frances Parsons in Dorset, England, and their first daughter, Marjorie Iris Millicent Webb, was born on 8 August 1906 in Plymouth, England. He was stationed at Lichfield in Staffordshire from 1908 to 1911, then at Shorncliffe in Kent, and finally Portland, where he remained until he and his family sailed for Malta on 22 November 1912. Edith gave birth to twins on 11 April 1913, but misfortune struck and both twins died in the same year. These two dearly loved children, Ethel Lillie (born 4 July 1913, died 8 September 1913) and Frances William Harold (born 4 July 1913, died 13 September 1913), were buried in Malta, their final resting place. William Webb was a talented musician and played the violin as well as other instruments. In August 1912, he was promoted to Band Sergeant and in June 1914 to Lance Sergeant. William Webb and his family returned to England in September 1914, one month before departing for the Western Front.

At that time the 2nd Battalion Royal Warwickshire Regiment, commanded by Lieutenant Colonel W L Loring, joined the 22 Brigade and were a part of the 7th Division commanded by Major-General Thompson Capper.[1] Lieutenant-General Sir Henry Rawlinson commanded the IV Corps of which the 7th Division formed the principal part. The 7th Division was a Regular Army division that was formed by combining battalions returning from outposts in the British Empire at the outbreak of the First World War (1914) and comprised entirely of serving regulars, which gave rise to its nickname "The Immortal Seventh."

1   Major-*General* Sir *Thompson Capper* KCMG CB DSO (1863-1915).

In October 1914 the 22 Brigade comprised:

- 2nd Battalion The Queen's Regiment
- 2nd Battalion Royal Warwickshire Regiment
- 1st Battalion Royal Welch Fusiliers
- 1st Battalion South Staffordshire Regiment
- 8th Battalion Royal Scots Fusiliers (joined 11 November 1914)

William Webb at age 34 years, landed in Zeebrugge Belgium on 6 October 1914 with the 2nd Battalion Royal Warwickshire Regiment and started writing his journals so that in event of his death, his family would understand what he went through each day. His three diaries cover the period from 6 October 1914 until 16 January 1916 and were written in pencil. The years have taken their toll on the legibility of the writing but I have attempted to record these treasured memories in his words as he wrote them. My only alterations are my having omitted the repetitions that occurred that may make for tedious reading and a few grammatical corrections. History records that the regular soldiers of the original British Expeditionary Force had suffered ninety percent casualties in the first few months of the war from late 1914 to January 1915. The few who were left held the line through the Flanders swamps throughout the winter. These men, like Lance Sergeant William Webb, fought in atrocious weather conditions, rain, snow, ice, bitter cold and trenches that were often flooded and knee deep in mud. They were ill-equipped and short of supplies and ammunition but, without consideration for themselves, they fought to prevent the Germans advancing and waited for the milder weather of spring to arrive. William Webb worked with the Medical Staff and a group of stretcher bearers, roaming the front line trenches and no man's land under fire to bring back their wounded and dead comrades to dressing stations, often set up in fields or barns that were constantly bombarded by the German artillery. He was in the front line during the First Battle of Ypres, the battles for Messines Ridge, Neuve Chapelle, Aubers Ridge, Festubert, Givenchy and Loos.

In November 1915, after the Battle of Loos and many months in the front-line trenches, suffering from bronchitis and a poisoned hand, he was transferred to the Base Camp at Le Havre. During the Battle of Loos he was mentioned in Sir John French's Despatches for "gallant and distinguished service in the field." From early 1916 until the end of the war in November 1918, we cannot be sure where he was serving; therefore I have followed the movements and actions of his beloved 2nd Battalion Royal Warwickshire Regiment. If William Webb was not with them in body, he certainly was with them in spirit as often he wrote in his diary, "I wish I was back with my regiment."

Finally, I would like to express my admiration and highest respect for William Webb, and for the service he carried out for his country over a period of 25 years. His love for his wife and family is warmly expressed in his diary as he ends each day with the words "Goodnight and God bless you my loved ones.

Gerald W Buxton
New Zealand 2014

Acknowledgements

There are a number of people who have made the publication of this manuscript possible and I would like to offer my appreciation to each of them, but most importantly, my thanks to William Webb for writing his diaries, without them his story could not be told.

My thanks also to his grandchildren Victor Woodfield, Diana Webb, Deirdre Pooley, Sandra Buxton, Cheryl Davey, Clive Horsnell and Tania Barton, who kindly provided me with fond memories of their grandparents, and permission to publish their story. A special thanks to my wonderful wife, Sandra Buxton, for her ongoing support, and to my family for understanding the importance of getting this book completed.

To my publisher, Duncan Rogers, for the opportunity, to my editor, Dr Michael LoCicero, for his support and advice, and to all the staff of Helion & Company Ltd who were involved, my sincere appreciation. I would also like to acknowledge the following sources for information:

C T Atkinson author of *The Seventh Division 1914–1918*
The National Archives for the War Diaries of the 2nd Battalion Royal Warwickshire
    Regiment
Chris Baker's website *The Long, Long Trail,*
The Imperial War Museum (IWM) for their collection of photographs.

Introduction
William Webb Service Number 4361 2nd Battalion Royal Warwickshire Regiment Service History (1894–1914)

William Webb joined the 2nd Battalion Royal Warwickshire Regiment on 26 September 1894 at the age of 14 years 4 months, one month later he was transferred to Ceylon where he served until he returned to England in March 1896.

On 11 October 1899 the Second Boer War started, following a Boer ultimatum directed against the reinforcement of the British garrison in South Africa. The crisis was caused by the refusal of the Transvaal, under President Paul Kruger, to grant political rights to the primarily English population of the mining areas of the Witwaterstrand and the aggressive attitude of Alfred Milner (British High Commissioner) and Joseph Chamberlain (British Colonial Secretary). An underlying cause of the war was the presence in the Transvaal of the largest gold mining complex in the world, beyond direct British control.

On 26 November 1899, the 2nd Battalion Royal Warwickshire Regiment sailed on the freight ship *Gaul* from Southampton, arriving at Cape Town on 16 December 1899. They were immediately ordered to the Britstown—DeAar district in the Cape Colony to put down the uprising of the rebels. The 2nd Battalion Royal Warwickshire Regiment joined the 18 Brigade of the main army in the Orange Free State on 17th March 1900 under Major General T E Stephenson.

On 16 April 1900 a new division, the 11th Division under Major General R Pole-Carew, had been formed of the Guards Brigade (Ingo Jones) and the 18 Brigade (Stephenson) which included the 2nd Royal Warwickshire Regiment, 1st Yorkshire Regiment, 1st Welch Regiment, 1st Essex Regiment and other support companies.

On 22 April 1900 Pole-Carew engaged the enemy at Paadekraal and a bitter fight ensued with Major General Stephenson first in contact with the enemy. Together, the 1st Welch Regiment and the 2nd Battalion Royal Warwickshire Regiment, advanced in gallant style and drove the enemy out of the strong position they held on a high kopje, which they abandoned with the loss of their ammunition. By 30 April 1900, the main army under Lord Roberts had secured Bloemfontein and were preparing for the march to Pretoria.

The greatest misfortune of the campaign began with the occupation of Bloemfontein, when enteric fever broke out among the troops. For more than two months the hospitals were choked with sick and dying men, one general hospital with five hundred beds held seventeen hundred sick men and a field hospital with fifty beds held three hundred and seventy cases. The total number of cases were about six or seven thousand and the military hospitals sufficed, after a long struggle, to meet the crisis. At Bloemfontein alone, as many as fifty men died in one day and more than 1,000 new graves in the cemetery testify to the severity of the epidemic. The officers and men of the medical service truly served their country and those who went through the epidemic never forgot the bravery and unselfishness of the nursing sisters who set an extremely high standard of devotion to duty. William Webb was lucky enough to survive this tragedy.

Early on the morning of 3 May 1900 Lord Roberts, who was 70 years old, left Bloemfontein at the head of his army for the long advance north to Pretoria, the capital of the Transvaal. Between the two cities lay nearly three hundred miles of rolling country, crossed by many rivers and a series of low undefined positions defended by the Boers, which created strong lines of resistance for the British Army. At the Zand River, Kroonstad, the Vaal River, Johannesburg and Pretoria itself were strong lines of resistance and the Boers fought hard to prevent the British advance.

At 5:00 a.m. on 5 June 1900, Pretoria was formally handed over and the British took possession of the Transvaal capital. The troops had marched in excess of 300 miles (483 kilometres), averaging approximately 7 miles (11 kilometres) a day over endless prairies. They marched in the blazing sun, with hot choking dust storms, bitter cold winds and icy hail storms. Fording rivers and floundering through sand with scanty food and shelter-less bivouacs made their journey even more difficult and they had little but hope to sustain them. The country itself added to the monotony of the journey and often there was nothing to be seen but their own long ranks, no sound to be heard but their own footsteps. Nevertheless, their toil was finally rewarded and the fall of the Boer capital crowned their efforts with honour and shocked the Boer rule in South Africa. William Webb was now 20 years old.

While Lord Roberts paused for a few days to adjust the disordered city of Pretoria, the Boers fell back in dejection toward the east. Many Boers made for their homes, many surrendered, the remainder, about seven thousand men with twenty guns, assembled fifteen miles eastward of Pretoria. Lord Roberts' field army, depleted by the wastage of his long march and by garrisons and railway guards dropped on the way, numbered now no more than sixteen thousand men. At 12:45 p.m. on 12 June 1900, the order for the attack on Diamond Hill was given, and the enemy upon it, shaken beyond endurance by the incessant downpour of shrapnel, fell away on either side pursued by the mounted cavalry.

Fighting continued on the 25 August 1900 to secure Belfast and on 24 September 1900 Pole-Carew entered and occupied Komati Poort. The 2nd Battalion Royal Warwickshire Regiment moved with the 18 Brigade to establish their Headquarters at Barberton and to protect the railway from Komati Poort to Waterval Onder.

William Webb left from Cape Town, South Africa on 29 May 1901 aboard the ship 'Armenian', together with the 2nd Battalion Royal Warwickshire Regiment (5 officers, 184 men) and 936 Boer prisoners of war. They arrived in Bermuda on 3 July 1901 and carried their duties guarding POWs until 17 November 1902.

The last of the Boers surrendered in May 1902 and the war ended with the Treaty of Vereeniging signed on 31 May 1902. The war had cost around 75,000 lives, 22,000 British and allied soldiers killed (7,792 killed in battle, the rest through disease), between 6,000 and 7,000 Boer fighters killed, and in the concentration camps between 20,000 and 28,000 Boer civilians (mainly women and children). The Horse Memorial in Port Elizabeth is a tribute to the 300,000 horses that died during the conflict.

William Webb, now 22 years old, returned to England where he was stationed until he left for Malta on 22 November 1912. When the First World War started in 1914 he returned to England with his regiment and on 4 October 1914, age 34, he left for Belgium and France.

2 Lance Sergeant
William Webb
c. 1918.

Part I

First World War Diary (1914–1915)

War Diary:
Landing in Belgium October 1914

Sunday 4 October 1914: Lyndhurst Camp

We received orders to proceed to France at 2:30 p.m. and moved off at 5:00 p.m. marching to Southampton docks and arriving at 8:40 p.m. The 2nd Battalion Royal Warwickshire Regiment[1] embarked on the ship HT *Cymrie* at 11:30 p.m. It was an awful trip, I couldn't find anywhere to sleep but at last I found a bunk and tired out, I finally went to bed at 2:30 a.m.

Monday 5 October 1914: At Sea

We set sail about 7:30 a.m. and sailed around the coast of England arriving off the coast of Dover at 6:00 p.m., the sea was calm. A Torpedo Destroyer came alongside at 9:45 p.m. and I heard the officer of the Torpedo Destroyer ask our Captain 'when were we going to move.' The Captain said 'he was waiting for written orders from Admiralty.' We eventually set sail at 9:45 p.m. German submarines were believed to be in the area but, thanks to the protection from the Royal Navy, we arrived safely in Zeebrugge, Belgium.

Tuesday 6 October 1914: Zeebrugge

I awoke at 2:30 a.m. and was told to be ready to disembark at 3:45 a.m. We started to go into the harbour at 6:00 a.m. and just as we were entering the breakwater a steamship called *Kutnivida* ran right across our bows and missed us by about 4 yards (3.6 metres). We pulled alongside the breakwater at 6:40 a.m. and there were a lot of Belgium soldiers and officers in their peculiar dress, they looked a smart lot of men. I saw one describe a dead soldier, he drew his hands across his knees and bowed his head. This place is called Zeebrugge and we disembarked at 9:30 a.m. but had to

---

1 The National Archives (TNA) WO 95/1664/3: 2nd Royal Warwickshire Regiment War Diary. The Battalion's embarkation strength was 1,002 of all ranks. However, William's diary of 7 November 1914 records the strength on arrival as 1,126.

hang about in the drizzling rain and cold until about 1:00 p.m. when we moved off by train to our billet at Bruges ten miles away. A Belgium soldier brought us post cards to send to England. I wrote a short letter to my wife Edith and then I sent a post card of a boat leaving Zeebrugge harbour. I wondered if she would guess that we landed here. The people cheered as we arrived at Bruges about 2:30 p.m. The station was crowded, the Red Cross ladies served out bread, meat, wine and lemonade. The Belgium soldiers gave us their bread and butter from out of their haversacks. I would like to say a few words about the journey from Zeebrugge to the town of Bruges. As we were passing, the people looked at the train and you could see astonishment on their faces, then all at once it dawned upon them that we were English troops, it was worth a five pound note to see the change on their faces. They cheered, they danced, in fact they did almost everything to show their joy, shouting *"Viva Anglais"* I don't know if I have wrote *"Viva Anglais"* correct but that is how it sounded to us. At Bruges town station, a very large place, the gates of the station were shut but I should say everyone in the town must have been there, shouting and jumping, girls throwing kisses, our men throwing penny and halfpenny coins, it did our hearts good to think that we were Englishmen, helping such a weak nation. Then we saw the other side of the picture, as we were leaving the station a train came in from Antwerp with the refugees all crying, they had been given twenty four hours' notice to leave Antwerp. When we were travelling to Bruges, I saw an old lady, I should say she was between 50 and 60 years of age, she shouted, clapped and danced, then took from around her neck a long muffler and started to wave, and to crown it all, she tried to run to keep up with the train. We dis-entrained the Royal Scots Fusiliers at Bruges and our regiment went further inland to a place called Oostkamp,[2] arriving about 4:00 p.m. We were naturally the curiosity of all the people there, they were talking to us, of course we couldn't understand one another but we managed somehow to relate to each other. At 8:30 p.m. I moved off to my billet, it was in a big house called '*The Sey Lugge,*' Sergeant D Armouce and Sergeant Shoemaker slept in the room with me. The people of the house did everything they could for us, they gave us bread and butter, milk, and they were pleased to have us stay in their house. A lot of the men slept in a barn with straw for a bed, of course we didn't have beds, but we slept well, that was everything. I saw one of the Belgium soldiers from the Fort of Namur. Goodnight love.

Wednesday 7 October 1914: Oostkamp

I got up early at 6:00 a.m. today and fell in for roll call at 7:30 a.m. We saw six Aeroplanes fly over this morning but we did not know whether they were German or British. We heard that the Germans are only 35 miles (56 kilometres) away and also heard a rumour that a boat with troops aboard following us struck a mine, I hope to

---

2   The name Oostkamp comes from the medieval 'Orscamp', which means 'place of the horses.'

God that it is not true. Later we heard that it was a grain ship and not a troop ship. This morning we had a lot of people visit us to watch us cooking and they were very pleased to see us. This afternoon one of the aeroplanes flew over from the direction of Antwerp, again we didn't know who it belonged to but it dropped a message. The Royal Welch Fusiliers came in this evening and I expect the South Staffordshire Regiment was with them, we don't get much news, no one is allowed to leave his billet after 6:00 p.m. It is 9:50 p.m. now so I am off to sleep. Goodnight love.

Thursday 8 October 1914: Oostcamp

Lieutenant Brown arrived at 5:00 a.m. for the Sergeant Major and we moved off at 8:30 a.m. We marched through Bruges and the place was crowded with people cheering and wishing us good luck. They gave us tobacco, cigarettes, matches and apples as we marched along and we could hear big guns firing. We marched 23 miles (37 kilometres) to Ostend carrying the stretchers and in full marching order, how our shoulders ache and how long the road seemed to be. We passed a lot of Belgium soldiers just returning from Buslam, some of the soldiers had their wives and sweethearts with them. It's now 5:00 p.m. and we are still marching, how tired we are, we arrived at our destination at 6:30 p.m., a place called Zandvoorde. I slept in a barn and it was very cold during the night. Goodnight love.

Friday 9 October 1914: Ostend

We had Reveille at 5:00 a.m. and were ready to move off at 7:30 a.m. We had to hand our ammunition in and put our packs on the cart and then we marched, halting for about four hours outside Ostend. As we rested outside Ostend we saw the refugees from Antwerp, people old and young, children toddling along catching hold of their mother's aprons and others with all their belongings on a wheelbarrow. I saw one old couple, a proper Darby and Joan, as they passed us they said 'good morning.' We moved into Ostend at 8:00 p.m. and believe we are on route for Antwerp, leaving at 9:45 a.m. I saw a lot of wounded Belgium soldiers on the platform and I managed to buy the *Daily Mail* in Ostend for twopence halfpenny. We went by train to Ghent and on the way we had to go through Bruges again where we saw a lot of our sailors who had been fighting. We arrived in Ghent[3] at 5:30 p.m., it is a very large place and the people cheered and shouted "*Viva Anglais*," England for ever, giving us apples, cigars and matches. It is a joy to see their faces as we pass by them and waited in the streets

---

3   C T Atkinson, *The Seventh Division* (Uckfield: Naval & Military Press reprint of 1926 edition), p. 11: Lieutenant-General Sir Henry Rawlinson (GOC IV Corps) decided to move two brigades with some artillery to Ghent to support the French Marines who had now arrived there, covering the withdrawal from Antwerp. The movement which began early on 9 October 1914 took some time, for although the distance was only 40 miles (64 kilometres) there was much confusion and congestion on the railway.

to be billeted. We have just received orders to move outside the town to support the French and so we went about 2 miles (3.2 kilometres) and bivouacked in a field, no blankets, how cold it was. At 10:00 a.m. the adjutant asked for anyone who could use a telephone. I volunteered and took Harrison with me, we found a telephone in the Burgomaster's house. He was there with his wife and daughter to greet us, how kind they were, they had lit a fire, made us coffee and gave us cigars, everything to make us comfortable. This is what they think of an English soldier. Goodnight love.

Saturday 10 October 1914: Kleyhoek

The adjutant came for us at 1:00 a.m. and we were disappointed as we thought we were going to stop the night. It was raining when we got back to the regiment and we moved off at 1:30 a.m. We marched about 5 miles (8 kilometres) and came across two men and one officer who had caught a spy. We heard a lot of rifle fire on our left which lasted all night and it was awful cold. We stayed until 5:00 a.m. and saw the Belgium Artillery pass us, after that we moved off and as we did the big enemy guns started firing. We walk about 6 miles (9.6 kilometres) and halted again about 4:00 a.m. We had a fatal accident about 9:30 a.m. when one platoon of the Royal Welch Fusiliers became lost and they were cleaning their rifles when a man let a round off and it struck Private J Swift (Service Number [S/N] 1136) from D Company straight through the head. We buried him in the church yard at 11:30 a.m., a Roman Catholic Priest officiated and two Belgium officers attended. We moved into action at 1:00 p.m., took up a position in a field, and at 8:45 p.m. we were under a terrific barrage of rifle fire which lasted about three quarters of an hour. I sent stretcher bearers out but luckily there were no casualties. The fire continued and kept up until 12:00 midnight when Corporal R Element (S/N 1721) was brought in shot through the knee. I would like to record the work that the stretcher bearers performed during the fight, they went along all the trenches every hour, and I don't know how they didn't get shot. Goodnight love.

Sunday 11 October 1914: Limberge

The firing has been going on all night and at 5:00 a.m. it ceased, we shifted our position again but nothing happened all day, we withdrew from the trenches at 8:30 p.m. and marched to Hansbeke via Ghent. Goodnight love.

Monday 12 October 1914: Hansbeke

We marched all night in the awful cold and frost until we reached a village at 6:00 a.m. We rested until 12:30 p.m. and then moved off again hearing that there were 10,000 Germans near Ghent. It is a beautiful day and we marched all the afternoon although

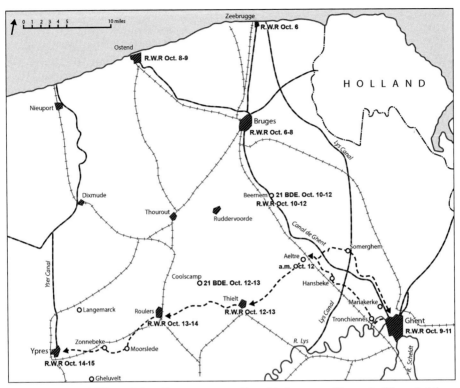

Map 1 Royal Warwickshire Regiment route from Zeebrugge to Ypres via Ghent 6–15 October 1914.

it was very cold. At 10:00 p.m. we reached our bivouac in a church at Thielt.[4] We were made very comfortable and shared a place with the French Marines. I wondered when I would get a letter from Edith, I had been thinking of her and Marjorie all day long but it is 12:00 midnight and so I am off to bed. Goodnight love.

4   Ibid., pp. 12–13: The information which came in seemed to indicate that the Germans were moving towards Ghent but, although both brigades reported contact with snipers and small parties of enemy, no attack developed. About 4:00 p.m. General Rawlinson issued orders to withdraw from Ghent after nightfall and make for Thielt, 8 miles (13 kilometres) beyond Aeltre. The 22 Brigade with Divisional Headquarters moved by Tronchiennes and Hansbeke to the south. Orders were issued that the march was to be made in strict silence and that if the enemy was encountered he was to be tackled with the bayonet. It was 9:00 p.m. before the march was started and the night was bitterly cold and the pavé very hard on the feet but, by daybreak, the troops had reached Hansbeke. Soon after midday the march resumed and it was nearly midnight before the rear guards crawled into Thielt. The men had covered over 26 miles (42 kilometres) in the previous 24 hours, most of them being short of food and sleep and greatly exhausted.

Tuesday 13 October 1914: Thielt

I had the best sleep for the last five days but was awaken [sic] this morning by a lot of rifle fire, our troops were firing at a German Aeroplane, which they shot down. We sent motor cars out to search for it and heard later that the aviator had been killed. We move off at 12:00 noon. I am writing this whilst sitting in a Belgium shop beside a fire and they are giving us coffee free, they are good to us, the women here wear little black bonnets which make them look like fairy grandmothers. It is now raining hard and has rained all the afternoon. We reached our bivouac in a town called Roulers at 10:00 p.m. feeling properly fed up. Good night love.

Wednesday 14 October 1914: Roulers

We arose at 4:00 a.m. and were ready to leave at 6:00 a.m. The men are tired, fed up and have to march 18 miles (29 kilometres) in the rain, how this palls on one, continual marching day after day. I see them limping along and thank God that I have got a good pair of feet. The roads here are little blocks of stone sloping to each side, you always seem to be marching on the side of your feet and to make matters worse we haven't had many hours of sleep this week. Can you wonder at men falling out, even the horses are dropping down, but I must stop writing like this and keep my spirit up. We have heard big guns firing all day, it is now 3:15 p.m. and we have just marched into a large town called Ypres.[5] I don't know how to write the names of these towns in English since I can only find their names in Flemish or French. There is an awful large force concentrated here and they told us as we entered the town that they had shot down a German Aeroplane with six officers in it. Later they shot two more down and captured a lot of German prisoners. We are bivouacked in a Convent for the night, it is 7:00 p.m. The mail came in today but I didn't get a letter from Edith. I expect she is off to the Freemasons Lodge tonight and Marjorie has been to the Juveniles. I shall think of them at 9:00 p.m. tonight. Goodnight love.

---

5   Ibid., pp. 14–17: On 13 October 1914 the Division resumed its march for Roulers, about 10 miles away, but matters were not improved by persistent heavy rain and muddy roads, and reports that the Germans were close at hand caused a covering position to be taken up. 14 October saw the first phase in the Division's operation completed. At 6:15 a.m. it was on the march again, making for Ypres some 15 miles away, in three columns, over bad roads and in steady rain. The men arrived at Ypres tired, their movement had seemed somewhat aimless, and they had not had the satisfaction of a serious encounter with the enemy or seeing Germans fall under their rifle fire.

War Diary:
First Battle of Ypres October–November 1914

Thursday 15 October 1914: Ypres

We left Ypres at 6:30 a.m. and marched to a position 2 miles (3.2 kilometres) further out with big guns and rifle fire being exchanged by both sides. On our left is the 22 Brigade and we are the covering party for them. When we left this morning we were not able to get anything to eat or drink, but on the way we stopped at a house by the roadside and managed to find something. We are expecting a big engagement, one of our men found a German officer's helmet, two were killed here yesterday. As we halted by the roadside, one of our men cut his comrades hair and they are both in full marching order. Before dusk we withdrew from our position leaving one company and several scouts on outpost and we bivouacked again in Ypres, but in another Convent this time. We got settled down about 7:30 p.m. after an easy day and went off to sleep at 9:00 p.m. Goodnight love xxx

Friday 16 October 1914: Ypres

We were awaken at 1:30 a.m. and marched off at 4:30 a.m. on a very damp, cold and misty morning, all along the road men from our outpost had felled trees to block the roadway. We marched 5 miles (8 kilometres) to a village called Zonnebeke located about 6 miles (9.6 kilometres) from the French border. We are full of praise for the Belgium people, they bring us hot coffee, especially the Nuns in the Convent. They brought us hot milk and chairs to sit down on. We walked through the village and I went into a house, made some tea, and had some bread and butter. At 9:30 a.m., it was still foggy and damp, a force of Germans were positioned close to our front line and so we sent out some troops with machine-guns and artillery. We heard yesterday that our General Capper was highly commended for the way he moved our division. I should add, the men should be highly commended for the way they marched. We remained in the village all day and at 7:30 p.m. we went to our billets, this time in a public house. It is a proper English November night, foggy, misty and damp, we have got to sleep with our equipment on, ready to turn out at a minutes notice. This diary is being kept especially for my wife's sake and I hope I shall be able to record a true record of our doings during this war. A spy was captured here today, it's now 8:30 p.m. and I'm off to bed. Good night love.

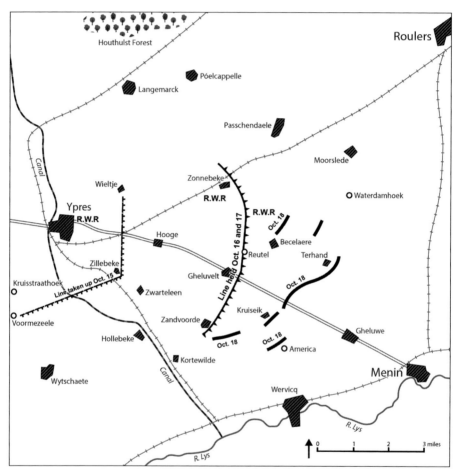

Map 2 Positions of the Royal Warwickshire Regiment during the First Battle of Ypres
15–18 October 1914.

Saturday 17 October 1914: Zonnebeke[6]

A cyclist orderly awoke me at 11:30 p.m. last night, the office at the outpost had sent for a stretcher. I sent a stretcher and four bearers out and waited for them to return, they got back at 12:15 p.m. A corporal had been taken ill and so I called the doctor but as I was sitting waiting for him a civilian burst into the room shouting "Deutsch." Our outpost at the time was fighting hard and the word "Deutsch" is Belgium for Germans. I eventually got to bed again at 1:30 a.m. but up at 4:30 a.m. standing to. We heard that 20,000 Germans are entrenching about 2 miles (3.2 kilometres) from here and we expect a big fight. I received a letter from Edith dated 5 October 1914, it was welcome and long overdue. We have remained in Zonnebeke all day but the 21 Brigade have been in action and wounded have come in as well as two German spies. We are having a well-earned rest, I shall soon retire to bed. Sergeant Smith returned today, he was reported missing, he was left with a cart in Ghent and managed to get on the last train that left leaving the cart behind. It's now 9:45 p.m. and I am off to bed picturing Edith out for the evening in Devonport on Saturday night. Goodnight love.

Sunday 18 October 1914: Zonnebeke

Reveille sounded at 4:00 a.m. and we were ready to move off at 5:35 a.m. We marched for about 3 miles (4.8 kilometres) into a wood in Veldhoek and had orders to keep under the trees so that Aeroplanes couldn't see us. The 20 Brigade are in action just in front of our position and the Royal Welch Fusiliers captured an enemy outpost. At 3:30 p.m. they brought in some wounded from the Bedford Regiment, they had been wounded with shrapnel. They were passing a windmill when the same old trick was done, that is, turn the wings of the mill three times, which shows that the troops are in range, then bang comes the shrapnel. They caught the man this time, he was a German sergeant and of course they made short work of him. We left the wood at 5:30 p.m. and marched to a village called Becelaere arriving at 4:30 p.m., we are billeted in a brewery. This marching at night is awful, fancy walking along at night, not a sound only the tramping of feet, never knowing when you are going to be attacked. I walk along thinking of my wife and child. Its 9:30 p.m. and I am off to sleep. Good night love.

6   Ibid., pp. 19–20: On 15 October 1914 General Capper had issued orders for the occupation of a defensive line from Vormeezeele on the right to Zillebeke, with outpost pushed well forward. The night of 15–16 October passed quietly, apart from a little sniping. Very early next morning an advance was made; the 20 Brigade pushed out to Zandvoorde and entrenched a line running eastward to Gheluvelt, whence the 21 Brigade carried it on to the north past Reutel, while the 22 Brigade (Royal Warwickshires) moved up on the 21st left and continued the line beyond Zonnebeke.

3 First wounded of 7th Division, Ypres October 1914. (IWM Q57209)

Monday 19 October 1914: Becelaere (Battle for Dadizeele and Kleythoek)

We got up at 4:00 a.m. and moved off at 5:30 a.m. toward Menin, there was no break-fast for half the men. We marched about three miles (4.8 kilometres) and then got into fighting order to attack the enemy at Dadizeele. An order was given out that anyone who owns a windmill with the wings moving when the troops are moving, the owner will be shot at once. We moved off into action at 8:30 a.m. and as we passed through a town the people gave us cigars, pears, tobacco and chocolate. I am going into action smoking a cigar and had only been in the firing line about half an hour when we had 12 men wounded with shrapnel. At 1:00 p.m. we had to advance up a road to collect the wounded, my God, what a time, shrapnel was bursting right down the centre of the road, and as we heard it coming we fell headlong into the ditch by the roadside. It was hell, I said my prayers my darling and prayed to God to preserve me from the fire, for I never thought I would come out of it alive. I had just moved by some houses when a shell burst, Harrison and I fell into the ditch, and poor White, who was about 5 yards (4.5 metres) behind me was killed and Laishley wounded. I saw the door of a house open, Harrison and I dived in and just as we slammed the door to, shrapnel struck the wall. Oh it was awful, we got out the back of the house and moved into another to find Laishley who was hit in the thigh. He told us White had been killed, we went to see but could not do anything for him. We waited for some time and then we carried Laishley back about 2 miles (3.2 kilometres), Oh, how he did hang on our shoulders but he bore his pain bravely. We came to a town and I collected a lot of wounded and put them into a hotel. Then we followed some more troops and at last we found our regiment at Zonnebeke. Oh my love, pray for me and ask God to protect me, I am dead tired but I will wish you good night when I go to bed love. I just heard that they have brought Laishley to this place at 8:00 p.m., so that is alright. It's 9:25 p.m. and I am off to bed, so Good night my darling and God bless you. xxx

PS. I found afterwards that my stretcher was all ripped with shrapnel from the same shell that killed poor White, it could have been me.

Tuesday 20 October 1914: Zonnebeke

Reveille at 4:00 a.m., it's a cold wet day and we march off at 5:15 a.m. We went to a field and stayed about one hour and then we moved into a wood, the road is crowded with refugees and it is pitiful to see them walking along. Your heart bleeds for them and I find it hard to describe, it is awful. Our big guns are shelling the German positions. We moved off again at 1:00 p.m. to Zonnebeke and when we arrived into town our big artillery guns were shelling the German positions and our naval armoury train came up and also started shelling, it was deafening. A lot of rifle shots came over, at last the Germans had found our position and shelled us with their heavy guns, we had to shift quickly and move further back. We went in front of our guns to find Colonel Loring, our Regimental Commanding Officer, he was wounded in the foot but still carried on fighting. Our regiment was behind a house and so we took refuge in a barn to escape from the rain. I have lost most of my equipment and top coat, I have only what I stand up in, and so I am off to bed at 9:00 p.m., Goodnight my love and God bless you. xxx

Wednesday 21 October 1914: Zonnebeke

I have hardly slept all night with the cold but at least the guns were quiet some of the time. Yesterday the Royal Welch Fusiliers captured seven guns and 200 rounds of ammunition, and five guns were captured this morning. Today at 6:00 a.m. our big guns relocated behind the barn I was in and their range was too short for the shells to clear the roof, so they knocked the top of the barn off and a brick hit me on the foot. This place has changed over the past two days and everyone has evacuated. It's now 4:30 p.m. and we have been bombarded all day long, we have been shelled out of three places. This morning we had the wounded coming in, a lot of the Queen's Regiment and our own Royal Warwickshire Regiment, we were busy all day taking care of them and patching them up. We had Captain Synachan and Whaley report wounded, this is something awful and they say this is worse than Mons. Where is General French with his troops, they say we have got to hold our position and clearly we are paying for it. Our Regiment has an awful lot of casualties and we had to do another run to rescue them. The Germans are using shells they call 'Jack Johnson'[7] and it is awful to see the wounded hobbling in and we can't do anything to stop it. We can't get near the trenches to attend to the wounded, poor Captain Methuan and Sergeant Garvey have been killed, it has been worse than hell. The Germans shelled a church which I think is sinful, we moved right back and waited and at last we had the order to advance about 1:00 p.m. and tend to the wounded. How silently we go along, it is dark, and firing is still going on. At last we get up to a bomb proof shelter where they had put the wounded and we started work to clear it. Oh what a sight and sound, poor men moaning with pain and the terrible sight of it by a flash lamp, still we struggled on. We had got all the men but eight back to two houses about a quarter mile away when a terrific rifle fire broke out, and we had to wait for almost one hour before we could move. At least we got most of the wounded away and then I went with the doctor to the house to await for the ambulance, it made my heart bleed for the wounded. There they were in a dimly lighted room on the floor packed together moaning with pain, we couldn't get an ambulance up to take them away. We sent Talmond to try to find it on a bike and at 1:00 a.m. eight stretchers came up, they had left the ambulance about a quarter of a mile down the road. We went back then to a railway crossing about 2 miles (3.2 kilometres) away, bitter cold and no blankets, so now Goodnight or rather Good morning and God bless you my love. xxx

Thursday 22 October 1914: Zonnebeke

I did not sleep all night and at 5:00 a.m. we moved to another place south west of the railway crossing and entrenched. Our big guns were firing on each side of us and we had to help to dig trenches.[8] The casualties for our regiment for yesterday were 235 killed, wounded or missing but today we have only had a couple of shells drop amongst us and no casualties, thank God. I am off to bed early and sleeping in a stable. Goodnight my love and God bless you xxx

---

7   A Jack Johnson was a large calibre artillery shell – the power and amount of dark smoke given off by these big shell explosions were evocative of black heavyweight boxing champion Jack Johnson (1878-1946).

8   Ibid., p. 44: Even a day of relative "Quiet" like 22 October 1914 was a severe strain on the endurance of the troops. Practically every officer and man was in the firing line or in close support and few got any chance of sleep or rest. One officer wrote "the terrific din of firing went on without ceasing, shells, guns and rifles all going at once made one's recollection of the Boer War fire seem like crackers at a picnic."

4 7th Division ambulance horse wagon October 1914. (IWM Q57213)

Friday 23 October 1914: Zonnebeke

I was awake at 5:30 a.m. disturbed by rifle fire that had been going on nearly all night and the big guns have just commenced firing. I have lost everything, I can't shave, I have to borrow a towel to wash and to make matters worse I have run out of cigarettes, tobacco and cigarette papers. At 8:34 a.m. I received postcards from my dear wife and Mrs Slivey, which cheered me up. Everything was quiet until about 11:00 a.m. when the big guns and rifle fire opened up on our right and it continued all day. At 4:30 p.m. the French advanced on our left and we supported them with artillery fire, it was a terrific din and it made my head ache. The Germans fired a lot of shells that landed close to our position but we were fortunate not to have our place blown up. At 6:00 p.m. we were ordered to move and we marched toward Zonnebeke but we heard that the Wiltshire Regiment had been severely cut up and so we moved back to our original position. It is 10:20 p.m. and so I will try to get some sleep. Goodnight and God bless you my love. xxx

Saturday 24 October 1914: Battle of Polygon Wood[9]

I arose from my shelter at 4:30 a.m. and moved out into the firing line, at 6:30 a.m. we moved into a house on the edge of the wood to make a dressing station. My God it was terrible, the Germans were mowing our men down like sheep. A couple of 'Jack Johnsons' came over and one passed over the top of the house, these shells make a hole that is deep enough to bury a horse and cart in. One sergeant of the Royal Engineers was in the house, he had been buried alive in the trenches and some men had dug him out. We sent the stretcher bearers out and they started to bring the wounded men back, you never saw such sights in your life, they were torn to pieces. I don't know what shells the Germans are using, but men came in with pieces torn out of their chest and body, this isn't war, it is scientific murder. Oh my God, what a terrible life this is. I had my coat off and sleeves turned up, patching my poor wounded comrades as best we could but many were beyond help. If the people in England could only see the battlefields. We had just got into action when a Belgium soldier came running down shouting "we are captured," the Germans are through our lines. Our regiment … were engaged in very heavy fighting and were held up at a farm where a large body of Germans offered a most desperate resistance, using machine-guns with great effect. Lieutenant Colonel Loring (our Commanding Officer) still kept on charging straight into the wood, then as they came out they met the enemy with their machine-guns, but still they kept charging on to take the farm (brave men). Oh how our men did fight, but the enemy force against us must be ten to one, and the spies are innumerable. Our stretcher bearers kept on working, carrying the wounded men back to our dressing station where we continued to patch them up and the Royal Army Medical Corp [RAMC] field ambulances kept taking them away. The house we used for the dressing station kept on getting full as more and more wounded men arrived. We have heard that our colonel has been killed, he is the bravest and coolest man I ever saw. Oh God, we have suffered again. Our regiment is now about 600 strong and we have lost

---

9   Ibid., pp. 24–29: Battle of Kleythoek orders were issued for the attack on Menin to be started at 6:30 a.m. on 19 October 1914; the move was to be carried out in three phases. The first, an attack from the north on Kleythoek by the 22 Brigade (Royal Warwickshires), secondly two other brigades were to attack Gheluwe and finally, all three were to attack Menin. One great difficulty was that the undulating and thickly wooded country presented a nasty problem for the artillery and they could not give the infantry effective support, being unable to locate accurately either the enemy trenches or gun positions. However, the 22 Brigade moved off on time and advancing by Strooiboomhoek to Dadizeele deployed there. The Royal Warwickshires were on the right with their left on the Menin-Roulers road, the Welch Fusiliers being on the left beyond the road, the South Staffords in support and the Queen's in reserve. At 10:30 a.m. the attack was vigorously pressed. Some parties of Germans cleared off as the troops pushed forward and machine-gun fire covered their advance, silencing rifle fire from behind a hedge which was threatening to check the Welch Fusiliers. On the right the Royal Warwickshires did really well, making good use of favourable ground.

about 16 of our officers (50 percent of our landing force remaining). Our men captured some German prisoners and you should have seen them, one was about sixteen years of age, and the others varied from that up to fifty five years old. They did look a poor miserable lot. We have had another brigade, The Queen's, come up to support us and we needed them, for we couldn't hold out much longer. One Brigadier said that the Warwickshire Regiment had saved the situation but we had 100 casualties.

Oh love, I can picture you in Devonport dreaming what we are doing, but pray for all our soldiers. We have had orders to go back to rest and another brigade of the 6th Division has come to relieve us. The woods are piled with German dead. The stretcher bearers made another effort to try to recue some more wounded, and when we had reached the end of the wood, the Germans fired two maxims at us and so had to retreat quickly and couldn't get them.

We saw a pitiful sight, the Royal Engineers digging graves to bury the dead and they were making crosses out of the branches of trees to put on each grave, God help them and their families. I wrote this on Sunday as yesterday was too horrible to write and so Goodnight and God bless you my love. xxx

Sunday 25th October 1914: Veldhoek

Last night I slept until 4:30 a.m. under a tree in a wood close to the Menin–Becelaere Road with no top coat, only a sack to cover me, and the big artillery guns and rifles firing all night. They say that this is one of the biggest attacks in history[10] and if it is successful we are going back to base to refit our brigade, and we need it. A big battle is in process on our front and we laid in the woods all day, in reserve, with a very big artillery battle in progress. A lot of German prisoners have been brought in and we had a letter from General French read out congratulating the troops for their bravery in battle. CSM Reeves was reported dead but he came in tonight and we were happy to see him. I wrote to Edith, Flo and Harold and as soon as I had sent Edith's letter, I received one from her. She told me she was going to put Marjorie to learn the piano. I am off to bed for an early sleep if I can. Goodnight and God bless you my love. xxx

Monday 26 October 1914: Veldhoek

I have been awake all night and it rained, I haven't got a top coat and so I use a sack to cover myself, then a very big night attack started. It was awful laying in a wood and expecting every minute to start fighting. I dropped off to sleep but at 11:30 p.m. last night I woke up again to hear high explosive shells screaming overhead. It was pouring with rain and I got very wet and was glad when we had to get up. Captain

---

10   TNA: WO 95/1664/3: 2nd Battalion Royal Warwickshire Regiment War Diary, 25 October 1914: General Sir Henry Rawlinson told the 2nd Battalion that they had saved the line on the previous day.

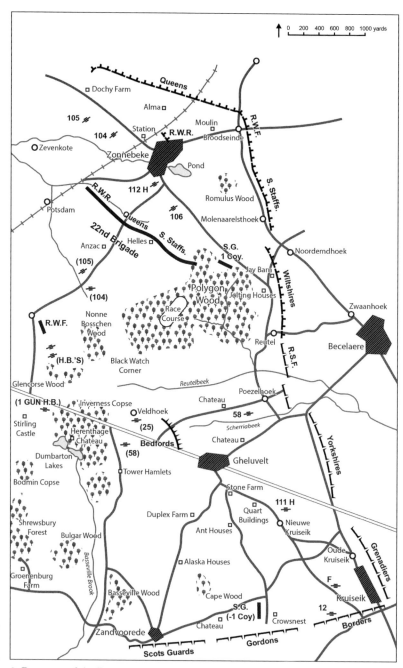

Map 3 Positions of the Royal Warwickshire Regiment during the Battle for Polygon Wood
21–24 October 1914.

Foster is now in charge of our battalion and our casualties in the fights last week were about 480 killed, wounded or missing. We were ordered to 'Stand to Arms' at 4:00 a.m. and advanced a short distance up the Menin–Becelaere Road but soon came under shellfire, so we stayed a short time and then moved off again only to come under more heavy shellfire, 'Jack Johnsons' and shrapnel. We hardly knew which way to turn so we had to fall back with shrapnel falling all around us until we reached a road and could advance again. We reached the side of a wooded area and as we moved into it the shelling with shrapnel started again, thank God none took effect. Then we had to dig trenches and at 10:30 p.m. we were off again, walking with no sleep the night before, dead beat, and marched until 3:00 a.m. when we found a little barn and tried to get some sleep. A little later we were awaken by a German Aeroplane flying over us and it was just like an English Aeroplane, it had the Union Jack and it hovered over our position, dropping shells, so we fired at the Aeroplane and hit the petrol tank setting it on fire, the pilot fell out, and the machine crashed into the ground. I said my prayers on the march, I said, Goodnight and God bless you my love. xxx

Tuesday 27 October 1914: Veldhoek

I was too cold to sleep last night and about 6:00 a.m. the enemy snipers got to work. Our stretcher bearers had to recover four dead men from the Salisbury Regiment and at 8:45 a.m. our first wounded man came in, shot in the back. Yesterday our reinforcements from England joined us, Sergeant Cleverly and Sergeant Luckman with 97 men, all desperately needed. I haven't had my boots or putties off for ten days and my feet are very sore. About 9:30 a.m. the Germans started to shell us with 'Jack Johnsons' and soon found our direction and location, knocking the house down and forcing us to move quickly, my God it was awful. You can hear the shells singing through the air, then they land with an awful thud and throw the dirt yards up in the air just like a great explosion. We all got out safe and moved back to another farm. It has started to rain and it is very cold, the shrapnel is still falling around us and I had to send stretcher bearers out to recover the wounded.

About 2:00 p.m. some men came down wounded, they had been behind a house when a Jack Johnson knocked it down on top of them. At 4:00 p.m. they started to shell us again and at last they found our farm, the shells going over the farm and missing the top by inches but nothing was damaged. I had to send more stretchers out and they brought two German wounded prisoners in. At 8:00 p.m. the doctor had left us and we were with the Colonel of the Queen's Regiment who told me to take my bearers away to the main road. For a while we were lost and at 1:00 a.m. I found General Langdon who used to belong to our regiment. I explained my situation to him and he gave me some biscuits, a billy of tea and sugar for the ten men I had with me. He knew me well and found an empty house for us to bivouacs, so I am just off to bed at 3:00 a.m. Good morning and God bless you my love. xxx

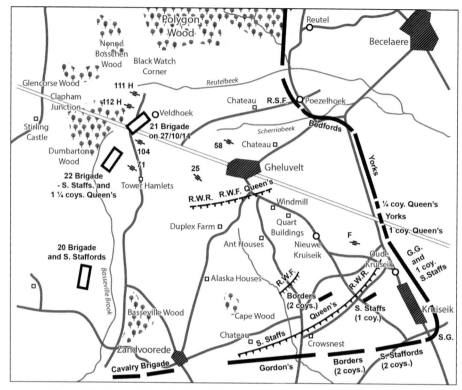

Map 4 Position held by the Royal Warwickshire Regiment 27 October 1914.

Wednesday 28 October 1914: Zandvoorde

We got up at 6:00 a.m. and made some tea, then I found a Medical Officer who was going to 1 Brigade Head Quarters, so I followed him and at last we found our regiment. The first thing we heard was that a soldier of our regiment was cleaning his rifle when it accidently went off killing one man and wounding another. The Commanding Officer brought us back into a wood to give us a rest, we don't know how long we shall stay. Our casualties for yesterday were 5 killed, 20 wounded, 3 men killed and 15 wounded by that 'Jack Johnson' I mentioned when it knocked the house down. We stayed here all the day, an aeroplane passed over us and the troops all fired at it. I went to bed early so Goodnight and God bless you my love xxx

Thursday 29 October 1914: Zandvoorde near Zillebeke

We tried to sleep but were kept awake by the freezing cold. At 4:30 a.m. we had 'stand to' and fell out again at 6:00 a.m. having orders to be ready to move off at any time. We moved off at 11:00 a.m. with a terrible artillery duel going on. At 11:30 a.m. we went into action, it was terrifying being back to where we were two days ago. The wounded started to come in immediately, they were nearly all from the Yorkshire Regiment that had been under very heavy fire when all at once the enemy sent twelve shrapnel shells in rapid succession over the house they were sheltering in. We treated many of the men and at 3:00 p.m. we advanced to another farm and on doing so we were under very heavy shrapnel and rifle fire. Again we treated many of the wounded men but the firing of the big guns and rifles was deafening, it was the biggest battle that has been fought so far and after staying about two hours we moved further along to another empty farm. Then we started to sweep the country for the wounded, but to make matters worse it started to rain, so the stretcher bearers persisted and soon returned with the wounded. We filled the barn up and started on the house but soon filled that up also. Some of the injured had been lying in the trenches since 9:30 a.m. in the morning, poor men, lying on wet, cold ground, wounded and unable to shelter from the heavy rain. We finished about 10:00 p.m. thoroughly tired out. We had Lieutenant Warren join us at 2:00 p.m. and Lieutenant Calderon, who only joined us at 11:00 a.m. this morning, was wounded at 3:30 p.m. Our casualties were roughly 1 killed and 20 wounded, we had to take another position up and so we moved off at 10:30 p.m. in the rain and cold. We couldn't have any tea and so with everyone treated, we went to bed, very tired, cold and hungry. Goodnight and God bless you my love. xxx

5 Wounded soldiers being loaded into an ambulance wagon October 1914. (IWM Q57215)

Friday 30 October 1914: Zandvoorde

We arose at 5:30 a.m. and at 7:00 a.m. a very heavy gun fire started, shells were bursting all around us, I am positive that everyone will be glad when this war is finished and I am trusting in God to return safely to my family. We shifted out of the farm house and into a ditch on the side of the road, surrounded by exploding shrapnel bombs. My God it's awful, can anyone ever get out of it without being killed or wounded and to make matters worse it is raining and we had to lay down in the ditch which was half full of water. Then the Germans moved to a position on our flank and started firing machine-guns and rifles at us, the bullets were whizzing all around us. Just opposite us a young officer was climbing on the bank when he was shot, we shouted "keep your head down sir" as they were still firing at him. Corporal Ashton crept over to him and put a bandage on him, we laid like that for about two hours, simply hell. Later it got so bad that we had to get out of it and so the doctor, myself, and two stretcher bearers made a dash and thank God we got out safe (Oh Edith, how I did think of you at these times). We passed a bomb proof shelter that we were in the day before, and I saw the most horrible site I have ever seen in my life. There were about fifteen men in the shelter and a 'Jack Johnson' struck close by it and they were all killed except one and I think he must have been out of his mind. The men had died as they sat, I saw one man with a big hole in the top of his head, by God this isn't war, its' murder. Can people wonder why some soldiers are callous? We moved through a wood targeted by snipers to collect a lot of wounded soldiers and carried them back to the safety of the dressing shelter. It was impossible for us to get back to our regiment so we stopped where we were until we could locate them. About 5:00 p.m. we started to move off and we reached the regiment at about 6:30 p.m. We were shelled on the way, poor Bill Inebury and Patterson were hit. Our casualties were 2 killed and 15 wounded. I got to bed thanking God about 10:00 p.m. so Goodnight and God bless you love. xxx

Saturday 31 October 1914: Veldhoek

I was awaken at 12:00 a.m. to get our rations and then again at 5:00 a.m. to move off with the doctor. Oh how tired I feel never having my boots or putties off all this time, now thirteen days and we can't make any tea. We moved back a short distance to a farm just in front of our heavy guns and at 6:15 a.m. they started to bombard the Germans, but the enemy immediately replied with their 'Jack Johnsons.' I thought yesterday was bad enough but today was worse, they simply dropped all around us and many, many wounded came in. How terrifying this is and we stuck it for five hours until they got the range of our farm and swiftly poured shells at us, we never expected to get away, so we had to make a mad dash. One dropped a little back from us and it covered us with mud and dust besides wounding some of our men, so we had to run again. It was hell, these shells make a hole big enough to put a cart in, and we expect one to hit us every minute, but again thank God we got through the day, it has been

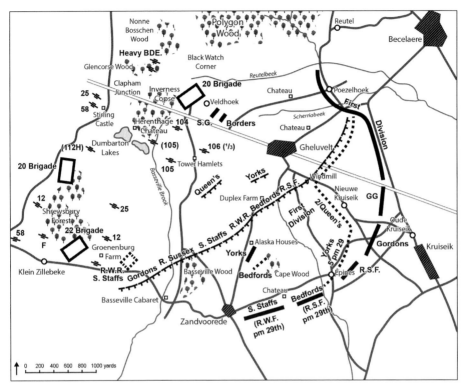

Map 5 Positions of the Royal Warwickshire Regiment 29–30 October 1914.

awful, a terrible battle, my poor head-aches through the big gun fire, oh how glad we are when night comes. We couldn't find the battalion anywhere and so we billeted for the night. It's 10:00 p.m. and the battle is still raging, guns firing, I shall be so glad when this is finished. Goodnight my love may God bless you. xxxx

Sunday 1 November 1914: Veldhoek

I got up at 5:30 a.m. after the best night's sleep I have had for a fortnight. We tried to find our regiment and I met the Quartermaster who gave us directions, but as we set off, we were bombarded with 'Jack Johnsons' and shrapnel shells which landed in front of us blocking our way through, so we had to come back. I sent the stretcher bearers out to find the trenches and they started to bring the wounded in, we haven't had any rations for two days or washed and shaved for four days, we feel awful. We had just got our wounded away in ambulances when the 'Jack Johnsons' started again to fall all around us, so we had to get out quickly. A lady doctor came up with the ambulance motor to fetch our wounded, she was dressed just like a man, trousers and putties. It's a nice warm day and so we stayed outside a farm for some time, but the same old thing, we had to quit when the shelling started, so we got a bit further down the road and everything was quiet for a while. We seem to be holding our own although this is a very big battle, some of the stretcher bearers found our trenches and all that was left of our regiment was Second Lieutenant Richardson and 120 men, although we must have a lot of men that have got lost from the regiment. To think we came out four weeks ago with 1126 men and all we can muster is 120 men, all tired and hungry. They are talking of making our brigade into one regiment, there being so few soldiers left alive. They brought 44 German prisoners in today, I wonder how many casualties they have suffered. We haven't had any rations for two days, so the doctor of the Scots Fusiliers managed to get some from their regiment for us. I had just moved away when a Jack Johnson fell by the stretcher bearers and our man of the Queen's was hit, it was a good job he had a bandolier coat on, for a piece of the shell struck him and cut his coat in half and took a piece out of his arm. It seems strange, it doesn't matter where we go we have these big shells after us, and thank God we have escaped them so far. I shall be very glad when I can have a good night's rest but we can never be sure that that will happen. I think of my wife every night and I try to picture what she is doing, that helps me to stay alive. We haven't had a church parade since we have been out here, and we have been fighting for fifteen days and hearing nothing else but the screaming of shells through the air. We are now sheltering in a house and cannot move outside, the risk of getting shot is too great. Goodnight and God bless you my love. xxx

Monday 2 November 1914: Veldhoek

We got up at 5:30 a.m. and I had a fair night's rest but I couldn't sleep after 4:00 a.m. We moved up about one mile (1.6 kilometres) and made a dressing station but a terrific artillery battle has been going on all day and heaps of wounded have come in, it makes our head ache to hear so many guns firing all the time. Our brave men are fighting well, we must have an awful strong enemy force against us and we heard last night that the Kaiser had come up to take charge of the German Army. It's 3:00 p.m. and the battle has been continuous, our stretcher bearers have been on the go all day long, I can't say how our regiment stands now but we brought in ten of our wounded men and dozens from other regiments including French Officers. The time now is 9:15 p.m. and the fighting still continuous, we heard that the Germans had made five night attacks and had been repulsed heavily by our troops. I shall try to have a sleep now, so Goodnight and God bless you my love. xxxx

Tuesday 3 November 1914: Veldhoek

I was working up until 11:00 p.m. last night and I was just going to lay down when eight more wounded men came in and so I had to take care of them and get them off to hospital. I was just going to lay down again when I heard an awful noise, someone said the Germans had broken through our lines but it was a false alarm. I finally got to bed at 1:00 a.m. and at 3:00 a.m. I was awake again, I couldn't sleep for the noise of shells exploding around us and rifle fire which continued throughout the night. I got up at 5:30 a.m. and although the Germans had been continuously bombarding all around us, our casualties were very low. The lady doctor I mentioned in my Sunday notes was Lady Dorothy Fielding.[11] A lot of reinforcements came up today for the various regiments and we need them. Colonel Webb and Private Collins was wounded yesterday and they were replaced. I managed to get a pair of socks, the first since I left England, but I cannot change my shirt and I haven't had a shave for five days. This is a terrific battle, nothing but fighting day and night, it is such a terrible strain and one never seems to get a minute's peace from the continuous roar of shells whistling through the air. The German bombardment today knocked down a beautiful Villa, and most of the villages are nothing but ruins. I have just received a letter from Edith and she says that Marjorie is going to knit me a scarf, how nice that will be. Goodnight and God bless you my love. xxx

Wednesday 4 November 1914: Veldhoek

I got up at 6:30 a.m. and did not have a very good night's rest due to indigestion. It's a very misty, cold, damp morning, our artillery started firing very early and the Germans replied, my head aches with the terrific noise from the guns and exploding shells. A lot of wounded were brought in and so we have been busy again, what awful sights we have to look upon, poor maimed men but heroes everyone, you wonder how they bear their pain. We treated one man the other day and there was hardly a sound piece of flesh upon him and not a murmur from him, except to say "sorry to cause you so much trouble," that is pluck if you like. My God, I had to stop writing, our bearers brought Private Perind of A Company in, he was hit in the neck with shrapnel and as he got out of his trench to come away, he got hit again with shrapnel in the leg. My God what a wound, it absolutely tore his leg apart, I never saw such a wound, but we patched him up. It has started to rain and my stretcher bearers have gone out again to search for the wounded, as they left, the enemy started a terrific rifle fire. Edith says she has sent me some cigarettes and I shall be pleased to get them. It is Lodge night tonight, I shall be thinking of her at 9:00 p.m. Goodnight and God bless you love. xxx

Thursday 5 November 1914: Veldhoek

I got up at 5:00 a.m. and stayed all day in the same position, we were shelled all around us, but thank God we were not touched. We had an awful lot of wounded come in,

11   Lady Dorothy Mary Evelyn Fielding, the second daughter of the 9th Earl of Denbigh, was born in 1889. With the declaration of war in August 1914, she volunteered for the Munro Motor Ambulance Corps, and spent four years on the Western Front as an ambulance driver. She had the distinction of being the first woman to be awarded the Military Medal for bravery as well as the French *Croix de Guerre* and the Belgian Order of Leopold.

we had one man killed and ten wounded. I had a big room full and three poor fellows died from wounds, it is so hard, having to sit and watch our brave men die. Picture me in a very large room full of wounded men, dimly lit by one solitary candle and poor men moaning with pain whilst others pass away, it is awful. We had orders to move back to have a rest, we started back about 8:00 p.m. for Ypres and arrived there about 9:00 p.m. The Germans were shelling all the roads and so we stopped in the Town Hall which is a magnificent building. Goodnight and God bless you my love. xxx

Friday 6 November 1914: Dickebusch

We had hardly been in bed an hour before they started to shell the Town Hall. One shell went into where the Queen's and Staffords were sleeping, killing two and wounding sixteen, so we stopped for a bit to help, then we had to go, we got through alright but they were still shelling the town. We went by omnibus to a place called Dickebusch and made breakfast and then we had to come back about 3 miles (4.8 kilometres). We heard that we were going down country to refit and recuperate, but no such luck, the 20 and 21 Brigades were going, but not ours. The General inspected us and gave us a lecture, he said how pleased he was and that we might stay two or three days before going back in the firing line. What a disappointment at 5:00 p.m. when we had orders to go as reinforcement to the firing line, so off we started, a very foggy cold night. We walked along the railway for about 3 miles (4.8 kilometres) and then had to stop, so everyone laid down trying to sleep, but it was too cold. I said my prayers and wished you Goodnight and God bless you my love. Xxx

6 The 2nd Battalion Royal Warwickshire Regiment passing through Dickebusch
6 November 1914. (IWM Q57328)

Saturday 7 November 1914: Zillebeke

I was awake all night with the awful cold but I had a tin of cigarettes and sweets from Edith yesterday and so I ate nearly all the sweets. We got on the move at 5:00 a.m. and it was very misty and cold, we walked about 2 miles (3.2 kilometres) and prepared for an attack on the enemy lines. Our brigade moved into a wood and were immediately in action, they charged the German trenches taking them and six machine-guns. We made a dressing station in front of our two artillery batteries which were firing shells all the day long, my poor head ached and was ready to burst. Yesterday we were able to get our regiment together and when we saw what remained of it we were shocked and I could have cried. We came out 1,126 strong and we have had two reinforcements, 94 and 43, that makes 1263, and we are 230 strong now, so we have lost 1033 men.[12] I have been in the Warwickshire Regiment for twenty years, and the fine regiment of men that we brought out with us no longer exists. I looked at the men and I hardly knew any of them, for they were nearly all reservist. Well to go on with today's fighting, it has been a terrific fight, fighting as hard as we could for the Germans were trying to break through our lines, but our men held them back. We have had 3 officers wounded, a major and two second lieutenants they lent us from another regiment, so we have only one second lieutenant out of 28 officers, 31 including the 3 wounded yesterday. Our 22 Brigade is the same, we can't make one regiment out of the whole lot. We have the Brigadier General and 4 officers left in the whole brigade. The brigadier has lost the whole of his officers and his staff. Poor Sergeant Luckman was killed today, our casualties being 2 killed and 20 wounded. We went back into a field to try to sleep at 10:30 p.m. Goodnight and God bless you my love. xxx

Sunday 8 November 1914: Gillebeke

Last night we had just got off to sleep when the shelling and rifle fire started again, bullets started to come over us and we had no cover to get behind so we remained there and hoped we wouldn't get hit. We got up at 5:00 a.m. to a very cold foggy morning but still we mustn't grumble, we are having very good weather considering the time of the year, but we haven't had a blanket for over a month and a top coat is not much cover. We laid in the field with the shells going over our heads and about 3:00 p.m. they started to come nearer, all at once one dropped about 50 yards in front of me and then they started to come closer but we kept clear, we don't know what we are going to do yet. At 5:30 p.m. we formed up for a church parade, the first one since we

12   Atkinson, *The Seventh Division*, p. 108: Casualties for the Royal Warwickshire Regiment in the First Battle of Ypres totalled 28 officers and 787 men, made up of 19 officers and 430 men killed or missing with 9 officers and 357 men wounded. The Seventh Division's total casualties were 364 officers and 9,302 men. These casualty figures differ from those recorded in William Webb's Diary on 7 November 2014, they include men temporarily missing.

have been out here. It is a scene that has and will make an everlasting impression on me. Now just try and picture the scene, an open field and the troops drawn up in three sides of a square, it was pitch dark, the Parson in the centre and he gave a hymn out "Fight the Good Fight". An officer had a pocket flash light which he held while the Parson read out the first verse of the hymn and the troops sang it, then he read out the other verses in the same manner, all the time this was going on shells were screaming through the air and the bullets were striking all around, then we sang "Jesus lover of my soul" and then we had a short sermon and sang "Abide with me". Of course, we had to sing softly, we had a lot of French Troops standing round, it did seem strange hearing the Parson preaching and we couldn't see him. The troops showed reverence, it was something sacred. We were about to lay down to sleep when we received orders to move, they say we are going back to rest, we are utterly shattered, we started out at 9:00 p.m. and marched to a place called Loker about 9 miles (14 kilometres) away, we arrived at 2:00 a.m. on 9 November 1914. We had to sleep in a field but I managed to get in a house and went to bed at 3:30 a.m. very, very tired. Goodnight or rather Good morning and God bless you my love. xxxx

Monday 9 November 1914: Loker

I had the best night's sleep for 21 days and got up at 7:30 a.m. to a letter from Edith, we moved off at 11:00 a.m. and marched further back to a place called Bailleul, a fine big town in France. We are stationed in a school and it is good to be in a peaceful town and not to hear the noise of the artillery guns and rifle fire. We were told that the Royal Warwickshire Regiment saved the situation on Saturday and if we gave way the whole of our line would have had to retire. We had Generals inspection and he read a telegram congratulating us on the way we took the German trenches and machine-guns on Saturday. It is good to have had a quiet day, be able to take my boots off with no danger of being called out in the night, so I am off to bed. Goodnight and God bless you love. xxxx

Tuesday 10 November 1914: Bailleul France

I got up at 7:13 a.m. after a restless night but it was good to take my boots off. We had orders to move off at 9:30 a.m. but it was 10:00 a.m. before we started. Our new Commanding Officer Major R H W Brewis joined us and we marched 6 miles (10 kilometres) to a place called Merris, we could hear the big guns quite clearly and we think we are going to stay there for a couple of days. It is good and something to be thankful for to be able to walk peacefully along a road without any shells coming over and to see people in the houses. It is a proper November day, cold and misty, and I had a post card from Mrs Slivey. It is something to be thankful for to see the men's faces, instead of being serious, they are laughing and singing, and showing the relief from the strain of battle. I am off to bed early tonight, billeted in a house with nine other sergeants, so Goodnight and God bless you my love. xxxx

Wednesday 11 November 1914: Merris France

I arose at 5:30 a.m. today and we have started to hold regular parades at three hour intervals starting at 7:00 a.m. so we are not getting much rest. It is a proper winter's day today, I had a letter and pencil from mother and a letter from Edith saying Marjorie has caught chicken pox, also saying Alf Merton was in Leicester Hospital wounded. I read it in the Warwick paper mother sent out to me. It is hard to realise that we are at war, haven't heard any guns today and so I wrote to Edith and my mother, I shall think of her at Lodge tonight at 9:00 p.m. We have had 150 reinforcements arrive from England today, had a good feast of roast pork, cabbage and potatoes, Sergeant Hawtin was the cook and we congratulated him on his cooking skills. I never had much sleep last night as I slept in the same room as CQM Moon, who is not well and was up nearly all the night, so I volunteered to stop with him. We have just had a French soldier come into the house to tell us to cover the windows up as our light are showing (prevention is better than cure). I must now close for the night. Goodnight and God bless you my love. xxx

Thursday 12 November 1914: Merris France

We had a parade at 6:45 a.m. today, it's a bitter cold morning and Major General T. Capper inspected us. In a lecture he told us that perhaps we may not realise the good work we had done, but when the history of the First World War is written, the good work we had done will then be known, and he complimented us on the work we had done the day Colonel W L Loring was killed. We had about 300 reinforcements join us today, but we are still short of officers. We had a good dinner today, fried chops and vegetables followed by custard and jam, what a luxury. I am afraid our happy mess will have to be broken up as we have too many sergeants with the increase today. You would laugh, as I am writing this, the woman in the house is putting tucks in my shirt sleeves, I received a new shirt but the sleeves are too long. It is a miserable day so I wrote a letter to Harold, Goodnight and God bless you my love. xxxx

Friday 13 November 1914: Merris France

I arose at 5:30 a.m. to a cold winter day, raining and sleet, no parade today we are fitting the men up with new equipment and heard that we have got to be ready to move by 7:00 a.m. tomorrow. It is still raining hard and thankfully I have been given a new suit, putties, underclothes, and cigarettes. We have seen the article in the papers about the 2nd Battalion Royal Warwickshire Regiment and Colonel Loring's death in the battle of 24 October 1914, how proud we all feel. I'll bet Edith is proud, but when I think of our old regiment and what has become of them, I could cry, but still we are proud men. We have had some more reinforcements join us and four gentlemen from the Artists Corp join as officers.[13] It's still raining and cold, so Goodnight and God bless you my love. xxxxx

Saturday 14 November 1914: Merris France

At 4:30 a.m. I arose to an awful bustle as men prepared to march off at 8:00 a.m., it's very cold and raining. Our battalion marched about 10 miles (16 kilometres) to a place called Sailly, we passed through some villages and it was shameful to see the church ruins, blown to pieces by artillery guns. We are relieving the 19 Brigade but I would have liked to have stopped at Merris until after Sunday so that we could have had a church parade. We can hear the guns and passed a lot of French troops on the way, stopped in a field for about two hours, then moved off again at 4:00 p.m. walking a further 5 miles (8 kilometres)) across clay fields to the front line trenches. We missed the doctor in the trenches and so we came back on to the road and into a farm house where I met a sergeant of the Yorkshire Regiment, he said their time here was very quiet, I hope we have a similar experience. Goodnight and God bless you my love. xxxxx

Sunday 15 November 1914: Fleurbaix

I was up in the night to draw rations, I couldn't sleep much on account of the bitter cold and we haven't any blankets to keep us warm. It is snowing and the snipers are on the go again as we went out to dig dug-outs just below the farm in case we were shelled. We seem to get a good supply of cigarettes and matches now, helps to keep us going. We had one man killed yesterday and four wounded today. It is awful cold, wet and miserable, went to bed at 10:30 p.m. Goodnight and God bless you my love. xxx

Monday 16 November 1914: Fleurbaix

I have been up most of the night with one or another casualty coming in but managed to get our wounded away about 6:30 a.m., it is still raining and the snipers are still targeting us killing one of our men today, I only gave him a drink of tea a few hours before. We had some shells pass right over us and into a village beyond setting fire to a house. Again we went out digging dug-outs for dressing stations and had eight wounded today. Off to bed at 10:30 p.m. Goodnight and God bless you my love. xxxxx

13   TNA WO 95/1664/3: 2nd Battalion Royal Warwickshire Regiment War Diary, 13 November 1914: The officers on probation from the Artist Corps were; Lieutenant B A Standing; Lieutenant P F W Herbage; Lieutenant V V Pearce; Lieutenant G B Monk.

Tuesday 17 November 1914: Fleurbaix

I was up most of the night again tending the wounded, I never seem to get a good night's rest. The weather is very bleak and a lot of big guns are firing but luckily not our way, this is a lot better than what we have been used to. I had a letter from Edith today and heard that Corporal Sydenham has been captured and poor young Ted had died, I replied and hope that my sister will bear up with God's help. We heard today that Lord Robert died of pneumonia at St. Omer, France, on 14 November 1914, I am full of sadness for I served under him during the Second Boer War and the Royal Warwickshire Regiment rode with him on the advance to Johannesburg in 1900. Edith says she has sent me the muffler that Marjorie made and cigarettes so I expect I shall get them in the mail delivery and I shall prize them. There is a lot of firing going on here when it gets dark and that is when our men get hit, we had two wounded today. I am off to bed at 9:49 p.m. hoping I get a good night's sleep. Goodnight and God bless you my love. xxxxxx

Wednesday 18 November 1914: Fleurbaix

I slept well last night and was awaken at 4:00 a.m. to send stretcher bearers out to recover a wounded man. They couldn't bring the man in as he was making an awful row and they were told to leave him because our trenches are only 150 yards (137 metres) from the enemy, so they bandaged him up and left him until later. It is very cold again today, nothing much doing but we recovered three wounded men. Goodnight and God bless you my love. xxxxx

Thursday 19 November 1914: Fleurbaix

I had a good night's rest and again today it is very cold, our feet are in a terrible condition. Edith asked me in her letter if I would like a fountain pen for Xmas, so I am writing back to say I would. It was prophesied that the war would finish today, it doesn't seem likely as the big guns were firing away all night, also terrific rifle fire. It has been snowing all day long, freezing cold and the snow is laying on the ground. It has been quiet today, wrote to Edith and sent her an account of our clearing the wood on 24 October 1914. I have read the newspaper article about Lord Roberts' death, how sorry the men are and I feel very sad. We are having some good feeds now, Private Black is the cook and we get some fowl and pig to eat. The doctor asked us where we got them from, and I told him they came in and surrendered. An order has been given out that nothing is to be taken, but the farms are deserted so I don't see anything wrong. I am off to bed early so Goodnight and God bless you my love. xxxxx

Friday 20 November 1914: Fleurbaix

I was awaked during the night to attend a wounded man with a finger blown off, and I suffered tooth ache all night and all day today. We were relieved by the 2nd Queen's Regiment at 7:00 p.m. tonight and moved to billets in a village called Rue de Batrille, it was 5 miles (8 kilometres) back and it was awful walking the snow covered roads, we were sliding all over the place. We arrived at our billet at 9:00 p.m., a barn, not as good as we left, but a relief for the men in the trenches. We recovered one wounded man today. Goodnight and God bless you my love. xxxx

War Diary:
'Splendid Hotel' Boulogne Hospital November–December 1914

Saturday 21 November 1914: Fleurbaix

Having suffered all night with terrible tooth ache, I reported sick to the Regimental Doctor who sent me to see Second Lieutenant Monk, our regimental Dental Surgeon. Second Lieutenant Monk received a commission from the Artists Corp[14] and was a Dental Surgeon in civil life. He thought I would have to have my teeth removed and would need to travel tonight by field ambulance to Sailly. The journey was about 5 miles (8 kilometres), it was awful cold and we got there about 9:15 p.m. Many of our men are suffering with frost bitten feet and I saw Sergeant Gibson of the RAMC, I had met him before. They gave me some hot soup which was very welcome, then I opened a parcel from Edith with the muffler and cigarettes that she promised and put the muffler on straight away. Goodnight and God bless you my love. xxxx

Sunday 22 November 1914: Outside Sailly

I awoke at 5:20 a.m. after the best night sleep I have had for some time. The doctor saw me and said I would have to go and have my teeth seen to by a specialist. I saw Sergeant Fraser, Hutchings and others of the RAMC that I knew, they were working. A Red Cross motor car came to fetch me and the doctor, who is a civilian, gave me a bar of chocolate to eat and took me to a big town where I boarded a train, I don't know where I am going, but I think I will be away for several days. We picked some more men up further down the line and a Sister came round in the train and gave us all cigarettes and beef tea, we arrived in Boulogne at 10:16 p.m. We were put into a motor ambulance and taken to a hospital, what a treat to be in a good bed and able to

---

14   The Artists Rifles was a popular unit for volunteers. Having been increased to 12 companies in 1900, it was formed into three sub-battalions in 1914, and recruitment was eventually restricted by recommendation from existing members of the battalion. It particularly attracted recruits from public schools and universities; on this basis, following the outbreak of the First World War, a number of enlisted members of The Artists Rifles were selected to be officers in other units of 7th Division.

sleep without any fear of a 'Jack Johnson' or shrapnel bomb landing on us. I went to bed at 1:00 a.m. Good Morning and God bless you love. xxxx

Monday 23 November 1914: Boulogne Base

It was glorious to be able to sleep with my clothes off and I got out of bed at 6:45 a.m. following a good night's rest. I slept in a room with Sergeant Juby of my regiment and a wounded German prisoner of war, they asked us to look after him. You would think by the way they crowded around him that they hadn't seen a prisoner before, he gave me a button for a souvenir. The doctor came round and he wrote 'W' on my diet sheet, I don't know what that means. Fancy, it is only one and a half hours sailing to England, how tempting. Lieutenant Criton of the RAMC is here, this is a very large hotel converted into a hospital and it is called the 'Splendid Hotel.' Some of the men have returned to England and some have gone to a convalescent camp, I wonder where I will be going? I shall write a letter to Edith as soon as I know, so Goodnight and God bless you my love. xxxx

Tuesday 24 November 1914: Boulogne Base Hospital

Another good night's rest, it is a luxury to be able to sleep in a comfortable bed and get up at 7:00 a.m. I bought the latest edition of a London evening paper for one and a half pennies, but it was worth it. I saw an incident today which I shall always remember, a French woman was scrubbing the rooms out when the German prisoner walked passed her; she immediately pulled herself away from him and the look of hate in her eyes I shall never forget. Later in the day I was disappointed to be sent to the convalescent camp about one and a half miles away, it was under canvas. I am off to bed on the floor, it is bitter cold, so Goodnight and God bless you love. xxxx

Wednesday 25 November 1914: Boulogne Convalescent Camp

Arose at 7:00 a.m., it poured with rain in the night, went on parade for roll call at 7:20 a.m. and saw the doctor at 9:30 a.m. He simply asked me 'what was the matter.' I would rather be back with my regiment, even though they are in the trenches. I think it is a shame, hardly any of the men have been examined by a doctor since we came down country and some of the men can hardly walk. I shall wait another day before I write to Edith and then perhaps I can tell her something definite, off to bed early, I am thinking of you at 9:00 p.m. Goodnight and God bless you love. xxxx

Thursday 26 November 1914: Boulogne Convalescent Camp

Arose at 7:00 a.m. and parade as usual. I went and saw the doctor this morning to see if they are going to do anything to my teeth to ease the pain. I told him that I would rather be back with my regiment than hanging about here doing nothing. Later in the day I went for a two and a half mile walk and visited a large monument that marked the place where Napoleon gathered his troops to make his attack on England, the other side is a monastery, the monks burnt it down when this war commenced. I sent a post card to Edith, I want to know what they are going to do before I write, so Goodnight and God bless you love. xxxx

Friday 27 November 1914: Boulogne Convalescent Camp

After morning parade I went to see the doctor again, he asked me how I was, so I told him I only wanted my teeth fixed and then I would go back to my regiment. He said there wasn't any dentist here but I could stop here on a staff billet. I told him I didn't want that, I only want my teeth done, he replied, he would send me to Base Camp today. We went down to what they called Base Camp, it is just outside the town of Boulogne. We walked through Boulogne which is a very nice place, I fancied I was in England. You would laugh, we are billeted in a place they are building for burning rubbish, it is only half completed, needless to say, it is a bit drafty, what homes we do get to sleep in. Goodnight and God bless you love. xxxx

Saturday 28 November 1914: Boulogne Convalescent Camp

Arose at 8:00 a.m. after a good night's sleep, went for a walk for about two hours, then saw the doctor who sent me to see the dentist, 2 miles (3.2 kilometres) away. He is a splendid man for extracting teeth, he was taking the men's teeth out like lightning. I have to go again on Monday and he is going to kill the nerves and fill the teeth. I wrote to Edith today, I bet she is surprised to get a letter from here. Goodnight and God bless you love. xxxx

Sunday 29 November 1914: Boulogne Base

We are having a very easy time here, went to an English Church this morning, it was good to go to church. We had to go into the centre of Boulogne and on the way a small French boy caught hold of my hand and wouldn't let go, he walked with me for about a half mile. There is a night watchman at the building we are billeted in tonight and he invited another Sergeant and myself to his room and gave us tea, but it was amusing, he couldn't speak English and we couldn't speak French, but we manage to get along alright. Goodnight and God bless you love. xxxx

Monday 30 November 1914: Boulogne Convalescent Camp

Arose at 8:00 a.m. and went to see the dentist, he took one of my nerves out, it pained a bit, he said to me 'I bet you have suffered with this one.' I have got to go tomorrow and he is going to treat the other tooth. I had orders to report to the major in command of the Sanitary Section and he wanted to employ me in the office. I told him plainly, I want to get back to my old regiment. King George V came here today and it rained all day. Goodnight and God bless you my love. xxxx

Tuesday 1 December 1914: Boulogne Base

Arose at 6:00 a.m. for parade at 7:00 a.m. I feel miserable and want to get back to my regiment, I don't know what to do with myself. I went to the dentist and he put some more stuff in my tooth, he wouldn't touch the other one as he thinks it was the one he took the nerve out affecting the others. It's raining hard so I went to see Sergeant Goble this evening. Goodnight and God bless you my love xxxx

Wednesday 2 December 1914: Boulogne Base

Today I saw Captain Wright our Regimental Medical Officer, he was going on leave to England with the regiments Non Commissioned Officers (NCO's) and I am deprived of my leave because I had to come and have my teeth done. I would have tolerated the pain for another month if I had thought leave was coming. I saw the Major in charge here this afternoon and I asked him to send me straight back to my regiment. The Major said he couldn't send me straight back but would send me to the Base, and would give me details tomorrow. Goodnight and God bless you love. xxxx

Thursday 3 December to Sunday 6 December 1914: Boulogne Base

After morning parade I went to Base and reported to the doctor. I told him, if he would send me home on leave I would pay for my teeth. He told me to make out an application for leave, and he would sign it tomorrow, saying it would benefit me to go to England to have my teeth fixed. On Saturday my application for leave came back and the Base Commander told me I had to see the dentist here, but I am still going to try to get my leave so that I can see Edith again. On Sunday I received ten Francs pay in the morning, then went to church where the Bishop of Khartoum delivered the sermon. Later I went to the Soldiers Home and to church in the evening. Goodnight and God bless you love. xxxx

Monday 7 December 1914: Boulogne Base

I saw the doctor this morning and I have to go to the dentist tomorrow morning and that will decide if I go on leave or back to the front line. It has been raining hard again today, my thoughts are with our men in the trenches and how uncomfortable they must feel. Yesterday we had 1 man killed and 5 wounded in the Fleurbaix trenches. Goodnight and God bless you love. xxxx

Tuesday 8 December 1914: Boulogne Base

The dentist told me today that he couldn't recommend me to go home as he wasn't allowed to, so he is stopping one of my teeth. I asked him to send me back to the front, it is hard for I thought I was going to see you love. I went to a meeting to help form a Masonic Lodge.[15] They asked me to take the chair, it was just like old times, I made a proposal that it should be called 'The Hope of the Field,' it was carried. The meeting was held in the English Wesleyan Chapel and the Minister is going to join. Goodnight and God bless you love. xxx

Wednesday 9 December 1914: Boulogne Base

Routine as usual, I went to the dentist and he took the stopping out on my tooth and put some more in. Jim Cusack was sent up to me this morning with a parcel from Edith, it was good to see someone from home, he told me about Edith and Marjorie. I am back to the front tomorrow to join my regiment and so I spent a couple of happy hours with him, he was sorry I was leaving and wanted to load me with all sorts of things, but I couldn't carry them. A sergeant of the Royal Artillery was there and he knew who was travelling to Rouen tomorrow so I shall have someone I know. Goodnight and God bless you my love. xxxx

Thursday 10 December 1914: Abbeville

Awoke at 6:00 a.m. and after parade I caught the 7:15 a.m. train to Abbeville where I had to change trains but it was difficult to find which train went to Rouen, I couldn't talk French and the officials couldn't talk English. At last I found the Divisional Road Transport office who told me to go by the 12:55 p.m. train to Rouen, but it was too full and so I had to travel with my party by a supply train in a truck, it was awful cold and the journey was uncomfortable as the truck jogged along the roadway. Goodnight and God bless you my love. xxxx

Friday 11 December 1914: Rouen

We arrived in Rouen at 4:00 a.m. and stopped in the truck till 7:00 a.m., made tea and had to parade at the Divisional Road Transport office for instructions. A guide took us up to the camp which was about 3 miles (5 kilometres) away, what a surprise, I found Cudly, Turfy Smith, Wilken Widwood, and a lot of men from my regiment. It was raining hard so I spent the day with Cudly and we went to see Billy Weaver on guard. Goodnight and God bless you my love. xxxx

15   A Masonic Lodge is the basic institution of Freemasonry.

Saturday 12 December[16] to Thursday 24 December 1914: Rouen

Arose at 7:00 a.m. on Saturday, awful wet day, received twenty Francs pay and had a yarn with Billy Weaver. On Sunday I went to church, it was raining all day and we went digging and cleaning the camp of mud. The next two weeks were very boring spent mostly on fatigue duty or on standby with the reinforcement party, I shall be glad to get back to my regiment and return to my duties. On Tuesday 22 December 1914 we heard that our commanding officer Major R H W Brewis[17] and Captain Brownfield[18] were killed on 18 December 1914, Lieutenant Mark Campbell and

16   TNA WO 95/1664/3: 2nd Battalion Royal Warwickshire Regiment War Diary, 12 December 1914: The battalion strength had been restored to 22 officers and 939 other ranks.

17   Atkinson, *The Seventh Division,* pp. 118–122: The first fortnight of December 1914 was rather quiet for the 7th Division, the ground was getting waterlogged and much had to be done to drain and improve the trenches. The strength of the 7th Division rose gradually, not only through the arrival of drafts, but from the addition of new units. During December 156 officers and 5,111 men joined the 7th Division; battle casualties came to 36 officers and 1,079 men and total wastage to 77 officers and 2,775 men, a net gain of nearly 1,500 of all ranks. Most of the casualties occurred on the night of 18/19 December 1914 when the 7th Division attacked the German trenches in an attempt to recover the Messines Ridge. The points selected for the 7th Division's attacks were near La Boutillerie and Rouges Bancs. At first the Warwickshires, supported by the Queen's, were to attack at 4:30 p.m. on 18 December, their attack being preceded by a quarter of an hour's artillery bombardment. It was to be followed at 6:00 p.m. by the 20 Brigade's attack using the Scots Guards and the Borders and then, if this attack was successful, the 21 Brigade would follow with the Yorkshires leading. The 22 Brigade was attacking just west of the pronounced salient in its lines at Well Farm near La Boutillerie. The Warwickshires were to form up in these lines on a front of 200 yards and advance on the close of the bombardment, the Queen's and South Staffordshires opening covering fire as they went forward. By 4:30 p.m. on 18 December 1914 it was practically dark and it became impossible to know what was happening; all that was known was that the Warwickshires had gone forward resolutely in face of a very heavy fire from rifles and machine-guns and had been lost to sight in the dark. About 5:00 p.m., however, their NCO came back and reported that the Warwickshires were held up short of the German trenches, had lost heavily and needed reinforcements. A company of the Queen's and two other platoons went forward to help, but the bombardment had inflicted little damage on the German wire and had not prevented them from manning their parapets in force and opening a heavy fire directly on our troops as they got near. Major R H W Brewis was killed at the head of his Warwickshire Regiment within a few yards of the German wire, and several other officers were shot down close to him trying to work their way through the wire. The losses had been heavy: besides Major Brewis the Royal Warwickshire Regiment had 8 officers and over 300 men killed, wounded and missing.

18   TNA WO 95/1664/3: 2nd Battalion Royal Warwickshire Regiment War Diary, 18 December 1914: The battalion was ordered to advance in three lines at 4:30 p.m. on 18 December 1914 to attack and take the German Trenches that were in front of Le Malsnil. The attack was proceeded by a heavy artillery bombardment by our artillery to which the enemy made hardly any reply. The attack was started by B Company 2nd Battalion

another officer wounded, but we have not heard how many casualties in the rank and file, our poor regiment. On 24 December 1914 I received orders to return to my regiment at 5:30 a.m. Goodnight and God bless you love. xxxx

Royal Warwickshire Regiment on the right led by Captain Haddon, advancing in two lines. A company advanced on the left in two lines with D Company in the centre. C Company formed the third line with entrenching tools. A machine-gun was on each flank. Immediately the attack was started the enemy opened a very heavy rifle and machine-gun fire. The battalion advanced under this with steadiness and suffered very heavy casualties. The 2nd Queen's sent a company in support and although our dead were found only a few yards from the German trenches, the attack failed to achieve its objective. What remained of the battalion subsequently retired into our trenches. Shortly after daylight the enemy came out and started examining our dead. Parties went out of our line and buried some of the officers and collected disc from some of the men killed. Owing to two officers of the Queen's and several small parties of the battalion when engaged in carrying our wounded from the enemy's lines being made prisoners, and also owing to Lieutenant Bower, South Staffordshire Regiment being killed while helping to collect our wounded, the informal armistice terminated. Lieutenant Colonel Brewis was found killed about 40 yards (36 metres) from the enemy's line. Captain Brownfield, Lieutenants Monk, Tucker, Campbell and Bert together with 34 men were found a few yards from a German machine-gun. From evidence available, it is apparent that Captain Brownfield though previously wounded continued to lead the attack on the gun. On the morning of 19 December 1914, the battalion mustered in the trenches, their strength reduced to 149 NCOs and men. The 2nd Queen's Regiment, who had come in on support the previous day, remained to occupy the line. Casualties were officers killed: – Lt. Col. Brewis; Captains Hodsson and Bromfield; Lt. Bernard; Second Lieutenants Monk, Tucker, Campbell, Standling, Pearce; Officers wounded: Captain Mulgrue; Lieutenant Richardson; Officers missing: Captain Haddon (POW; other Ranks: 96 killed, 91 wounded, 109 missing. Lieutenant Colonel Brewis and Second Lieutenant Standling are buried in Sailly Churchyard.

War Diary:
Christmas in the trenches December 1914

Friday 25 December 1914: Merville

We left Rouen on Christmas Eve and travelled all night in cattle trucks, 40 men in each truck, it was very uncomfortable and my feet were very cold and painful. On Christmas morning[19] we sang a song called 'Christian Awake' and silently remembered our family and friends at home. We reached Merville at 2:30 p.m. and brewed tea in a field, then we marched to our billets in a nearby barn. My feet were very swollen and I could hardly walk. Goodnight and God bless you my love. xxxx

Saturday 26 December 1914: Merville

At 6:00 a.m. we marched to meet our regiment about a half mile (0.8 kilometres) down the road, the stretcher bearers were glad to see me back but gave me some terrible news. Last Friday 18 November 1914 they made a night attack on the German Trenches at Messines Ridge and casualties were very high with 8 officers including Lieutenant Rellie and 375[20] men killed, wounded or missing. I believe it was hell for the men and I am glad to be back with my regiment. I had a few letters, cards and a parcel for Christmas from my family and friends. Goodnight and God bless you my love. xxxx

27 December 1914: Merville

We were awaken at 11:30 p.m. last night by very heavy artillery fire, we went up to our old trenches expecting an attack quite like the old times. At 3:30 p.m. we marched

---

19 Atkinson, *The Seventh Division*, p. 126: An informal armistice, started by mutual consent on the morning of 25 December 1914 and continuing till the next afternoon, did not meet with approval in higher quarters and its repetition was forbidden in the future. It did, however, afford the opportunity for burying and identifying many of those killed in the attack of 18 December 1914.

20 This figure includes men missing temporarily, hence higher than the 300 men mentioned in the earlier footnote.

back with the German artillery still firing shells at us but there was no attack. The Germans were firing star shells and when they explode in the sky, a star appears followed by a brilliant light which illuminates the countryside just like daylight. It is another very cold day, the ice is thawing, but thankfully we saw no action. I forgot to mention yesterday that my Cousin Arthur Bench of the 1st Battalion Royal Warwickshire Regiment came to see me, I was surprised to see how tall he had grown. Goodnight and God bless you my love. xxxx

Monday 28 December 1914: Merville

Late last night a very heavy artillery bombardment started, we had to sleep with all our equipment on ready to go out again. At 6:00 a.m. we were assembled and ready to move out, it was raining hard and it continued all day. I went round with the doctor to see which men wanted to be inoculated. At 4:00 p.m. we received orders to move to the reserve trenches and moved off at 5:00 p.m., still raining and blowing a gale. I wrote to my wife Edith today, and received the Princess Mary Xmas gift.[21] Goodnight and God bless you my love. xxx

Tuesday 29 December 1914: Merville

Last night we had a violent storm, strong winds and heavy rain flooded the low lying trenches, in places to a depth of two feet (0.6 metres) or more. Many of the communication trenches were so bad with mud and water that the men had to risk the snipers to go above ground. There was heavy artillery fire this morning but during the day the weather cleared up and the firing ceased. We have cut a lot of new trenches today, a proper maize, and they have called them by names like Maconi Lodge and Charing Cross. It's a moonlight night and I received a Christmas card from my brothers Jim and Harry. Goodnight and God bless you my loved ones. xxxx

Wednesday 30 December 1914: Merville

Today the Germans were shelling the road that D Company were walking along and a shell dropped on the rear of the company killing 2 men and wounding 7 others. Casualties would have been greater if the shell had struck the centre of the company. Goodnight and God bless you my loved ones. xxxx

21   The British soldiers received a Royal gift from Princess Mary containing cigarettes or pipe tobacco and chocolate for non-smokers.

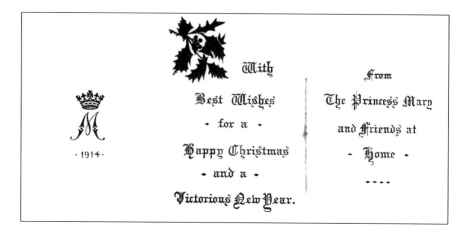

7 Princess Mary's Christmas card sent to the British troops.

Thursday 31 December 1914: Merville

I had a good night's sleep and awoke to a very wet and windy day with the big guns firing on our right. Today I received a parcel of cigarettes from some little school children from Copenhurst School in Chester with a letter from Linda Mckee. I answered it and also wrote to my mother. Goodnight and God bless you my loved ones. xxxx

War Diary:
Trench warfare in winter January–March 1915

Friday 1 January 1915: Merville

After a good night's rest I awoke to a cold winter morning. We had 76 become sick this morning, in the afternoon Corporal Crisp and I walked about 5 miles (8 kilometres) to Sailly to get a fresh supply of tablets. I met Sergeant Frash, on the way back it started to rain and a very strong wind blew against us making it difficult to walk. We arrived home about 6:30 p.m. drenched to the skin and very tired. The trenches are in a fearful state, full of water and the mud is knee deep. The Germans are sending those star shells up on our right and heavy gun fire has started, they are frightened of the Gurkhas[22] creeping up to them in the night. I received a letter from Edith, so Goodnight and God bless you my loved ones. xxxx

Saturday 2 January 1915: Merville

About 11:00 a.m. last night one of our officers came back from the trenches, he had been lying in a trench which was half full of water, when he tried to get out the Germans were sniping at him, keeping him pinned down for hours. We managed to give him a dry shirt, drawers, socks and body belt, he stayed all night with us while we dried his clothes. I did feel sorry for him, he was shivering uncontrollably so I rubbed him down with a towel. It rained torrents all the day, the trenches are in a fearful state, and the men are covered from head to foot in clay. I received a message to send aid to a man who was hit in the stomach, I sent Lance Corporal Gumbly, he bandaged him up, but we are unable to bring men down in the daytime. I received orders to send two stretchers up at dusk, the man hit in the stomach had died and another man had been hit with a hand grenade, my God what a wound, the doctor and I went to patch him

---

22 The sturdy little Gurkhas from the hill country of Nepal were tough fighters proud of their skill with their razor sharp kukris, a lethal weapon with a curved blade which they thought were better than any rifle. One favoured story told of a German soldier looking over the parapet just as a Gurkha crawled up. The kukri swished and the German sneered and said, "You missed, Gurkha." The Gurkha replied "You wait German, until you try to nod your head!" This summed up the spirit and character of these tough hill men from Nepal.

up, he had a compound fracture of the leg. The doctor told me that he would have to remove his leg, so we didn't finish work until 10:00 p.m. I had a letter from Edith and my daughter Marjorie which I read before going to bed. Goodnight and God bless you my loved ones. xxx

Sunday 3 January 1915: Merville

It is a fearful day, raining, windy and bitter cold. We had a man killed by the same grenade that wounded the other man yesterday at Wells Farm. Last night the French guns on the right started a very heavy bombardment at 11:00 p.m. and we found out that they were shelling the German ammunition column. The trenches are in a terrible state, the men are up to their knees in water, I had to send a stretcher out in these impossible conditions to retrieve a man from the Royal Engineers but he was dead when they brought him in. I wrote to Edith and Marjorie before I went to bed. Goodnight and God bless you my loved ones. xxxxxxx

Monday 4 January 1915: Merville

A sergeant from the Royal Engineers arrived at 5:30 a.m. to find out where we were going to bury their man, Crisp showed him and two of his men came and dug the grave. The Parson came about 1:00 p.m. and we buried him in a field by the side of four other artillery men, it was raining hard but we gave the poor man as good a burial as we possibly could. Just picture very heavy artillery fire, the dead Royal Engineer on a stretcher carried by four of our men, he was followed by two Royal Engineers, the doctor, myself and Private George. The doctor is Lieutenant Button and he is a fine gentleman, he sits with us in a room, reading and talking, he received a parcel from his young lady, he gave me a mince pie and told me that she had taken a first class prize in a cooking class. We have had a suspected case of enteric fever, so we had to clear the barn of straw and tomorrow we are going to disinfect it. Wrote to my sister Flo and my brother. Goodnight and God bless you my loved ones. xxxxxx

Tuesday 5 January 1915: Merville

Today we disinfected the barn which had been occupied by D Company on account of suspected enteric fever? We came out of the trenches and moved to reserve billets at Rue Delpierre, it's raining very hard and we had more reinforcements today. Sergeant Wicton joked with me about putting my request for furlough in at Rouen, but I had a laugh, he was due to go on leave the day after he received orders to come up here. Goodnight and God bless you my loved ones. xxxxx

Wednesday 6 January 1915: Merville

I have got an awful cold in the head which kept me awake all night long. It is raining again, the roads are ankle deep in mud and for the next four days we are in reserve billets at Rue Delpierre, about 2 miles (3.2 kilometres) from the trenches. I found two letters from Edith in our orderly room box, thanks to Sergeant Spencer. I wrote to Edith and will think of her at 9:00 p.m. tonight when she goes to her Lodge meeting. Goodnight and God bless you my loved ones. xxxxxx

Thursday 7 January 1915: Merville

A very wet morning raining torrents, the trenches are swamped. We had one man killed and one man wounded today, it was accidental, they sent for a stretcher and I ran up but was too late, he was shot through the brain. His name was Private Franks S/N 5798, I bandaged him up and we buried him in a field. We heard that the Germans brought two very big guns up and a man could sit in the muzzle to eat his dinner. I wrote to Flo and mother, had a parcel from Mrs Hall in Malta containing two body belts, four packets of socks and two packets of mitts, I gave a packet of socks and mitts to Black and Lieutenant Tillson. Goodnight and God bless you my loved ones. xxxxxx

Friday 8 January 1915: Merville

My cold is a lot better today so I went to see Sergeant Weaver at the house he is billeted in. When I went inside I noticed twin boys in a cradle and it made me think of our twin babies that we lost in Malta, so I had to rock them, then I sent my Princess Mary's gift to Mrs Hall, our friend who lives in Malta. Goodnight and God bless you my loved ones. xxxxxx

Saturday 9 January 1915: Merville

We had 94 men come in sick this morning and heard that Sergeant W Owen died on 24 December 1914 in hospital. We moved back to our reserve trenches at 4:30 p.m. in the rain and cold, the roads are flooded and the carts can't move, they are stuck in the mud. They have condemned our advanced dressing station, so our local one has become the advanced one. We tramped back through the water, our feet got wet very quickly and we finished up with B Company, then occupied a small house for seeing the sick. I must find a proper place for the sick and wounded tomorrow. I was walking down the road when three shrapnel shells went over my head, lucky for me I escaped the blast. Major H C Hart joined us today as the new Commanding Officer for the 2nd Battalion Royal Warwickshire Regiment and he recognised me. Goodnight and God bless you my loved ones. xxxxxx

Sunday 10 January 1915: Merville

Most of the night I lay awake after having a terrible dream that my daughter Marjorie was here but lost somewhere. In the house where I am staying there is a little girl that is the image of Marjorie and I think this made me dream of her. In the morning I went hunting for a billet for our stretcher bearers and at last I found a suitable house. I received a letter from mother and parcel from Edith with a cake, chocolates, fags, sweets, and a pocket book. I also received a reply to the letter that I wrote to the little school girl Linda McKee, she sent me a photograph of herself. Corporal Moon and Mason went on furlough today, roll on when it's my turn. Later I saw three little refugee children who had lost their mother and father, some other people were looking after them, they looked so sad. It rained all night and we had sent 350 men out on a working party repairing trenches. Goodnight and God bless you my loved ones. xxxx

Monday 11 January 1915: Merville

Had a good night's rest and awoke to a fine sunny day. Last night we had 1 man killed (he had 14 bullets in him) and 1 man wounded from our working party. The women here have told us that 240,000 English soldiers are gathered at Merville, less than 1 mile (1.6 kilometres) from here, we can see the town clearly across the countryside. We are sheltering in a house with a man who is the image of my brother Jim, he is up to all sorts of tricks and he makes us laugh. Goodnight and God bless you my loved ones. xxxxx

Tuesday 12 January 1915: Merville

We had a draft of 100 men this morning and they had just paraded for inspection when the Germans fired some 'Jack Johnsons' at our billets, we had to scatter quickly, it was a good start for them but no damage was done. In the house where I am stopping there are three women and two children, they were so frightened when the shells came over but, when they saw that I didn't move and no damage was done, they were alright. Goodnight and God bless you my loved ones. xxxxx

Wednesday 13 January 1915: Merville

We moved to the advanced trenches at 5:30 p.m. today to relieve the South Staffordshire Regiment, it is cold and wet, and the trenches are in an appalling state. I had a letter from Edith with a photograph of Marjorie, she is eight years old, I do miss them so. Goodnight and God bless you my loved ones. xxxx

Thursday 14 January 1915: Merville

At 10:30 a.m. the doctor told me to go and clean the barn out as we had a suspected case of enteric fever. We had just finished at 12:30 p.m. when the Germans started to fire 'Jack Johnson' at us, they dropped shells all around us, over the top of the house, in front and to the side, but thank God they never touched anyone. Further up the road they dropped a shell on a house and it killed one of the Royal Scots and wounded two of our men, one of them had half of his arm torn away. Up in the trenches we had 1 killed and 5 wounded but thank God I am alright. Goodnight and God bless you my loved ones. xxxx

Friday 15 January 1915: Merville

Last night I kept going until 11:30 p.m. taking care of the sick and wounded as they arrived, the last being an officer who came in sick. The Germans started shelling at 11:10 a.m. searching for one of our batteries. A little later a man came for a stretcher, they had a man hit in nine places with shrapnel, he was lucky to be just out of range of the full explosion. The doctor went up to the trenches and found men hit everywhere, one man killed, another one hit in four places, and one of our chap's was hit about twenty times, he was an awful sight. We got him to the dressing station, the doctor tried his utmost and worked hard to save him, but he died. Our casualty list for the day was 2 killed and 2 wounded. Goodnight and God bless you my loved ones. xxxxx

Saturday 16 January 1915: Merville

I woke up at 5:00 a.m. and went to bury the man with multiple shrapnel wounds at 9:00 a.m. but the Parson didn't arrive, so I waited. A messenger came down from the top dressing station to inform us that some men were hit so the doctor with all the stretcher bearers went up to help. Five men of the South Staffordshire Regiment were hit so they brought them down and just as they arrived, two 'Jack Johnsons' fell just by the house forcing us to move further up the road. We had to shift all the men and equipment, some poor men fell into a ditch full of water, so we had to strip them and I managed to get some of their clothes dry. At 4:10 p.m. the Parson still had not arrived so we buried the man, wrapped him up in a blanket and put him in the grave. I said the Lord's Prayer and as we were covering him in, the Parson arrived, I told him what I had done and he read the memorial service over him. Picture eight of us standing around one poor comrade with the Parson reading the service, it was nearly dark, raining and the coffin was half covered with fill. We couldn't do anything more for him and I hope I did my duty to him. Our casualties today were 2 wounded and 1 killed. Goodnight and God bless you my loved ones. xxxx

Sunday 17 January 1915: Merville

A very rough night in the trenches, wet and cold but quiet until 3:00 p.m. when the Germans started shelling our trenches. Our guns returned fire and knocked out one of the German guns, they replied but no damage was done. At dusk we came out of the trenches, relieved by the Queen's Regiment, and moved back to the local billets at Rue Delpierre to get some rest. Our casualties were 1 man killed and one man gassed during relief. Goodnight and God bless you my loved ones. xxxxx

Monday 18 January to Monday 25 January 1915: Fleurbaix

It is snowing this morning, large flakes of snow and very cold. We have to rub the men's feet and treat their open sores and blisters, they suffer Trench Foot[23] through standing in the wet trenches and their feet swell to twice the normal size. We had a draft of about fifty men from England, they were very welcome and will help to rebuild our regiment. On Wednesday I refereed a football match, it was wet and muddy but great to see the men relax after being in the trenches. The Queen's came out of the trenches on Thursday, they had been knee deep in mud. We have had some cases of enteric fever again, the arrival of a special Sanitary Section will help improve the conditions for the men. On Saturday a German aeroplane flew over and dropped bombs on us so our aeroplanes went after them and they cleared off. We have heard that our brigade will go down for a rest when we come out of the trenches the next time, probably on the 29 January 1915. On Sunday a man from the South Staffordshire Regiment came in with his nose broken and eye brow cut open, he said someone had thrown a stone at him (doubtful), I sent for the doctor, then I had to go down to D Company to treat a sick man. On Monday I went up to the trenches in the evening to check the men, there are still rumours of going down country on the 29 January 1915. Goodnight and God bless you love. xxxx

23   Trench Foot is a medical condition caused by cold, wet and insanitary conditions; affected feet may become numb, turn red or blue as a result of poor vascular circulation. Feet may begin to have a decaying odour due to the possibility of the early stages of necrosis setting in. As the condition worsens, feet may also begin to swell. Advanced trench foot often involves blisters and open sores leading to fungal infection. If left untreated, trench foot usually results in gangrene, which can cause the need for amputation. It can be prevented by keeping the feet clean, warm and dry. Application of whale oil was a standard army remedy.

Tuesday 26 January 1915: Fleurbaix

I never had a very good night's rest, rather cold, very quiet all morning. At 1:30 p.m. all our artillery started to shell the German trenches. I went up the artillery observation post to watch it and saw our shells bursting right over the German trenches. The Germans sent a few 'Weary Willies'[24] over but no damage was done. Later I had to send stretchers up to the trenches, we had 4 killed and 4 wounded in the afternoon. We heard that the Scots Guards had inflicted heavy losses on the Germans but became isolated and had to retire from their trenches. Goodnight and God bless you my loved ones. xxxx

Wednesday 27 January to Sunday 31 January 1915: Fleurbaix[25]

At 6:00 a.m. this morning our artillery bombarded the Germans, they did not reply. Tonight we buried Lance Corporal Haas and the other men from my Regiment who were killed yesterday, the Reverend Peel came up and conducted the service. We had one man from A Regiment killed today and we heard that Sergeant Reeves had been awarded the DCM. Our doctor had a narrow escape today, the German snipers had a go at him and he had a bit of skin knocked off one of his fingers. I thought we would be relieved today Friday 29 January 1915 but I don't think we will. We had 1 killed and 1 wounded today, we got back to our billets at 7:30 p.m. and found Frank O'Dell waiting for us from the 1st Battalion, who came to see us. It has started to snow and I have a fearful headache. A draft of 60 arrived on Saturday but they consisted mainly of old men. Our regiment played a league football match with the Northumberland Hussars and drew two goals each. I awoke on Sunday after a good night sleep to

24 A 'Weary Willie' is a German shell passing safely, albeit rather slowly, overhead. The expression was first used in 1914, from a pre-war *Comic Cuts* character of the same name.

25 Atkinson, *The Seventh Division*, pp. 126–128: Trench Warfare, Well Farm near La Boutillerie: January 1915 saw little change in the situation except that the water problem grew increasingly serious. Trenches and dug-outs filled with water and, by the end of the first week of January 1915, half the original trenches had been abandoned. It was decided to start constructing posts on areas of high ground in the rear for use in case floods should compel the evacuation of the front line. By damming short stretches of trenches and pumping vigorously it was possible to maintain garrisons in parts of the front line. By heightening the parapet and constructing wooden platforms above the water level, these garrisons could be kept more or less out of water. However, on the whole the labour devoted to fighting the water was wasted and would have been better spent on the construction of breastworks, which proved satisfactory. With so much water about a serious attack was out of the question and, even patrol activity was much reduced. The month of January passed away and with little activity for the division, the casualties were reduced to 2 officers and 68 men killed, 6 officers and 193 men wounded and 1 officer missing. However, the sick-list of 33 officers and 1,613 men admitted to hospital proved conclusively that the weather and conditions of the trenches had caused more serious wastage than the enemy.

a very cold morning, it was snowing. We played a football match with 21st Field Ambulance, it was awful muddy and we had just started the second half when we received an order for everyone to stand too. Just picture playing football with the big guns firing and all you can hear is the whiz of the shells. Goodnight and God bless you my loved ones. xxxx

Monday 1 February 1915: Fleurbaix

Our Regiment played the RAMC in the divisional league at football and won 1-0, it was strange watching a football match and hearing the whizzing of the shrapnel shells bursting about 100 yards (91 metres) away. My cousin Arthur Bench came over from the 1st Division Royal Warwickshire Regiment to see me, Culman went on furlough. Goodnight and God bless you my loved ones. xxxx

Tuesday 2 February 1915: Bois Grenier trenches

Last night at 11:30 p.m. our Artillery started to fire very rapidly and we learnt that the 8th Royal Scots are unfit for the trenches. At 5:45 p.m. we moved to new trenches to relieve the 1st Battalion Royal Welch Fusiliers, they were further away from Fleurbaix towards the left. It is a cold wet night, the wind is howling and we have secured a school for a dressing station. Goodnight and God bless you my loved ones. xxxx

Wednesday 3 February to Sunday 14 February 1915: Bois Grenier trenches

I hardly slept a wink last night, I had an awful headache and felt poorly all the morning. Our artillery continues to bombard the German defences and I went through our trenches to remove the sick and injured men. On the morning of Thursday 4 February 1915 our artillery bombarded the Germans and they replied shelling right down the road. Later in the day I went up to treat the sick and had just returned to the dressing station when another German bombardment commenced and our artillery replied, it was just like hell for about three quarters of an hour. One of our men was badly hit in the head and as I was treating him shells were dropping close to us shaking the panes of glass out. They were shelling our transport and hit one man, I went up with the doctor to see if there were any other men wounded men, but there were none from this shelling. Our total casualties today were 1 man killed and 3 men wounded. One of the wounded, Private Ive, had 16 shrapnel wounds. I received several parcels and letters from Edith and my family and replied to them before retiring for the night. On Friday 5 February 1914 the Germans were very quiet but our artillery continued to bombard them. We move back into billets at Rue Bataille tomorrow night. Private Pitt S/N 8747 was shot at 7:30 a.m. on Monday 8 February 1915 for desertion. On Tuesday 9 February 1915 we played a football match in the rain with the 22nd Field Ambulance, we lost 2-1. We had General's inspection on Wednesday morning and moved back to the trenches at Bois Grenier around 6:00 p.m. to relieve the 1st Battalion Royal

Welch Fusiliers. On Friday 12 February 1915 the Germans dropped a shell into our Headquarters but there was little damage. The German bombardment continued on Saturday and Sunday, apart from the shelling things were quiet in the trenches. Our casualties on Saturday 13 February 1915 were 4 men killed and 2 men wounded, we buried the dead on Sunday 14 February 1915 at 7.00 a.m. The Parson stood in between the graves and read the burial service, it was raining and very windy. We expected a night attack but nothing turned up, however, we hear the bombardment of Le Basse every day, it is a short distance across the countryside. We were relieved by the Welch Fusiliers and moved out of the trenches back to our billets at 5:30 a.m. on Monday 15th, an old billet at Rue Delpierre, we are all tired out. Good morning and God bless you my loved ones. xxxx

Monday 15 February to Friday 19 February 1915: La Roulette

I never went to bed, we arrived at our billet too late on Monday morning and the big guns continue to fire all day long. It is a wet and cold morning and our doctor came off leave last night so I had to meet with him. On Tuesday 16 February 1915 we had a draft of thirty men arrive and a Canadian Regiment has arrived at Fleurbaix. On Wednesday the big guns were firing all night, a very heavy bombardment towards Le Basse and we heard that the troops there have advanced 4 miles (6.5 kilometres). Thursday was a cold day and the Germans have been shelling all round us, they dropped three little 'Weary Willies' on our football pitch at Fleurbaix breaking our cross bar on the goal post. We move out of our billets at 2:00 a.m. on Friday morning and arrived at the Bois Grenier trenches at 3:00 a.m. to relieve the Royal Welch Fusiliers. I had one hour of sleep but awoke with an awful headache due to the heavy shelling, we had one man wounded. Goodnight and God bless you my loved ones. xxxxxxxx

Saturday 20 February 1915: Bois Grenier trenches

Last night about 10:30 p.m. the German artillery started shelling again. At 6:30 a.m. this morning Corporal Crisp came down and said a dug out had fallen in and buried some of our men. We all went up and found three men unconscious and two men semi-conscious. We sent the latter down to the dressing station and we started artificial respiration on the other three. We worked for three and a half hours but couldn't save them, we were awful distressed and downhearted over it. The shelling continued all day so we buried the men at night, picture us, a moonlight night and eight of us standing around three graves with the Parson saying the burial service by memory. It was awful sad, we were filling the graves in when the shells started to fall around us forcing us to run for cover, but we went back and finished our work. We had some Canadian Artillery Officers join us today observing the enemy lines. In the evening I wrote post cards to Edith and my mother. Goodnight and God bless you my loved ones. xxx

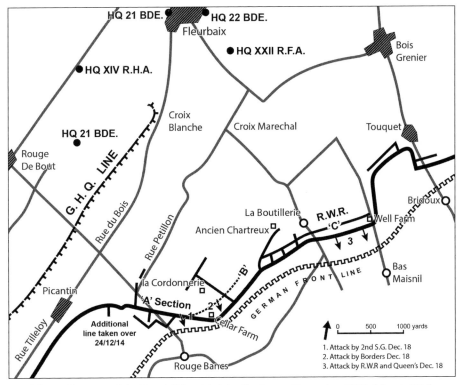

Map 6 Position of the Royal Warwickshire Regiment November 1914–March 1915.

Sunday 21 February 1915: Bois Grenier trenches

Had a good night's sleep, frosty and cold this morning, a very thick mist and very quiet. The Canadian Officers lectured our artillery men on the new shrapnel shells and they exploded one as an experiment, but it only just blew the shrapnel out, we picked some of it up. About 9:30 p.m. last night an awful bombardment of German artillery guns and rifle fire started and I am waiting to see if there are any wounded. Casualties for today are 2 men killed, one from the artillery and one from our regiment. Had a letter from Edith and a parcel of books from Mr Stebbing. Goodnight and God bless you my loved ones. xxxxx

Monday 22 February 1915: Bois Grenier trenches

I got to bed at 12:30 a.m. and was up at 5:30 a.m. to a very cold and misty morning. We buried our comrades at 3:00 p.m. today and moved back to our Rue Bataille billet at 8:00 p.m. dead tired so I am off to bed. Goodnight and God bless you my loved ones. xxxx

Tuesday 23 February to Friday 26 February 1915: Rue Bataille

We were on the go all day long tending the sick and wounded, assisted by stretcher bearers Wilkins, Underwood and Lumer. I met Dick Smith with the Canadian Scottish Regiment and we had another draft of 40 men arrive. It was very quiet for the next few days giving us a welcomed break from the incessant shelling, but returned to the Bois Grenier trenches on Friday night. Goodnight and God bless you my loved ones. xxxxxxx

Saturday 27 February 1915: Bois Grenier trenches

I was awaken at 2:45 a.m. to attend to a man who was shot in A Company trench, sent the stretcher bearers to pick him up and he was brought in at 3:30 a.m. I sat up with him all night, he was shot in the abdomen. I must have caught a cold in my eyes through jumping straight out of bed and going out into the cold night air. I heard that we move out of the trenches on Monday night and go back for rest, our place is being taken over by the Canadians. Goodnight and God bless you my loved ones. xxxxxxx

Sunday 28 February 1915: Bois Grenier trenches[26]

The Germans shelled our position all night hitting the house in front of us, we were lucky to escape, only one man wounded. The Colonel of the Canadians came tonight to take over, we are being relieved tomorrow. Goodnight and God bless you my loved ones. xxxx

Monday 1 March 1915: Fleurbaix

The Canadians[27] relieved us at 7:00 p.m. tonight and we reached our billets at 9:00 p.m. The Germans dropped some heavy shells in Fleurbaix today which killed 2 men

---

26   Ibid., p. 129: February 1915 saw little change in the situation but there was an increase in artillery activity and sniper fire. Water continued to be a serious problem and more was done to drain and reclaim the old front line. Casualties for the month of February were again low: 6 officers wounded, 72 men killed, 213 men wounded, 2 missing, under 300 in total.

27   Ibid., pp. 130–132: On the evening of 1 March 1915, two Canadian battalions took over the left sector from the 22 Brigade and the division's withdrawal from the trench-line it had held for over three months ended a second phase in its story. It had reached that line in November, shattered and broken, but had been strengthened by reinforcements that it had welded together into coherent and effective units. In March 1915 the proportion of veterans of 'First Ypres' in the ranks of the 7th Division was very low, especially in the infantry units, but enough had been done as the next few days would show to render the division once again an efficient and effective fighting unit. These months of dull monotony and toil had been of great value.

and wounded 11 others. I believe it was through the foolish idea of running to see where the shells were falling. Goodnight and God bless you my loved ones xxxxxx

Tuesday 2 March 1915: Fleurbaix

It was too cold to sleep last night, haunted by the thought that we are billeted by the place where those men were killed yesterday. In the morning I saw Atkin who used to belong to our band. We moved off to Laventie in the early evening and arrived at 6:30 p.m. after losing ourselves on the journey, we are staying in a restaurant at Fort D'Esquin. Goodnight and God bless you my loved ones. xxxxx

Wednesday 3 March 1915: Laventie

In the early morning I had to go through Laventie to find the Field Ambulance. The Germans have shelled this town beyond recognition, the beautiful church is completely ruined but one thing I notice is that all the crucifixes have not been touched. I saw a figure of the Virgin Mary which had fallen and was leaning out of the case with her

8 Crucifix still standing after bombardment Neuve Chapelle 10 March 1915.
(IWM Q56178)

hands clasped together, it seemed like she was praying over the door of the house. When I arrived back I was told that a civilian had split his head open, so I went to fetch him from his home and bring him to see the doctor, he had a very bad gash and we had to put two stitches in his head. Two of our companies are cut off from us, they can't get to us in the daytime because of the heavy shelling, but we had a draft of fifty men arrive. Goodnight and God bless you my loved ones. xxxxxx

Thursday 4 March 1915: Laventie

I was awaken this morning by a French woman shouting through the door, "any eggs." After we had attended to the sick, the doctor said "come on Sergeant Webb, we will go and visit the sick of D Company," who are cut off from us during the day time on account of the road leading to Laventie being dangerous, but anyhow off we went. Several shells passed over us on the journey and a few 'Weary Willies' dropped close to the barn where they were sheltered. Then he said "come on, we will go and see where our dressing station is at the trenches," so off we went to a point 300 yards (274 metres) away from the firing line. Nothing happened, the shells were whizzing over our heads all the time but we arrived back safely. I went to see the grave of three artillery men killed on 25 October 1914, they were blown up with their timber wagon and were buried in one grave with two broken timbers on each side, just as they were hit with the shell, a fine setting to the grave. I counted about forty 'Jack Johnson' holes in the field, it must have been terrifying. A large digging party had to go out tonight, so the doctor and a stretcher squad went with them, he didn't want me, so I am sitting up waiting for them to return, it is past midnight. I had a letter from Edith and wrote one to her, so Goodnight and God bless you my loved ones. xxxx

Friday 5 March 1915: Laventie trenches

I sat up till 3:00 a.m. when the doctor returned, wet and cold. The Germans shelled the billets occupied by the Sherwood Foresters, killing 2 men and wounding 5 others. We moved off to the trenches at 6:00 p.m. tonight and I had to stop at the dressing station, so I took the stretcher bearers with me to show them their place, it was pitch dark coming back, slipping and sliding in the mud of a ploughed field, finished up by falling down. Goodnight and God bless you my loved ones. xxxxxxx

Saturday 6 March 1915: Laventie trenches

The ambulance came at 5:30 a.m. and we went up to the trenches where one man had been killed. On the way back I slipped again, finished up laying on my back in the field, lovely and muddy, to make matters worse my boots are in need of repair, my feet are wet, and the Germans started to land shells right where we were located. Goodnight and God bless you my loved ones. xxxx

Sunday 7 March 1915: Laventie trenches

Had a good night's rest but awoke to another wet morning, shelling going on all day. Lloyd had a very narrow escape today when two shells went through the house he was in. He was cleaning a stretcher and the shell smashed the woodwork and ripped the canvas of the stretcher but never touched him, thank God. Goodnight and God bless you my loved ones. xxx

Monday 8 March 1915: Laventie trenches

A very cold frosty morning, a lot of big artillery gun fire from both sides, we had 1 wounded man and heard a rumour we are soon going to make an attack on the German lines. We were relieved by the 2nd Battalion Queen's in the evening and proceeded to our billets. I received a parcel from Edith containing chocolate, flash lamp, batteries, tea, sugar, milk and a letter from Marjorie. Goodnight and God bless you my loved ones. xxxx

War Diary:
Battle of Neuve Chapelle March 1915

Tuesday 9 March 1915: Laventie

We moved out of the trenches last night and the Germans shelled one of our billets today, C Company had six wounded, one man had fourteen wounds but survived. We had a paper issued about the attack we are going to make to capture Neuve Chapelle,[28] we move off at 4:30 a.m. tomorrow morning. Goodnight and God bless you my loved ones. xxxxx

Wednesday 10 March 1915: Laventie (Battle)

A cold, damp and misty morning, I was up at 4:00 a.m. and we moved off at 4:45 a.m. going a little to our right, we got into position for the attack at 5:30 a.m. At 4:30 a.m. our artillery started a terrific bombardment, the din was something awful, we were told that we have 500 guns here and I would agree. About 10:00 a.m. one of our aeroplanes came down and Major Hart asked me to go and see if they needed any help, so off I went. I had to jump over a big brook to get to the crash site and in I went, nice and cold, then I had to cross ploughed fields. I got there at last, saw the pilot and asked him if he was hurt, he said no, so I had a look at his machine, it was hit in the petrol tank and the wings. About 11:30 a.m. I was showing Jim Dawkins where it had fallen and suddenly I saw a German aeroplane dropping a bomb on our battery. All at once

---

28   Neuve Chapelle village is on the road between Bethune, Fleurbaix and Armentieres, near its junction with the Estaires-La Bassee road. The front lines ran parallel with the Bethune-Armentieres road, a little way to the east of the village. Behind the German lines lies Bois de Biez. The ground here is flat and cut by many small drainage ditches. A mile (1.6 kilometres) ahead of the British was a long ridge, Aubers Ridge, barely 20 feet (6 metres) higher than the surrounding area but giving an observation advantage. Some 15 miles (24 kilometres) to the south, this flat area is overlooked by the heights at Vimy Ridge. The German lines in the immediate vicinity were very lightly defended. The night before the attack was wet, with light snow, which turned to damp mist on 10 March 1915. See *The Long, Long Trail* <http://www.1914–1918.net/bat9.htm/> (accessed 8 December 2014).

there was one of our aeroplanes crumpled up, and falling from the sky, my God what a sight, so I told Major Hart and volunteered to go and see if I could be of any use. I went with four stretcher bearers across the fields as the German were firing shells over our heads. Just before I got to where it had crashed, I met a doctor from the Artillery who told us we couldn't be of any use. We have done well today, our men on the right took the trenches, set fire to the town and took about 2,000 prisoners.[29] It is 9:00 p.m. now, Lodge night, so I am thinking of Edith. Goodnight and God bless you my loved ones. xxxx

Thursday 11 March 1915: Laventie (Battle)[30]

I had a very little sleep last night, got up at 5:00 a.m. as the Germans started to shell us, they dropped 'Jack Johnsons' all around us and our guns replied. I saw two armoured cars with naval quick firing guns mounted on them, our progress has been good again. Had a letter from mother, and a paper from the Lodge, sent post cards to Edith and Flo. Goodnight and God bless you my loved ones. xxxxx

Friday 12 March 1915: Laventie (Battle)

I never got to bed until midnight and was up again at 5:00 a.m., a violent bombard-ment taking place again and it's very misty and cold. About 11:00 a.m. we received orders to advance to support the 24 Brigade.[31] As we were walking along the road it

---

29 Atkinson, *The Seventh Division*, pp. 136–137: The day selected for the attack was 10 March 1915. It began misty but cleared by 7:30 a.m. when the bombardment started on the German wire and trenches. The assaulting infantry went 'over the top' thirty five minutes later and most of them found the wire well-cut and the trenches and enemy garrisons very much knocked about. By 9:00 a.m. men of the 25 Brigade were in the ruins of Neuve Chapelle and establishing themselves on their objective but the 2nd Middlesex Regiment were mown down almost to a man in no man's land. All the other brigades found tough resistance and the day ended without the breakthrough that had seemed in the 7th Division's reach. Neuve Chapelle was a snipers' paradise; the houses, still mostly intact, were full of them firing in all directions from behind stout walls. The night passed quietly; the expected counter-attack never developed, though rifle fire was almost continuous and the Scots Fusiliers beat off a weak attack, probably only a strong patrol.

30 Ibid., p.142: At 7:30 a.m. on 11 March 1915 the attack continued but during the night the Germans had strengthened their lines and brought up many more machine-guns and reinforcements. Enemy fire was too heavy to allow substantial movement of troops by daylight and so the day ended with little gain.

31 Ibid., pp.145-146, 149-152: On 12 March 1915 the Germans, profiting by the check to the British advance, had brought up large reinforcements. These included the whole of the 6th Bavarian Reserve Division and the XIX Army Corps, as well as additional artillery, who were to support a counter-attack to recover their lost ground. The British received their first warning of what was to follow from the heavy bombardment which opened about 4:30 a.m. and went on with great intensity for half an hour. The Germans launched

was a perfect hell, 'Jack Johnsons' and shrapnel falling everywhere, how we escaped without casualties I don't know, but thank God we got through it safely. We turned a farm house into a dressing station, just over to the left was our battery which the Germans were shelling, it knocked two of our guns out. They dropped forty 'Jack Johnsons' in a small space around it, we had to run away from the house to some dug-outs as shells were coming too close to us. Then the wounded started to come in and I was very busy putting fresh bandages on the men. We had casualties from all regiments, some of my men had put four of our wounded into a house which stored rifle ammunition and hand grenades, a shell struck the house and they had to pick the wounded up and run for their lives, for the house was on fire. We were collecting our wounded up until 3:00 a.m. and about 2:30 a.m. on the morning of Saturday 13 March 1915, a 'Jack Johnson' struck the other side of our building and blew two men literally to pieces, we had to take care of our wounded and get them away to safety. Casualties were Second Lieutenant A A Owen and 9 other ranks killed, 36 men wounded. We captured three German wounded prisoners which we treated, then we had to move back to our billets properly tired and worn out. Goodnight and God bless you my loved ones. xxxxx

Saturday 13 March 1915: Laventie (Battle)

We had just reached our billet, completely worn out and tired, soaked in water and covered in mud, and we received orders to relieve the Yorkshire Regiment in the trenches. Oh how tired and cold I am, covered in blood from the wounded yesterday, we reached the trenches at 3:45 a.m. on Saturday morning and they are awful muddy trenches. I was sitting down when a big 'Jack Johnson' fell on the other side of the trench, it nearly deafened me. Oh God it is awful, as I am writing this the shells are screaming overhead, bullets are whizzing past us and I am tired and cold. At 11:00

their counter-attack about 5:00 a.m. and confused fighting went on at close quarters for some time before they were driven back and most of the lost ground recovered. Again the Germans counter-attacked all along the British line but were repelled and many German prisoners taken. The 22 Brigade kept the Germans under fire and the reserve battalion of the 22 Brigade, the Royal Warwickshire Regiment, who reinforced the Northamptonshire Yeomanry with one company, was now brought up and placed in the British lines between the Moated Grange and Chapigny in readiness to co-operate should the advance be renewed. Two companies of the Royal Warwickshire Regiment had been ordered to push forward along the Mauquissart road but, though one platoon advanced and established itself in no man's land just to the left of the captured part of the German front line, the British trenches were congested with troops and it was difficult to give adequate support to the advanced platoon. There was no prospect of the 22 Brigade being able to carry out the work originally assigned to it and, at 11:00 p.m., orders received for the Warwickshires and South Staffordshires to relieve the 21 Brigade. During the night something was done to sort out the troops, withdraw the most exhausted units and reorganise the line.

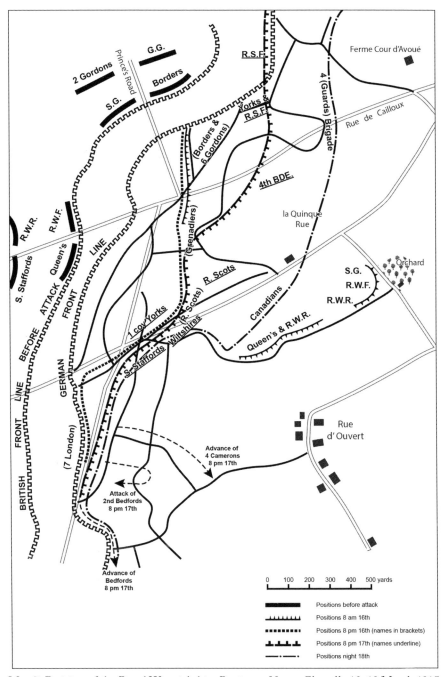

Map 7 Position of the Royal Warwickshire Regiment Neuve Chapelle 12–18 March 1915.

a.m. we had to move out of the trenches to make another attack and we were a part of it, we got it thick and hot, we had to lay behind a ruined house just by the German trenches we had taken yesterday. The dead are laying about all over the place and the Germans have just started to shell us here, my God it is hell again, shells falling all around us, how they missed us I don't know. We laid there for six hours,[32] we couldn't move, it is awful, no food, no water. The doctor told me that he had found a man of the Guards Regiment who had been laying out since 9:00 a.m. the day before, and so we went to bring him in at 4:00 p.m. However did the shells miss him, they were all around him and just as we reached him they started to shell again. I don't know how we got out of it but we got him back to safety, God only knows how we got him away. Then for the next twelve hours we collected the dead and wounded,[33] are we ever going to finish, the stretcher bearers are totally fatigued, the doctor told them to lay down. I kept on working until 6:30 a.m. on Sunday, but I am completely exhausted, I can hardly stand up, I shall be so glad when I can fall down and sleep. Goodnight and God bless you loved one. xxx

Sunday 14 March 1915: Outside Aubers

Still up I can't sleep, I am too tired, the doctor made me lie down and I had a sleep for about two hours. The Germans are still shelling us, how awful it is. The doctor came and told me that we have got another hard nights work ahead, where shall we finish, we are just outside Aubers at the moment. I started to collect the wounded at 1:00 a.m. on Monday morning and we are not finished yet.[34] I went up to the old German

32 Ibid., p.153: 13 March 1915 proved to be another day of disappointment and casualties with nothing to show for them. As before, the bombardments failed to silence the German machine-guns which frustrated every attempt to advance. The Warwickshires, moving across to the captured trenches to relieve the Wiltshires, had been considerably delayed owing to a mistake on the part of the guides, so that daylight found their last companies crossing the open north of the Moated Grange, unable to reach the old German front line to join their comrades.

33 TNA WO 95/1664/3: 2nd Battalion Royal Warwickshire Regiment War Diary, 13–14 March 1915: Casualties were: 1 officer and 27 other ranks killed; 2 Officers and 84 other ranks wounded; 14 other ranks missing.

34 The 7th Division's losses of 138 officers and 2,666 men, though not approaching those suffered in the long-drawn-out struggle at Ypres, were heavy enough for a four-day battle in which only two brigades had been seriously engaged, one of which had suffered most of its casualties before reaching the firing-line. In the 22 Brigade, the Royal Warwickshire Regiment alone had lost 3 officers and 126 men, nearly half the brigade's total. The result had fallen short of expectations but had demonstrated that the German lines could be stormed. The weeks that followed Neuve Chapelle were, for the 7th Division, marked by few outstanding incidents. Sir Douglas Haig's hopes of promptly following up Neuve Chapelle by a fresh attack at another point had had to be relinquished because of the shortage of ammunition. For the rest of March the 7th Division continued to occupy the trenches parallel with the Rue Tilleloy roughly from its junction with the Mauquissart

9 Battle of Neuve Chapelle – fire trench. (IWM Q380)

trenches to fetch eight wounded prisoners, we finished collecting them at 3:30 a.m. and we are going back to Laventie at 4:15 a.m. I am very tired, so good morning and God bless you my loved ones. xxx

Monday 15 March 1915: Outside Aubers

I finally got to bed at 6:00 a.m. but could not sleep and so I got up again at 8:00 a.m. We had a draft arrive with a lot of our old comrades amongst them, Adu and Gold came back. Everybody is talking about our doctor and I know how brave he is, he deserves the VC, and they are all praising the stretcher bearers for their brave efforts during the fight. I went and sewed Lieutenant Owens up and we buried him today.

road to the right of the old lines. One brigade held the line at a time, which gave the others a much needed rest and time to train new recruits. By the end of March most units were up to strength again, our lines considerably improved regarding drainage and several gaps were filled up. The British losses in the four attacking divisions were 544 officers and 11,108 other ranks killed, wounded and missing. German losses are estimated at a similar figure of 12,000 which included 1,687 prisoners. See Atkinson, *The Seventh Division, pp.* 154-154.

10 Neuve Chapelle after capture of the village 15 March 1915. (IWM Q47577)

I wrote to Edith, she will wonder why I haven't sent a letter for a day, so to bed, Goodnight and God bless you my loved ones. xxxx

Tuesday 16 March 1915: Laventie

It's a very cold day today, not much doing, so I got up at 8:00 a.m. with a very sore back, but I am getting on alright. I heard that we are going down for a rest, I wonder how many more times we are going to hear that. The Germans have just dropped a heavy shrapnel shell on Laventie Church and they shelled our digging party at the cross roads. I wrote to Edith and mother. Goodnight and God bless you my loved ones. xxx

Wednesday 17 March 1915: Laventie

I had a pretty good night's rest, a cold morning but it turned out beautiful. Had a letter from Edith and parcel from mother, wrote to Marjorie and Flo. Went to the trenches tonight, back in the mud and blood. Goodnight and God bless you my loved ones. xxxxx

Thursday 18 March 1915: Laventie (Trenches)

Had a wounded man come in at 3:45 a.m. with his finger blown off and so I treated him, then went to the dressing station where we collected the wounded. When we were fighting and the Devonshire Regiment were here, I saw a man that was attached to us when we were in Devonport. Moved out of the trenches to the other end of Laventie but I had to go right back to the other dressing station as some sick men were lost. I arrived back at 11:00 p.m., fed up. We heard that another attack is planned for Sunday, same place where we made the last attack the other day, it's called the 'street of hell.' Goodnight and God bless you my loved ones. xxx

Friday 19 March 1915: Laventie

Had a poor night's rest, went to Estaire (Town in France) and saw Sergeant Fraser and Sergeant Woolway, it was a treat to walk through a town. I have not felt too well today, it is snowing, cold, so I am off to bed. Goodnight and God bless you my loved ones. xxxxx

Saturday 20 March 1915: Laventie

Had a good night's rest and in the morning we had stretchers drill. Lieutenant Colonel V R Pigott arrived yesterday to take command of the 2nd Battalion Royal Warwickshire Regiment, relieving Major H C Hart. A German aeroplane flew over Estaire today and dropped a bomb killing 18 men and wounding 2 men. I wrote to Edith and Linda McKee, so am off to bed, Goodnight and God bless you my loved ones. xxxxxx

Sunday 21 March 1915: Laventie

I had a good night's rest and awoke to a beautiful day. We heard that the Royal Warwickshire Regiment have got to make the next attack. Played football today and wrote to Edith and mother. Goodnight and God bless you my loved ones. xxxxxx

Monday 22 March to Thursday 25 March 1915: Laventie

On Monday we had stretcher drill and Adjutants Inspection which we passed first rate. We heard of a big Russian Victory so I must find out more about it. On Tuesday at 4:15 a.m. the Germans started to shell the church in Laventie again, they dropped thirty six 'Jack Johnsons' and knocked all the pinnacles down except one, it is a shame. We heard last night that the Russians had taken Przemyst. We are still resting, training and planning for the next attack. Over the next few days we had demonstrations by our bomb throwers, Russian, Japanese, and all the Generals were present. Later I went to look at an armoured train. Goodnight and God bless you my loved ones. xxx

Friday 26 March to Wednesday 31 March 1915: Laventie

This afternoon the Germans shelled the church again killing 4 men and wounding 2 men. Two officers came galloping by and told us some men had been hit, so Lance Corporal Gumbly and I went down, but the Welch Fusilier doctor was there and did not need our help. On Sunday I refereed a football match, South Staffordshire Regiment against our regiment. As you walk along you hear an explosion just like a 'Jack Johnson' but it was the bomb throwers practising. The next few days were quiet and I had time to write to all my family and friends after receiving mail from them. I had a nice surprise on Tuesday, Teddy Paul came to see me from Estaires, he is in the Canadians and tomorrow he is going to bring me some spices. The doctor told us today that we are leading the next attack and we heard of a French victory today. I am waiting for the stretcher squad to return from digging. Goodnight and God bless you my loved ones. xxxxxx

War Diary:
Aubers Ridge Trenches and the Second Battle of Ypres April 1915

Thursday 1 April 1915: Laventie[35]

I did not sleep very well last night, but today the weather is fine. We had to go to Estaires to practice for the next attack, our battalion strength is 24 officers and 948 other ranks. We are preparing our assembly and communication trenches and improving the drainage using working parties at night. I saw Dick Smith and had a letter from Goodday, then wrote to my sister Flo and Edith. Goodnight and God bless you my loved ones. xxxx

Friday 2 April 1915: Laventie

Preparation for the next attack continued and Captain Bowley came to see the officers today, I saw him and he shook hands with me. I received a parcel from mother. Goodnight and God bless you my loved ones. xxxx

Saturday 3 April 1915: Laventie

Our doctor, Captain Button, left us today for England, we were so sorry to lose him and he was sorry to leave us, Lieutenant Powell took over from him. It is very quiet again, nothing going on and we heard that the attack has been postponed, the Germans are moving a lot of reinforcements up. We might get away from here for a while and our men are looking forward to it. At 10:30 p.m. a man came down to say that three of our men were hit by snipers in the trenches, I am sending for them.

---

35 Atkinson, *The Seventh Division*, pp. 160–161: On 1 April 1915 the Divisional Commander General Capper was injured by a premature explosion whilst watching some experiments with trench mortars. His injuries were serious and he was forced very reluctantly to relinquish his command. In his farewell order General Capper spoke with pride of the 7th Division's achievements and its spirit, and expressed the hope that he might someday return to it. Major General Gough from the 2nd Cavalry Division succeeded him, taking over command on 19 April 1915.

At 12:15 a.m. my squad came back, the men had been taken to the Guards dressing station. Goodnight and God bless you my loved ones. xxxx

Sunday 4 April 1915: Laventie

At 8:00 a.m. one of the wounded man came down and told me that Billy Weaver had been hit and had died. I was in an awful state about it so I went off to Estaires and found him alive in hospital, thank God. He asked me to write to his wife, he is badly hit, so I wrote a letter to her and received a letter from Edith. It's been raining heavy all day and we had a draft of 50 other ranks join the battalion for duty. Goodnight and God bless you my loved ones. xxxx

Monday 5 April to Saturday 10 April 1915: Laventie

Had a good night's rest, a very wet morning, raining all the time. We had Generals Inspection and then went on a long route march, it was wet but I enjoyed walking. The rest of the week was very quiet, nothing happened except we changed billets on Wednesday and had a sports competition on Friday. Goodnight and God bless you my loved ones. xxxx

Sunday 11 April 1915: Laventie (Trenches)

Had a good night's rest, a beautiful day. The Germans started shelling today and at 4:45 p.m. we went to the trenches to relieve the 2nd Queen's Regiment. We had one man wounded. Goodnight and God bless you my loved ones. xxxx

Monday 12 April 1915: Laventie (Trenches)

I was woke up at 5:00 a.m. by the stretcher bearers, they brought a wounded man in, poor old Hunt of the 22 Brigade. He was hit in the head and the bullet hadn't come out, I heard later that he died from his wounds. The Germans have been shelling very heavily all around us today and we had a second man wounded in the head. Had a letter from mother and Mrs Stebbing and sent a post card to Edith. Goodnight and God bless you my loved ones. xxxx

Tuesday 13 April 1915: Laventie (Trenches)

I was woke up at 12 midnight, a man of the Borders was wounded, and so I dressed him and sent him to hospital at 5:00 a.m. The Germans shelled us again today, we had one of our men and one man of the Artillery wounded. Goodnight and God bless you my loved ones. xxxxx

Wednesday 14 April 1915: Laventie (Trenches)

The Germans shelled our trenches today and I picked up a live fuse, it was solid brass. We had two men hit near our dressing station. We moved out of the trenches back to Estaires and arrived at our billets in La Gorgue at 1:00 a.m., properly tired out. I had a letter from Edith, it is her Lodge night tonight. Good morning and God bless you my loved ones. xxx

Thursday 15 April to Sunday 18 April 1915: Estaires

Had a good night's rest although our billets are very poor. Jack Blackwell came with a draft of 20 men and we are still practicing for the next attack. The next few days were very quiet and on Saturday we were asked to bring our mouth organs on parade. There were only four of us who could play but we had a laugh and managed to get through a tune. On Sunday we played a football match with the Welch Fusiliers, lost 3-2, but it was a beautiful day. Good morning and God bless you my loved ones. xxx

Monday 19 April 1915: Estaires La Gorgue

Heath had a letter from Francis who is a prisoner of war, he is starving, so we collected some money, about one pound (£1.0.0), sent it to Edith to buy things to send to him. Goodnight and God bless you my loved ones. xxxx

Tuesday 20 April 1915: Estaires La Gorgue

It is a beautiful day and we went for a bath, it was grand and there was every convenience. They employ a lot of French women to repair the clothes and sew the buttons on, wish there was one behind every line. Wrote to mother and Flo, Goodnight and God bless you my loved ones. xxxx

Wednesday 21 April 1915: Estaires La Gorgue

I didn't get into bed until 11:00 p.m. last night and arose at 5:00 a.m. to a very cold morning. We were inspected by Field Marshall Sir John French this afternoon, the whole of the brigade. Each regiment was drawn up in a three sided square, and he addressed each regiment separately. He told our regiment he was proud of them, he knew of the enormous losses and he thanked us for our part at Ypres and Neuve Chapelle. We are going into the trenches at Neuve Chapelle on Friday. Had a letter from Edith and answered it. Goodnight and God bless you my loved ones. xxxxx

Thursday 22 April 1915: Estaires La Gorgue

We had Generals Inspection today, he congratulated the men of our regiment who were awarded the Distinguished Conduct Medal.[36] The West Yorkshire Territorials came here today, they are a fine body of men. I played a football match today and received a letter and cigarettes from Billie Weaver, he is going on well. Goodnight and God bless you my loved ones. xxxx

Friday 23 April 1915: Estaires La Gorgue

Had a good night's sleep, awful cold, east wind. Had a letter from Edith, answered it, very quiet, so Goodnight and God bless you my loved ones. xxxx

Saturday 24 April 1915: Estaires La Gorgue

At 6:30 p.m. last night we had the orders to be ready to move off at any minute. The Germans had used poisonous gas[37] on the French and they say their casualties were 3,000 men[38] and they lost 36 guns. It is now 10:00 p.m. and we are still standing too, so I am off to bed. Goodnight and God bless you my loved ones. xxxxx

Sunday 25 April to Tuesday 27 April 1915: Estaires La Gorgue

We were not disturbed last night and heard this morning that the Canadians had taken the trenches and guns back, that the French lost at Ypres.[39] A few quiet days, played the 1/8th West Yorkshire regiment at football and beat them 2-0. Heard that one force have landed in Gallipoli. Goodnight and God bless you my loved ones. xxx

---

36   TNA WO 95/1664/3: 2nd Battalion Royal Warwickshire Regiment War Diary, 22 April 1914: The Distinguished Conduct Medal (DCM) was awarded to the following: Sergeant Norman S/N 2060, Sergeant Reeves S/N 8594, Sergeant Johnson S/N 787, Corporal Weston S/N 1233, Private Russell S/N 1222 (Killed in action).

37   Opening of Second Battle of Ypres (22 April-25 May 1915). See below.

38   The combined casualties for French and Colonial troops were far worse than the 3,000 French casualties quoted.

39   Second Battle of Ypres (22 April–25 May 1915 was fought for control of the strategic West Flanders town of Ypres in Western Belgium in the spring of 1915. It marked the first time Imperial Germany successfully deployed poison gas. Consisting of four separate engagements, Ypres and its eastern environs was defended by British, Canadian, French and Belgian divisions. The 7th Division, including the 2nd Battalion Royal Warwickshire Regiment, was held in reserve and did not take part in these battles.

Wednesday 28 April 1915: Estaires

At 10:30 a.m. we had orders to move off at 12:30 p.m. but we don't know where we are going, probably Ypres. During the march we had a lot of men fall out, we marched through Merris and stopped at a place called Méteren, Belgium. We had to hunt for a billet, you would have laughed, there was the adjutant, the doctor and me going into civilian houses and of course we couldn't speak French, so we couldn't be understood. We sent for the interpreter, found a beautiful furnished house and the woman who owns it lived next door, she made us welcome. She can talk English and was telling us what it was like when the Germans were there. The doctor is stopping here with us and the woman found me a bed to sleep on, so I am off to bed. Goodnight and God bless you my loved ones. xxxxx

Thursday 29 April 1915: Méteren Belgium

Had a good night's rest and it is a beautiful day, very quiet. We are here as reinforcements, just in case we are needed at Ypres. Sergeant Major Daukins and I went to see the graves of the men of our 1st Battalion Royal Warwickshire Regiment that were killed taking this place. They are buried in a trench with a simple cross in memory of the 1st Regiment killed in action. We went into a cottage owned by an old man and his wife and they showed us where the bullets from the Germans had come through their cottage when our men were advancing. I forgot to mention that yesterday we had to make gags[40] to fit over our nose and mouth on account of the Germans using poisonous gases on us. Goodnight and God bless you my loved ones. xxxx

Friday 30 April 1915: Méteren Belgium

Had a good night's sleep, it's a beautiful day and we went for a route march. I heard that the Indians had been cut up but have no details. Had a letter from Edith, mother, Mabel, and Linda, wrote to Edith. Goodnight and God bless you my loved ones. xxxx

---

40   After the first German chlorine gas attack, Allied troops were supplied with masks of cotton pads that had been soaked in urine. It was found that the ammonia in the pad neutralised the chlorine. The pads were held over the face until the soldiers could escape from the poisonous fumes. Other soldiers preferred to use handkerchiefs, a sock or flannel body-belt, dampened with a solution of bicarbonate of soda, then tied across the mouth and nose until the gas passed over. Soldiers found it difficult to fight like this and attempts were made to develop a better means of protecting men against gas attacks. By July 1915 soldiers were issued the more efficient Hypo Helmet gas mask.

War Diary:
Battles of Aubers Ridge and Festubert May 1915

Saturday 1 May 1915: Méteren (France)

At 1:40 a.m. an orderly woke me up to warn me that we were going on a route march at 8:00 a.m. It is a beautiful day, we returned from the route march at 12:00 noon to hear that our 1st Battalion Royal Warwickshire Regiment has had a severe shaking. Our battalion strength is 23 officers and 1017 other ranks. I received a parcel from Edith, papers from Flo, and wrote to Marjorie, Flo and mother, so Goodnight and God bless you my loved ones. xxxx

Sunday 2 May1915: Méteren (France)

I had a good night's rest and in the morning attended church service held in a field, it was a very impressive service. Afterwards I showed some of the stretcher bearers the graves of our fallen comrades of the 1st Battalion Royal Warwickshire Regiment, they look nice now our men have banked the long graves up and enclosed them with painted white post and wire. Smith, the pioneer, made a beautiful cross and painted on it "In Remembrance of the 1st Battalion Royal Warwickshire Regiment, erected by the 2nd Battalion," it was 13 October 1914 when they all got killed. I had a letter from Edith and wrote back, also wrote to Linda McKee, Bill Goodday, and Mabel. Goodnight and God bless you my loved ones. xxxx

Monday 3 May 1915: Méteren (France)

We had to get up at 4:30 a.m. and went for a route march, it was very hot and we heard very heavy gun fire at Ypres. I feel very uneasy today, something has happened to my brother Bob and I can't find out how serious his injuries are. We played football in the afternoon, Royal Garrison Artillery (RGA) versus our regiment, we won 2-1. Good night and God bless you my loved ones. xxxx

Tuesday 4 May 1915: Méteren (France)

My brother Bob has been wounded and the losses today for the 1st Battalion Royal Warwickshire Regiment was 7 officers killed, 5 wounded, 1 missing, 578 other ranks killed, wounded and missing. We went on a route march this afternoon, then wrote to mother. Goodnight and God bless you my loved ones. xxxx

Wednesday 5 May 1915: Méteren (France)

Today a very heavy bombardment is taking place at Ypres. We played a football match during the day, 4th Division Supply Column versus our regiment, we lost 4-2. We had orders to move back to La Gorgue departing at 9:00 p.m. but it was 10:00 p.m. before we got going. While we were waiting to move off the troops started singing, just picture a thousand men singing in a street of a dark town, soldiers are always singing love songs, such as 'Men were deceivers, every girl is a nice girl.' It was awful marching, we arrived at La Gorgue at 2:30 a.m. on Thursday morning, properly tired out. Good night and God bless you my loved ones. xxxx

Thursday 6 May 1915: Lavente La Gorgue (France)

I got up at 8:00 a.m., nothing doing all day. I had a post card from mother telling me that Bob is at Colchester Hospital and letters from Edith, Jim and Flo. I heard today that Sergeant Gibbs had died from his wounds. We go into the trenches tomorrow night and we heard that we are making an attack on Saturday, please God help me to come out of it safely. Goodnight and God bless you my loved ones. xxxxx

Friday 7 May 1915: Lavente La Gorgue (France)

I had a good night's rest, then spent my time preparing to go to the trenches tonight for the attack tomorrow. It is grand to see the spirit of the men, you hear them say, "well, let's get a move on, it isn't any good staying here, for this will never finish the war." I heard men talking, one said, "well good luck Jack, hope you will come through safe" and the other man said "same to you." We have improved our gas mask and I wrote to Marjorie and Jim. We just heard the attack has been cancelled for 24 hours on account of the rain that has started, so I am off to bed. Goodnight and God bless you my loved ones. xxxxx

Saturday 8 May 1915: Lavente La Gorgue (France)

I had a good night's rest and awoke to a beautiful day, then had a good bath and wrote letters to all my family. We are going to the trenches tonight at 10:00 p.m. to prepare for the attack tomorrow morning. I hope and trust in God to come through it safe. Goodnight and God bless you my loved ones. xxxx

Sunday 9 May 1915: Battle of Aubers Ridge[41] (France)

We arrived at the trenches at 12:30 a.m., it is a very cold night and I couldn't get any sleep. The bombardment started at 5:00 a.m., it wasn't as heavy as Neuve Chapelle. We started to advance toward the German lines at 6:30 a.m. under fire, as we crossed a road we received very heavy fire and the casualties started. We moved into a trench with our regiment and we had to remain there. The artillery was just behind us, my poor head, how it did ache. We lay in the trenches under fire all day, at 4:30 p.m. it was a bit quieter, but at 8:15 p.m. they started shelling again, it was awful. The trench was our only shelter, then we received orders to replace the 8th Division in their trenches. Their attack had failed and our regiment will have a difficult time if we have to advance. The Germans have brought a lot more big guns up and are shelling all the fields that we have got to cross when we attack tomorrow morning. Later the attack was cancelled and at 2:30 a.m. we went back to the dug-outs where we started from yesterday. Our casualties were 19 men. Goodnight and God bless you my loved ones. xxxxxxx

Monday 10 May 1915: Battle of Aubers Ridge (France)

We were shelled all the way back to our trenches and had just returned when a heavy shell burst about thirty yards to our left, poor young Smith was hit with a piece of shrapnel and it smashed his shoulder. The doctor thinks he will lose his left arm, we all

41   Battle of Aubers Ridge 9 May 1915: The British First Army's objective in the flat and poorly-drained terrain was the "Aubers Ridge," an area of slightly higher ground 2-3 kilometres south of Allied lines and marked by the village of Aubers, Fromelles and Le Maisnil. This same area had been targeted in the Battle of Neuve Chapelle two months earlier. The battle marked the second use of specialist Royal Engineers tunnelling companies, who deployed mines underground to disrupt enemy defence lines, through use of dug tunnels and large amounts of explosives at zero hour. The duration and weight of the British bombardment was insufficient to break the German wire and breastwork defences, or to destroy or supress the front-line machine-guns. Trench layout, traffic flows and organisation behind the British front line did not allow for easy movement of reinforcements and casualties. British artillery equipment and ammunition were in poor condition through overuse and faulty manufacture. It soon became impossible to tell precisely where the British troops were and so accurate close-support artillery fire could not be given. British casualties from the 9 May attacks continued to move through the Field Ambulances for at least three days after the attack. The battle was an unmitigated disaster for the British Army. No ground was won and no tactical advantage was gained. It is very doubtful if it had the slightest positive effect on assisting the main French attack fifteen miles to the south. The battle was renewed, the epicentre shifted just a little way south, from 15 May and was known as the Battle of Festubert. More than 11,000 British casualties were sustained on 9 May, the vast majority within yards of their own front line trenches. Mile for mile, division for division, this was one of the highest rates of loss during the entire war.

feel very sad for him, for he was a brave little lad. I went to see Quarter Master Andou at the transport depot, he is with the West Yorkshire Regiment. We arranged transport for young Smith but the enemy artillery fire is very heavy again. We have got to move tonight at 8:00 p.m. but we don't know where we are moving to. Eventually we moved to Bethune at 1:30 a.m. and laid in an open field in the bitter cold for the rest of the night. Good morning and God bless you my loved ones. xxxxx

Tuesday 11 May 1915: Essars (France)

The General told the regiment that we were going to attack and that we were to get the bayonet home, however we are not moving tonight. Goodnight and God bless you my loved ones. xxxxxx

Wednesday 12 May 1915: Essars (France)

Nothing doing all day but we did hear of a great victory at Ypres. The Germans used their gas during the attack but our men put their gas mask on and waited for them, when they got to the barbed wire our maxims and rifle fire mowed them down. Goodnight and God bless you my loved ones. xxxxx

Thursday 13 May 1915: Essars (France)

It is raining hard and so we had to shift from the open field to billets at Locon, about 2 miles (3 kilometres) away, a very heavy bombardment going on at the moment. Had a letter from Edith and wrote back to her telling her of the Band Masters brother's death yesterday. Goodnight and God bless you my loved ones. xxxxxx

Friday 14 May 1915: Locon (France)

We are on stand-by for the attack, but it is a very wet and cold day. Later we heard the attack was cancelled but we are going into the trenches for twenty four hours. We heard of a great French victory at Souchez. Goodnight and God bless you my loved ones. xxxxx

Saturday 15 May 1915: Battle of Festubert

I had a good night's rest and awoke to a beautiful day. I sent a letter of condolence to Mr Stebbing on the death of his brother and wrote to mother, Edith and Flo. We moved off tonight at 7:50 p.m. for the attack marching via Rue de Bois, Rue Le Pinette, and arrived at our support trench at 11:30 p.m. without any casualties. It is an awful cold night and we couldn't find a dug out, so we had to lay in an open field, the big guns and snipers were busy, so it was dangerous. Goodnight and God bless you my loved ones. xxx

Sunday 16 May 1915: Battle of Festubert[42]

At 2:45 a.m. our artillery opened a bombardment and the Germans replied, it was a very fierce artillery duel. Then, at 3:15 a.m. the attack commenced and within a quarter of an hour from the start our men had crossed no man's land and had taken the first row of trenches. There were plenty of wounded needing our attention but we did fine and about 700 prisoners were captured. The Queen's[43] suffered heavily, mowed down as they crossed no man's land, but they went forward line by line. We were working very hard to recover the wounded and did not finish until 2:00 a.m. on Monday morning. Then we had to push on to join our regiment in another trench further forward. Good morning and God bless you my loved ones. xxxx

Monday 17 May 1915: Battle of Festubert

The fighting is going on continuously, it is awful to see the dead lying about. I had laid down for about one half hour when they woke me to say we had some wounded men out in no man's land, so I went out and brought three men of our regiment back in safely. There are dozens of wounded here, we can't get them away, we have been working all day. I am just sitting in a dug-out and the shells are whistling overhead, we had 185 killed, wounded and missing yesterday. There are not many casualties today so far, but the firing is awful, the Reverend Pue was wounded yesterday, he was a brave man. It is now 7:30 p.m. and an attack has just started on our right, the 21 Brigade are attacking the German lines. There is a lot of rifle fire and I had to go through it to reach the other trench where a man was hit with a piece of shrapnel, no

---

42   The Battle of Festubert (15-19 May 1915) was undertaken to assist the French offensive near Arras by preventing German reserve troops from being available to move there. The attack was made by the British First Army against a German salient between Neuve Chapelle to the north and the village of Festubert to the south. The battle was preceded by a sixty hour British bombardment that fired about 100,000 shells on the front line defences of the German *Sixth Army*; however, the German lines were not significantly damaged. Although the initial night advance on 15 May made some progress in good weather conditions, further attacks during 16–19 May resulted in heavy losses and by the 19 May the British 2nd and 7th Divisions had to be withdrawn. The British forces then entrenched themselves at the new front line in conditions of heavy rain. The Germans now brought up more reserves to reinforce their lines. From 20–25 May 1915 the attack was renewed, resulting in the capture of the village of Festubert. The total offensive had only resulted in a one kilometre advance, at a cost of more than 16,000 casualties. French losses there were over 102,000 against German almost 50,000, including Festubert.

43   Atkinson, *The Seventh Division*, pp. 172–173: The day (16 May 1915) ended with the 7th Division consolidating a line far short of the advanced points reached, but continuous and defensible. The old German front trench had been consolidated as a second line of defence and was held by the Warwickshires, the Scots Guards, and the rest of the 2nd Gordons. The Queen's, who were reduced to under 300 of all ranks, had been taken right back to reserve.

hopes, he died. It is raining hard and very miserable, the Germans are shelling us with High Explosive shells and we are still tending to the wounded. I am totally exhausted and will try to get a sleep if possible, so Goodnight and God bless you my loved ones. xxxxxxxx

Tuesday 18 May 1915: Battle of Festubert

I could not sleep and so I sent a post card to Edith and my mother, it might be the last one I send. It was an awful wet night and we spent the morning burying the dead, what awful sights, we find the poor men laying as they fell.[44] The German trenches that we captured are full of dead Germans, three and four deep. Our artillery was marvellous, absolutely smashed the German trenches in. Another attack is planned for 9:00 a.m. if the weather clears up. It's now 11:00 a.m. and still misty, the attack has been delayed. The Germans are shelling us with 'Jack Johnsons' and heavy shrapnel, my God it is awful, it is enough to drive you mad. They have got the range of this trench to a nicety, they have just hit the top off the sand bags, you should see them fly but luckily nobody hurt. Poor Paddy Black was hit, what a lucky man, a 'Jack Johnson' came over the trench and burst a yard in front of him, it only wounded him slightly on the forehead, I was very close to him, it is hell. We were relieved tonight at 8:00 p.m. by the Canadians, oh what a relief to get out of this place, still we did well, we took about 1000 yards (914 metres), a glorious victory. At 11:00 p.m. we marched to a place outside Bethune, still wet, we are sleeping in a loft, so Goodnight and God bless you my loved ones. xxxx

Wednesday 19 May 1915: Outside Bethune (France)

I had a glorious sleep, the first since Saturday night, got up at 10:00 a.m., it's still damp. We have got to move into new billets further back for a week's rest. We started at 2:00 p.m. and marched through Lillers, I don't know the name of this place, right out in the country, you can hardly realise that a war is on. Had a parcel from Edith, and letter from Harry Goodday, so am off to bed, Lodge night, so Goodnight and God bless you my loved ones. xxxxx

Thursday 20 May 1915: Le Cornet Bourdois (France)

I had a good night's rest and it's a beautiful day, this is lovely, just like being in the country at home. Paddy Black was promoted to full Corporal for good work. I wrote

---

44   Ibid., p. 182: The 7th Division losses had been terribly heavy, 50 per cent higher than those of Neuve Chapelle, amounting in all to 170 officers and 3,833 men. The Royal Warwickshire Regiment casualties were 2 officers and 25 men killed, 47 men missing, 3 officers and 158 men wounded.

to Edith, Marjorie and all the family. Goodnight and God bless you my loved ones. xxxxxx

Friday 21 May 1915: Le Cornet Bourdois (France)

Brigadier-General S T B Lawford[45] inspected us today and he congratulated us on our brilliant victory. We had a nice day enjoying ourselves in the country, a very heavy bombardment going on, we can hear the guns quite clearly. Unfortunately a man shot himself tonight, overcome by the stress and fear of battle, poor soul. Goodnight and God bless you my loved ones. xxxx

Saturday 22 May 1915: Le Cornet Bourdois (France)

Our doctor left us today and we have a replacement. We also had a draft join us, Sergeant Ink, Corporal Grey and about 114 men. Goodnight and God bless you my loved ones. xxxx

Sunday 23–Monday 24 May 1915: Le Cornet Bourdois (France)

Today is a beautiful day, what a difference to last Sunday. I had a very busy time going around all the billets inspecting the men. On Monday we went for a one hour route march through the country, you wouldn't think a war was on, the women here do nearly all the work in the fields. We heard today that Italy had declared war. Goodnight and God bless you my loved ones. xxxx

Tuesday 25 May 1915: Le Cornet Bourdois, (France)

Five reporters came round today and when they had gone into our headquarters I talked to their chauffeurs. When the Major of the Staff came out, he said, "what telling them some experiences," I said, "no Sir, nothing to tell." He said, "You were at Festubert," I said, "Yes sir and at Ypres," but I am saving the stories up until I get home. He did laugh, we are not allowed to say anything about the fights. I had a birthday card from mother today, she is staying with Edith at Devonport, Plymouth. Goodnight and God bless you my loved ones. xxxx

Wednesday 26 May 1915: Le Cornet, Bourdois (France)

A German aeroplane flew over our way last night and dropped bombs on us, but I didn't hear it. Strangely enough, last night I was dreaming of the same thing, except

---

45   Brigadier-General Sidney Turing Barlow Lawford (1865-1953) GOC 22 Brigade; father of actor Peter Lawford (1923-1984).

the bomb fell near me and didn't explode. Today is my 35th birthday and so I am having a quiet day. Lodge night for Edith tonight, so Goodnight and God bless you my loved one. xxxxxx

Thursday 27–31 May 1915: Le Cornet Bourdois (France)[46]

On Thursday 27 May 1915, our regiment paraded with the brigade for inspection by the French Commander-in- Chief General Joffre.[47] General French accompanied him and a Special Order[48] was read out at the parade. After the parade I went for a walk into Lillers, it is very cold. On Sunday 30 May 1915 we had church service in the afternoon and a draft came up with Captain H L Matear, Lieutenant W L Witten and 60 men of other ranks. Goodnight and God bless you my loved ones. xxxxxx

46 For about 10 days after the withdrawal of the 7th Division infantry, including the Royal Warwickshire Regiment, the operations continued without any major gains. The heavy fighting and serious losses emphasized how formidable the German defences were and what difficult obstacles the Division had encountered.
47 General Joseph Jacques Césaire Joffre (1852-1931). French commander-in-chief August 1914-December 1916)
48 TNA WO 95/1664/3: 2nd Battalion Royal Warwickshire Regiment War Diary, 28 May 1914: Special Order: The following is a brief summary of the results of the operations on the front of the First Army since 16 May 1915: The enemy's line has been pierced on a front of about 5,400 yards (4938 metres), of this the whole hostile front line system of trenches has been captured on a front of 3,200 yards (2926 metres). On the remaining portion the front and second line of trenches have been captured. The total number of prisoners taken was 8 officers and 763 other ranks. 11 machine-guns are known to have been captured or destroyed and 15 more are estimated to have been damaged or lost making a total of 26. A considerable quantity of material and equipment was taken the exact amount of which has not as yet been ascertained. The General Officer Commanding (GOC) desires to express his satisfaction to all ranks of the First Army on their achievements and has much pleasure in publishing the following congratulatory telegram: From Field Marshal Commanding-in-Chief: "I think your summary of the results attained by the First Army from 16 May 1915 up to date is very satisfactory. Please convey my congratulations and thanks to Canadian and 47th Division, which have so well matured and extended the excellent work begun by the 2nd and 7th Divisions, who's services I have already acknowledged."

War Diary:
Battle of Givenchy June 1915

Tuesday 1 June 1915: Le Cornet Bourdois (France)[49]

At parade this morning we practiced fitting our gas mask on our faces. They are made from a piece of black crepe doubled and stitched each side of the mouth to make a pocket which is filled with cotton waste dipped in a solution. The mask fits over your mouth and you have to bite it to stop yourself breathing through your nose, the top piece covers your eyes. The whole thing is carried in a rubber bag slung around your neck. Goodnight and God bless you my loved ones. xxx

Wednesday 2 June 1915: Le Cornet, Bourdois (France)

We moved away from here today at 12:45 p.m. and marched just beyond the billets that we were in before the Battle of Festubert. Our battalion strength is now 21 officers and 1016 other ranks. It is a very hot day and some of the men fell out during the long march, we arrived at 6:15 p.m. and found our billets which are awful. Goodnight and God bless you my loved ones. xxxxxx

---

49   Atkinson, *The Seventh Division*, pp. 184–185: The shattered battalions of the Seventh Division were relieved from the front line on 20 May 1915 but had to return to the line on 31 May. Their relief period was all too brief for shattered battalions requiring rest and the chance to train their new recruits. The Royal Warwickshires and many other battalions had lost so heavily that they were quite disorganised and the officers left in command had little training or experience. It was very hard on them that they had been called back to the trenches, harder still on some of its units that they had been required to undertake yet another attack before June was out. The low-lying ground just north of Givenchy was left in an unsatisfactory state after the last offensive, while the captured trenches and redoubts were overlooked from the top of the bluff held by the Germans and were liable to be bombed from this enemy position at any time. On the bluff itself, it was hard to make out the exact enemy line in the maze of old trenches, shell holes and craters formed by mine explosions. This irregular ground gave chances to German snipers which led to many casualties.

Thursday 3 June 1915: Le Casan (France)[50]

Another very hot day today and there is a lot of large artillery gun and rifle fire taking place. We have a 9.2 inch (234mm) gun close by and we went to see it firing. I had heard that you can see the shells flying through the air, well that is true, we could see this shell just after it had left the muzzle, it was like a big football in the sky. I had a letter from Edith, a birthday card from Harold and Lillie, papers from Flo and I wrote to Edith, I don't feel so well today and so I am going to bed early. Goodnight and God bless you my loved ones. xxxx

Friday 4 June 1915: Locon (France)[51]

I don't feel much better this morning and tonight we are going into the trenches about five miles away. We arrived in the trenches at 12:00 midnight to relieve the 3rd Battalion Grenadier Guards, the Germans were constantly shelling our lines and all the houses were knocked down. Goodnight and God bless you my loved ones. xxxxxxx

Saturday 5 June 1915: Givenchy (France)

The Germans were shelling our trenches all night, it is a little misty and at 8:00 a.m. the 'Jack Johnsons' started to come over, they hit an old house about 20 yards (18 metres) away, but we survived. I went up into the trenches tonight to see the Medical Officer, it is the strangest firing line I have ever seen, a maze of old trenches, shell-holes, and craters formed by mine explosions. This is where Michael John O'Leary[52]

---

50 Ibid., pp. 185–186: The 20 Brigade was the first to take over the new front line, with the 6th Gordons on the right, the Grenadiers in the low ground opposite the southern end of Rue d'Ouvert and the 2nd Gordons on the left facing the northern end. On 3 June 1915 an attempt to improve their position on the bluff was made and the German lines were attacked following a mine explosion, which produced a big crater and did great damage both to the German trenches and their garrison. The assault was successful, capturing some 50 German prisoners. However, about 3:00 a.m. the Germans started counter-attacking in force, supported by trench mortars. For a time the Gordons kept the attackers at bay but before long their supply of bombs ran out and they were gradually forced back from the captured trenches. By 7:30 a.m. the Germans had recovered all their ground and occupied the crater, beating off two efforts by the Borders to retake it.

51 Ibid., pp. 186–187: On the night of 4–5 June 1915, the 22 Brigade took over from a battered 20 Brigade and for the next ten days there was constant shelling, intermittent bombing and sniping. With the very hot weather and so many unburied corpses lying about, clearing up the area was a particularly trying and dangerous task. The Royal Warwickshires in the centre did very good work in patrolling and bringing in valuable information. Their snipers were very successful, particularly two men who lay about 200 yards (183 metres) in front of the enemy line and shot ten Germans on one day.

52 Lance Corporal Michael O'Leary VC (1890-1961).

won his Victoria Cross on 1 February 1915. It's now 10:00 p.m. and our guns have been shelling the enemy lines all day, the Germans have been returning fire on our trenches. Goodnight and God bless you my loved ones. xxxxx

Sunday 6 June 1915: Givenchy Trenches (France)

I was up at 5:30 a.m. to a beautiful Sunday morning. The German artillery have been shelling all day long and our artillery have been returning fire, it is so strange that the heaviest shelling always takes place on Sundays. Sometimes when the shelling ceases for a few minutes and the birds start singing and flying about, I imagine we are not at war, all at once over comes another shell and my thoughts are quickly broken up as I crouch for cover. Two snipers were posted 200 yards (183 metres) in front of our front trench and shot ten of an enemy working party. We have had 4 wounded and 1 killed today and the French are starting an attack on our right. It is now 12:15 a.m. so Goodnight and God bless you my loved ones. xxxx

Monday 7 June 1915: Givenchy Trenches (France)

For about one hour the Germans shelled our trenches about 50 yards (46 metres) to our right with very heavy 'Jack Johnsons.' It is a very hot day and I received a letter from home to say that my poor mother had got cancer, telling me not to worry 'Gods work will be done,' I am upset. Alf Merton sent a letter with cigarettes for the stretcher bearers, it was very good of him and they came at the right time. Our casualties today were 4 killed and 5 wounded, but we did good work, our snipers were very successful. Goodnight and God bless you my loved ones. xxxxx

Tuesday 8 June 1915: Givenchy Trenches (France)

At 4:30 a.m. the casualties came in, 1 killed, 2 wounded. It is another hot morning but after dinner it rained and our artillery have been bombarding the German lines all day, it gives you a head ache. About 4:30 p.m. the Germans dropped a 'Jack Johnson' in the South Staffordshire's dressing station, it was located just in front of ours, but no one was injured, thank God. Our casualties at the end of the day were 1 killed and 4 wounded. I found time to write some letters to the family and so will try to get some sleep. Goodnight and God bless you my loved ones. xxxxx

Wednesday 9 June 1915: Givenchy Trenches (France)

At 4:00 a.m. a wounded man of the Kings Own Regiment was brought in. I did feel sorry for him, he hadn't got a stitch of clothes on him and he was hit yesterday morning, which was due to his inexperience. I must say that those stretcher bearers of the Kings Own Regiment deserve praise for the way they worked. We were supposed to move out of the trenches at 5:00 p.m. but it poured with rain, we were eventually relieved by the Royal Welch Fusiliers at 12:30 a.m. As we walked down the road we could see the flash from the explosions as our fellows and the Germans threw bombs at each other. We arrived at our billets at Marias, just behind the trenches, at 1:00 a.m. tired out. Goodnight and God bless you my loved ones. xxxxxx

Thursday 10–Saturday 12 June 1915: Gorre (France)

At 6:00 a.m. we were awaken by the rain pouring through the house we were billeted in, I had to laugh, someone said that a submarine had torpedoed us. The batteries of artillery are positioned right behind us and they fire their shells over our heads, they are firing all night, the Germans are trying to destroy these batteries and so we are bombarded from both sides. We sent 400 men digging trenches today and had one man killed and one man wounded. We moved off at 3:00 p.m. on Saturday and arrived at our billets at 6:30 p.m., on the march we met Teddy Paul who was wounded and he told us that Dick Smith of the Canadians was killed. The billets are situated in a very quiet spot at Mt Bernenchon but they are not good billets. I had a letter from Edith but I am too tired to write tonight, so Goodnight and God bless you my loved ones. xxxxxxx

Sunday 13 June 1915:

I had a good night's sleep but was awaken by our artillery bombarding the German lines and trying to destroy their wire defences. We are practising putting our gas mask on so that everyman knows exactly how to use them. Goodnight and God bless you my loved ones. xxxxx

Monday 14 June 1915:

Tonight we are shifting back to the Givenchy trenches, our division is going to attack the Germans lines on the evening of 15 June 1915. I had a letter from Flo with a certificate of young Thompson's father who is dangerously ill, I gave it to him and told him to show it to his officer. We marched off at 8:30 p.m. and arrived at Le Casan at10:30 p.m. tired out. Goodnight and God bless you my loved ones. xxxx

Tuesday 15 June 1915: Le Casan

The artillery have been firing throughout the night and continued all day getting more and more intense at 5:00 p.m. We have to be ready to move at 4:00 p.m. but we don't know for certain if we are required for the attack or will be held in reserve. I had a letter from Goodday and he said they were forming a divisional band[53] and the

---

53   William was promoted to Band Sergeant on 26 September 1915.

bandsmen in the trenches would get the first chance to join. The artillery is still firing and we heard that we have taken some enemy trenches. Goodnight and God bless you my loved ones. xxx

Wednesday 16 June 1915: Givenchy Reserve Trench[54]

We had orders at 1:45 a.m. to move up to support the attack and reached the reserve trench at 3:00 a.m. Our men [the Bedfordshire Regiment] took the crater but couldn't hold it, the German bombardment was too heavy and only a few men could attack it at a time. Our artillery bombarded the German trenches and parapets all day and the bombardment intensified at 4:00 p.m. The 21 Brigade made another attack at 4:45 p.m. getting into the crater and inflicted heavy losses on the Germans, but were bombed out and had to retire. We [22 Brigade] are moving up to the advance trenches now and taking over from the 21 Brigade tomorrow night. A bullet has just whizzed right passed me and we are being bombarded as we move through a 2 mile

---

54   Atkinson, *The Seventh Division,* pp. 188–194: On the evening of 15 June 1915 another attack was planned, following days of heavy bombardment to try to destroy the German wire. At 6:00 p.m. the troops went forward but the German defences were extremely formidable, the trenches were nine to ten feet deep and very narrow with well-protected, deep dug-outs. The German lines opened fire directly our advance started across no man's land, killing many before they got within fifty yards (46 metres) of the German trenches, but still the Yorkshires and Wiltshires persistently attacked, only to be cut down by machine-gun fire. A second attack was cancelled because the two battalions were too hard hit to be fit for another attempt. On 16 June another attack was made by the Grenadiers, backed by the Wiltshires and the Canadians, but again the assault failed and they were lucky to escape with only sixty casualties. Despite the lack of success, the Canadians, Scots Fusiliers and Bedfords commenced another attack at 4:45 p.m. on 17 June. Heavy bombardment during the morning and early afternoon was intensified three quarters of an hour before the attack but, two minutes after it stopped, the Germans manned their parapets in strength and opened fire, catching the Scots Fusiliers in the act of leaving their trenches. More than half the troops were killed or wounded before they passed the British wire; in one section five men out of thirteen were hit in their own trenches and very few managed to get more than fifty yards. Two subalterns pushed ahead and were shot on the German wire, but the two leading companies were almost wiped out before the commanding officer prohibited any further advances. The Canadians also had failed and, though the Bedfords got into the crater and made a gallant fight, they were ultimately bombed out. They had the satisfaction, however, of inflicting heavy losses on the Germans, who presented good targets for the two machine-guns as they covered the retirement. After dark, as the survivors of the attack crawled back, the authorities at last began to recognise that Givenchy was not a suitable place for a local offensive without a far heavier weight of guns and ammunition in support of it. On the night of 17–18 June, the 22 Brigade (including the Royal Warwickshires) relieved the 21 Brigade, who were over a thousand men fewer than before the attacks. They had ten days of rest before they were sent back to the front-line at the end of June 1915. The three months which followed the abandonment of the failed Givenchy assault were reasonably quiet and some rest and relaxation was, by army standards, permitted.

(3.2 kilometre) long communication trench to get to the advanced trench, we had 2 casualties. Goodnight and God bless you my loved ones. xxxx

Thursday 17 June 1915: Givenchy Trenches

I was awake nearly all night, pretty quiet so far, wrote to Edith and mother. At about 9:00 p.m. the Germans shelled us thick and fast and then our artillery returned fire. At 10:30 p.m. we had to go out to collect the wounded, we had 5 killed and 18 wounded, it is very difficult to get them out of the trenches which is nothing but a maize. I have seen some dreadful trenches but nothing like these. We finished at 4:00 a.m. and I nearly got hit twice by sniper fire, I had to see that everything was complete and then I laid down, but I was awful cold and couldn't sleep. Goodnight and God bless you my loved ones. xxxxxx

Friday 18 June 1915: Givenchy Trenches

Our bombardment was to take place at 2:45 a.m. but was cancelled. The Germans shelled us at 5:00 a.m. but it was very quiet afterwards. This is an awful position, I saw one of our aeroplanes chasing a German aeroplane today. At about 5:00 p.m. the Germans shelled our trenches and the wounded started to come in. I went up to the trenches to see if everything was clear and then took the doctor around, we had 2 killed and 30 wounded. As I am writing this an awful lot of rifle fire is going on, I am properly tired out and will try to get a nap in case anything happens. Goodnight and God bless you my loved ones. xxxx

Saturday 19 June 1915: Givenchy Trenches

A terrific bombardment started at 3:00 a.m. and at 3:30 a.m. I had to send stretchers up to the trenches to fetch the wounded out. I went up to B Companies trench to help clean out, I was the only one that knew how to get out to the other trenches and it was an awful struggle to get the injured and dead men out. We had to come across the open ground for 30 yards (27 metres) and of course we had to carry all the wounded on our backs. It remained pretty quiet up til 3:00 p.m. when the Canadians came up to relieve us, of course they were spotted by the German observation balloon and their artillery bombarded us with high explosive shrapnel and 'Jack Johnsons.' We had a lot more wounded and had to go out to bring them back, it is hell. I had a most marvellous escape going up to the trenches, I nearly got hit with a piece of shell that just missed me. Coming back I met the doctor and some stretcher bearers of the 22nd Field Artillery, we just got on to the road when I heard some shells coming. We made our dive and fell straight down just behind a house. My God, it was marvellous, for if we had been standing we should have all been killed. Then we had a job, a lot of men six yards (5 metres) away got wounded and so we dressed them up. Poor old Bert Gumbly got seriously wounded, we left at 11:30 p.m. for Les Chocqiaux and arrived at 2:00 a.m. tired out. I had letters from Edith, Jim, Marjorie, Ernest and Jack Tunes, another cake for the stretcher bearers from Smith's sister. Our casualties for the five days were 7 killed and 55 wounded. Goodnight and God bless you my loved ones. xxxxx

Sunday 20 June 1915: Les Chocqiaux

I was over tired and couldn't sleep but what a treat to have a quiet day. Captain Duke came back, he said to me 'you must be getting used to it now Sergeant Webb,' I don't think you can ever get used to this terrible life. Goodnight and God bless you my loved ones. xxxx

Monday 21 June 1915: Les Chocqiaux

I had a good night's sleep and awoke to learn that we are moving back to the trenches today. We moved off at 3:00 p.m. and arrived to the reserve trenches to relieve the Grenadier Guards at 6:00 p.m. Goodnight and God bless you my loved ones. xxxx

Tuesday 22 June 1915: Givenchy Trenches

Today is a very hot day and I did not sleep well last night, it is very uncomfortable in the trenches, I think this area is called Le Plantin. We are under continual bombardment and sniper fire but there are no attacks planned. I wrote to mother, Flo, and Billy Weaver. Goodnight and God bless you my loved ones. xxxxxxx

Wednesday 23–Friday 25 June 1915: Givenchy Trenches

It is pretty quiet today apart from the German bombardments and occasional outburst of rifle fire. We had a draft of sixty men arrive and Doctor Edmonds came with them. Thursday was quiet and on Friday we moved to the advanced trenches at 9:30 p.m. to relieve the 2nd Battalion Queen's Regiment. It had been raining hard all day and the trenches were in a fearful state. Goodnight and God bless you my loved ones. xxxxx

Saturday 26 June 1915: Le Plantin Trenches (North Givenchy)

It is a better day today but the bombardment from both sides continues all day long. As I write this in my diary, I am sitting by a village and it does seem a shame for there is hardly a house left standing and the fields are covered in shell holes. It must have been a pretty village, the birds are singing lovely and then, bang goes a big gun, and we are at war again. The Germans are trying to bomb our batteries which are located close by us and they have just fired sixty big shells, but no damage done. It's Sunday tomorrow, shelling day for the Germans. Had a letter from Edith with photo. Goodnight and God bless you my loved ones xxxxx

Sunday 27 June 1915: Le Plantin Trenches (North Givenchy)

I was awaken at 11:15 p.m. last night and at 1:45 a.m. this morning as the wounded came in, I treated three men. It is a cold morning and the Germans have started to shell at 8:00 a.m. wounding one man. Goodnight and God bless you my loved ones. xxxx

Monday 28 June 1915: Le Plantin Trenches

I dressed a wounded man at 1:45 a.m. this morning, it is a cold and wet day and we are moving out of the trenches later. The Germans shelled us heavily dropping shells just in front of us. At 12:00 noon, an Artillery Officer come to say that one of his men was testing the telephone wires on the road and was blown to pieces with a 'Jack Johnson.' I went up to fetch the poor chap, he was a sight, his back blown out, one leg blown off and the other leg shattered. At 11:30 p.m. they brought another wounded man in, we dressed him and moved off to our billets at Marias arriving at 1:00 a.m. Our casualties today were 5 wounded. Good morning and God bless you my loved ones. xxxxxx

Tuesday 29 June 1915: Gorre (France)

A quiet day today, I wrote some letters to my family and friends. Just outside my dug-out there three soldier's graves beside the road, some poor unfortunate unknown British soldiers, lost to their families forever. Goodnight and God bless you my loved ones. xxx

Wednesday 30 June 1915: Gorre (France)

We move tomorrow, further back into the country for a rest. I watched a fine sight today, three of our aeroplanes flying low over our billets and the Germans shelling them. Lance Corporal William Angus,[55] 8th Royal Scots Regiment has earned the VC. It was a fine deed, he went in the broad daylight to within a few yards of the German Trenches and fetched a wounded officer, receiving some forty wounds by bombs and rifle fire. Goodnight and God bless you my loved ones. Xxxx

Thursday 1 July 1915: Gorre (France)

I had a good night's sleep and it is a very quiet day. The Highland Brigade, Kitchener's First Army relieved us today, they are a fine body of men and came about 7:00 p.m. We moved off at 8:30 p.m., our battalion strength is back to 22 officers and 1009 other ranks. Goodnight and God bless you my loved ones xxxxx

---

55   Lance Corporal William Angus VC (1888-1959).

Friday 2 July 1915: Norrent Fontes (France)

We march all night and arrived at our billets at Norrent Fontes at 5:15 a.m. This place is near Lillers, a large village in France. I am dead tired, too tired to sleep but I laid down for a couple of hours, then put in for furlough which I think will be granted, so roll on Devonport, home to see Edith and Marjorie. Goodnight and God bless you my loved ones. xxxx

Saturday 3 July 1915: Fonte (France)

I couldn't sleep last night, it is very hot and I am overtired, dropped off about 2:00 a.m. I am anxiously waiting to hear if my leave has been approved, Corporal Crisp said he saw Rogerson in the Military Police at Lillers when he came on the billeting party. Had a letter from Edith with a photo of her and Marjorie, I replied to Edith and wrote to mother and Flo. Goodnight and God bless you my loved ones. xxxx

Sunday 4 July 1915: Fonte (France)

I heard that I go on leave tomorrow from 6th until the 12th July, I shall be so happy to see Edith and Marjorie, I am quite excited. Goodnight and God bless you my loved ones. xxxx

Monday 5 July 1915: Fonte (France)

I went to get my leave pass from the orderly room at 9:00 a.m. and found the time has been altered. We have gained on it, we leave Boulogne (France) at 1:00 a.m. on 6 July 1915 and arrive at Victoria (England) at 5:00 a.m. On the return trip we practically gain two days leaving Victoria at 7:15 p.m. instead of 8:30 a.m. on 12 July 1915. I spent the day preparing and left Lillers at 3:53 p.m. arriving at Boulogne at 2:30 a.m.

Tuesday 6–Sunday 11 July 1915: England (Leave)

Arrived Folkestone 5:30 a.m. and Devonport at 2:30 p.m. I am alright now, Edith and Marjorie met me and we had a good leave in Plymouth, England.

War Diary:
Back in the trenches July–August 1915

Monday 12 July 1915: Devonport (England)

I left North Road railway station in Plymouth at 12:30 p.m. to travel back to my regiment in France. I enjoyed my furlough and being with my family but I never kept a record, I left my first two diaries with my wife and will make a fresh start on my third diary. I arrived at Paddington station in London at 4:45 p.m. and then went to Victoria station where I met two ladies who spoke to me for about half an hour. They were on the look-out for Harry Goodwin but they didn't see him although there were quite a few men returning from leave. We left Victoria at 7:15 p.m. and a large crowd came to cheer us as we left the station. We arrived in Folkstone at 9:30 p.m. and left by boat at 10:00 p.m., the passage was good and we arrived in Boulogne at 12:30 a.m. to catch the 1:45 a.m. train to the front. Goodnight and God bless you my loved ones. xxxx

Tuesday 13 July 1915: Boulogne

We arrived in Lilliers at 6:10 a.m. and were given orders to proceed to Chocques where our brigade [22 Brigade] was located. What a pickle we were in, our regiment had moved and we couldn't find out where they had moved too. We boarded the divisional supply trucks that took us to Cologne where I found Corporal Gumbly, he put me on the right track and told me our regiment was at Vieille Chapelle. We finally reached the regiment at 2:30 p.m. and were then told to go directly to the trenches. We arrived at 10:00 p.m. very tired and so Goodnight and God bless you my loved ones. xxxx

Wednesday 14 July 1915: Richebourg L'Avone

It's a very wet day and we are back to the same old things, shells and rifle bullets, they have been shelling us all day long. I managed to write to Edith and mother during the bombardment. Second Lieutenant A Kinlock had a lucky escape although he was wounded, he was looking through his field glasses when a bullet went through them striking his finger. Tillson was sent to hospital tonight and I was made a paid Lance

Sergeant from 10 July1915. Major B P Lefroy DSO joined the battalion and took over command from Major J H Lloyd. Goodnight and God bless you my loved ones. xxx

Thursday 15 July 1915: Trenches at Richebourg L'Avone

It rained in torrents throughout the night and at 12:30 a.m. I had to go out to fetch a wounded man in, it was awful as we were up to our knees in water. It's a bitter cold morning and the Germans have been shelling us continuously all day. A dug-out with two stretcher bearers in it was blown in but they escaped. A man was hit in the abdomen with shrapnel, we are keeping him here to give him a chance. Goodnight and God bless you my loved ones. xxx

Friday 16 July 1915: Trenches at Richebourg L'Avone

The Germans started shelling us about 4:30 a.m. and after a short time it was very quiet, about 11:00 a.m. they started to shell us again and destroyed our dug-out, luckily no one was hurt. The man we kept here that was wounded in the abdomen is going on fine, I think we saved his life. The Germans enfiladed us with machine-gun fire tonight and the shelling is continuous. Our doctor returned from leave and I am waiting up for the ration party to return just in case there are casualties. It has started to rain again and the snipers are very busy, their bullets are hitting just in front of our trench. It's 12:45 a.m. and a very heavy bombardment has started on our right, I am thinking how peaceful it was at home last week. We had 3 men wounded today. Goodnight and God bless you my loved ones. xxxxx

Saturday 17 July 1915: Trenches at Richebourg L'Avone

I got some sleep last night but my feet are like ice, it is a bitter cold day and very cloudy. The Germans shelled our trenches during the morning, we had two men wounded and I managed to get them away at noon. In the afternoon the Germans started a heavy bombardment and I went around all the trenches with the doctor to check the men, another three wounded. Goodnight and God bless you my loved ones. xxxxx

Sunday 18 July 1915: Trenches at Richebourg L'Avone

At 12:00 a.m. I was sent to a man seriously wounded, he was hit in the head with a piece of shrapnel, a very bad wound. We had to carry him on our backs out of the trench, it was 2:00 a.m. before we got back to the dressing station. We had just finished dressing him when another man was hit in the liver, so I had to go out again and bring him back. It was 5:00 a.m. before I had a chance to lay down. The Germans shelled us very heavily about 8:00 a.m., the usual Sunday hymn of hate. We were relieved tonight by the 2nd Queen's Regiment and got back to our billets tired out at

11:30 p.m. Our casualties were 1 officer and 5 other ranks wounded. Goodnight and God bless you my loved ones. xxxxx

Monday 19 July 1915: Le Maisons

We had four men wounded from A Company today, they were shelled by the Germans. Thompson came off furlough and brought me a box of cigarettes from Flo, also Paddy Bremnire came off furlough and when he got here he found out that he had made a mistake and had come back a day before his time. You bet he didn't say anything to the other men. Goodnight and God bless you my loved ones. xxxx

Tuesday 20–Friday 23 July 1915: Le Maisons

It has been pretty quiet the last few days except for periods of heavy shelling. We moved ten miles further back to Carvin on Friday night, it was raining and we got wet through. Goodnight and God bless you my loved ones. xxxx

Saturday 24 July 1915: Carvin

General Capper returned today to resume command of the 7th Division, he was wounded on 18 April 1915. He inspected us and praised us, saying that we had always done our duty and he knew that the 2nd Royal Warwickshires Regiment would always do what was required of them. He then called out the men who came to Belgium with the battalion in October 1914, we mustered 153 men. I feel so sad when they form us up like that, my poor old regiment, we came out 1110 men strong and we are all that remain. Goodnight and God bless you my loved ones. xxxx

Sunday 25 July 1915: Carvin

I went to a church parade, it was very quiet but I enjoyed it. We heard that we go back into the trenches tomorrow. Goodnight and God bless you my loved ones. xxxx

Monday 26 July 1915: Carvin near Robecq

It is a nice day, we started to march at 3:30 p.m. and stopped at Vieille Chapelle for tea, stayed two hours and arrived at the trenches to relieve the 2nd Battalion Border Regiment at 11:00 p.m. We are located at Rue du Bois to the left of Festubert, I feel tired after our journey so am off to bed, Goodnight and God bless you my loved ones. xxxx

Tuesday 27 July 1915: Trenches at Rue du Bois

The Germans started shelling our trenches at 1:00 a.m. and then again at 6:00 a.m. The War Room sent for Heath to go on leave and when he got there, he discovered it was Harvey they required, we teased Heath about it. At 9:30 a.m. it started to rain and it was very cold, the shells were whizzing over our heads as the German artillery fought a duel with our artillery, we had one man wounded in the bombardment. Our airmen also fought a brave battle with the Germans, they kept flying over their front lines with the enemy firing at them but luckily, none were hit. Goodnight and God bless you my loved ones. xxxxx

Wednesday 28 July 1915: Trenches at Rue du Bois

At 7:30 a.m. the Germans shells started to land right next to our dressing station, they were using High Explosive (HE) shells but we escaped without injuries. We had a good laugh today when Wilkins and I tried to make a collapsible table, we finished up after seven hours by making a fixture that wouldn't collapse. I received letters from Edith, Flo and Mother, and I sent post cards in return. Later, I had to send our stretcher bearers to pick up some men of the Queen's, they were on the road and hit by machine-gun fire which killed one man and wounded two others. At 11:00 p.m. our artillery opened fire on a German working party, they retaliated by shelling our trenches. Good night and God bless you my loved ones xxxx

Thursday 29 July 1915: Trenches at Rue du Bois

Another artillery duel going on, the Germans are shelling close by on our right. They still fire at the old German trench where a lot of German dead bodies remain and some skulls, quite clean, the stench is bad. Corporal Crisp arrived back from furlough early and later Harrison was wounded and sent to hospital. The Germans turned their Maxim machine-gun on the road tonight which makes it difficult for us to transport the wounded to hospital. We had 4 men wounded today but I heard we are going to be relieved on Saturday night. Goodnight and God bless you my loved ones. xxxxx

Friday 30 July 1915: Trenches at Rue du Bois

Apart from the showers it is a nice day except for the continuous heavy enemy bombardment. At 11:00 p.m. this evening we had to go out to collect a man wounded in the leg, it was 12:30 a.m. before we got him back to safety. Our casualties today were 1 man killed and 7 wounded. At 1:00 a.m. we went out to collect the other wounded men, it was very difficult getting them back to the dressing station. I carried a man weighing about thirteen stone (83 kg) on my back, after that I called for more stretcher bearers and together we completed our work by 5:30 a.m. The Germans had spotted our working party and opened fire on us as we were bringing the wounded out, I am exhausted and tired out. I passed the old German trench, the stench is awful from the dead bodies, so I am off to have a sleep. Good morning and God bless you my loved ones. xxxx

Saturday 31 July 1915: Trenches at Rue du Bois

I felt a bit rough this morning when the doctor came to ask if we could collect the dead men and bring them out of the trenches. He thought it was too dangerous and I told him it was too much to expect of the men, for if the Germans see only two men in the communication trench, they shell it. Edith and Marjorie are on their way to Warwick now, wish I was with them. The shelling has been heavy all day, after dark we collected the dead men and eventually moved off at 12:15 a.m. marching all night to reach our billets at Cornet Bourdois. Goodnight and God bless you my loved ones. xxxxx

Sunday 1 August 1915:

After marching all night we stopped in a field for tea and something to eat, I felt very tired. Our battalion strength is 26 officers and 960 other ranks. I had to stay and bring a man along who fell sick, we got lost and didn't know which way to go so I decided to follow my nose until we found our billets. We are staying in the same house at Le Cornet Bourdois, the woman and her husband were pleased to see us again. I had a sleep from 1:00 p.m. to 4:30 p.m., then opened my letters and parcel from Edith and wrote back to her. Goodnight and God bless you my loved ones. xxxxx

Monday 2–Sunday 8 August 1915: Le Cornet Bourdois

I had a laugh on Tuesday, I never had any pockets in my trousers, so I asked the woman in the house to put two in for me. She had my trousers for about three quarters of an hour when they informed me that our Divisional General (General Capper) was coming around to inspect our billets, so I had to send for my trousers. After he had gone I gave them back to her, and she had just got all the seams open when we had the order to stand to. I was in a fix and had to wear my trousers with the seams open. The doctor had a good laugh, it turned out to be a practice drill. The remainder of the week was quiet except for route marches. On Saturday we had the Divisional Band[56] come to entertain us, it was very good considering they had only been together for a fortnight. It was Marjorie's birthday on Sunday 8 August 1915, we went to a church service where a man of the Queen's played a cornet for the hymns and it made

---

56   A welcome innovation during periods out of the line, the 7th Division Band was formed in July 1915. William was promoted to Band Corporal 4 August 1912 and to Band Sergeant 26 September 1915. He played the violin and trumpet, and also enjoyed performing with a mouth organ.

the service go twice as well. I wrote letters to all my family and to Linda Mckee. Goodnight and God bless you my loved ones. xxx

Monday 9 August 1915: Le Cornet Bourdois

Our 22 Brigade went on a route march today, it was very hot and I saw an airship flying in the distance. In the evening we had a boxing competition and heard that our troops had captured the trenches at Hooge. Goodnight and God bless you my loved ones. xxx

Tuesday 10–Monday 16 August 1915: Le Cornet Bourdois

Monday was a quiet day but very murky and close so I went for a swim in the canal. On Tuesday the Bishop and Lord Mayor of Birmingham visited us, they spoke to a lot of the men. The rest of the week was quiet except for the brigade boxing competition, where our regiment had three wins, and our field sports day. We move off at 5:30 a.m. on Tuesday 17 August 1915. Goodnight and God bless you my loved ones. xxxx

Tuesday 17 August 1915: Le Cornet Bourdois

I got up at 3:00 a.m. and we marched to Le Casan at 5:15 a.m. where we bivouacked in a field, during dinner it rained so we shifted into barns. We moved off at 8:15 p.m. and arrived at the local billets in Rue des Chevattes at 10:00 p.m. Our battalion strength is 24 officers and 975 other ranks. Goodnight and God bless you my loved ones. xxxx

Wednesday 18 August 1915: Trenches at Rue des Chevattes

Just a few yards from here a Major of the Highland Light Infantry and some of his men were killed the other day. It has been an awful cold and raining all day long. Goodnight and God bless you my loved ones. xxxx

Thursday 19 August 1915: Trenches at Rue des Chevattes

Today I had to send the stretcher bearers out with a digging party to clear some of the trenches. I read in the papers that one of our transport ships had been sunk in the Dardanelles, 600 men were saved and 1000 lost. Goodnight and God bless you my loved ones. xxxx

Friday 20–Saturday 21 August 1915: Trenches at Rue des Chevattes

The last two days have been very quiet but as I am writing this a terrific rifle fire has opened and our big guns have started firing. Goodnight and God bless you my loved ones xxxx

Sunday 22 August 1915: Rue des Chevattes

I had a poor night's sleep last night and today I don't feel very well. The doctor wanted to send me into hospital but I won't go. The Germans brought down a French aeroplane this morning, I ran over to see if anyone was injured, but the airman landed safely in a field. Lieutenant Richardson came back today and told us we are going into different trenches tonight. We arrived in the trenches at Rue du Bois at 8:30 p.m. to relieve the South Staffordshire Regiment. At 10:30 p.m. a private of the 6th Gordon's was brought in shot straight through the temple but still living. Our casualties today were 1 man killed, one officer, 2nd Lieutenant Stutter, and 2 other ranks wounded. Goodnight and God bless you my loved ones. xxxxx

Monday 23 August 1915: Trenches at Rue du Bois

The German bombardment was heavy at 5:30 a.m. today and our artillery replied. They brought a dead man in and it took two stretcher bearers to dig his grave. We had to carry the body 1½ miles (2.5 kilometres) to bury him, they have a large cemetery there and a Minister was present, we got back at 6:00 p.m. I started work immediately, Captain P K Wise was killed, Sergeant Melbury and Second Lieutenant W S de C Stretton was wounded, other ranks 2 men were killed and 2 wounded, and a man of the Queen's Regiment was hit with shrapnel, it's now 12:00 a.m. and I have just finished. Goodnight and God bless you my loved ones. xxxx

Tuesday 24 August 1915: Trenches at Rue du Bois

At 2:30 a.m. they woke me up to tell me a man had been killed, I never went to sleep again and took him down to be buried at 8:30 a.m. It's a nice day but the shelling is pretty heavy. Later another man was killed and we buried him at 4:30 p.m. It is a nice burial ground and it is good to think that theses brave men are buried decently, the shells as they whizz overhead seem to be a proper fitting. I sent a letter to Edith and mother, so Goodnight and God bless you my loved ones. xxx

Wednesday 25 August 1915: Trenches at Rue du Bois

I was awaken at 12:45 a.m. when a man was shot through his arm. At 7:00 a.m. they brought poor old Sergeant Wilson in, he was killed by an aerial torpedo, the first that has been used against us, it makes a bigger hole than a 'Jack Johnson' and an awful noise. We buried poor old Wilson at 4:30 p.m. after I sewed him up in a sack. It is now 7:45 p.m. and they have just started to use their torpedo bombs again. I have just had a letter from Edith and she tells me that Wilfred Moon was killed, so I went along the trench to tell his brother. When I saw him he was cheerful and appeared not to know anything about it, so I decided not to tell him now. The snipers are very busy and our trench mortars started firing at the German aerial torpedo, they made it cease firing.

It seems to be propelled by a jet of steam and so you can see it high up in the air, you have time to dodge it providing you see it first. Lodge night tonight, so Goodnight and God bless you my loved ones.xxxx

Thursday 26 August 1915: Trenches at Rue du Bois

I had a splendid night's sleep and awoke to a very quiet day although our artillery was very active. Charley Moon had a letter today to tell him of his brother's death so I went to talk with him for a couple of hours. I felt so sorry for him, he was so fond of his brother and when he saw me he started crying, poor chap. I had a letter from Edith asking me if we should adopt my youngest sister Adelaide's baby, I wrote back to Edith, also to mother and Uncle William. Goodnight and God bless you my loved ones. xxxxxx

Friday 27 August 1915: Trenches at Rue du Bois

Just as I was going to lay down last night at 11:00 p.m., we heard a cheer and then a terrific rifle fire, the bullets came over in hundreds and it kept up for about twenty minutes. I went up to the trenches to find out if there were any wounded but there wasn't any. The cause of the firing was the Germans cheered and then made an attempt to get out of their trenches, so our men let them have it thick and fast, they soon returned to their trenches. I went to bed at 2:30 a.m. and had a good night's sleep. Today is very quiet, our artillery bombarded the Germans but they did not reply. We are to be relieved tonight by the Indian Regiment, we hear that we are going to Givenchy, another warm place. There is a lot of firing tonight, it generally happens the night we are going to be relieved, our artillery fires on the enemy and they return the fire as we come out of the trenches. We got clear and arrived at our billets in Hinges at 12:00 mid-night. Goodnight and God bless you my loved ones. xxxxx

Saturday 28 August 1915 Hinges

I had a splendid bath today, it was glorious, then I walked around one of the barges that transport the wounded down to Paris, they are very wide and splendidly fitted with every comfort. We are shifting today to the reserve trench and marched off at 7:00 p.m. to Noyelles, arriving at 11:00 p.m. and taking over the General Headquarters Lines in the 1st Division area. We had to find places to sleep the best way we could and eventually got into bed at 1:00 a.m. Good morning and God bless you my loved ones. xxxxx

Sunday 29 August 1915 Sailly Labourse

The trenches here are fifteen feet deep in some places, they were dug into chalk to defend the village should an attack take place. It is surprising to see that the village and coal mines have not been touched, the Allemands (Germans) must have been very good when they got driven from here, but they did shell the church. Jim Hawkins was in the paper on Friday for receiving the St Georges Medal 1st Class (Honours given by the Czar of Russia). We are the only regiment from the 22 Brigade around here. I am writing this diary roughly, but God sparing me, after the war I intend to re-write it.[57] Every one went digging trenches tonight in the rain, we had a terrible time, poor old Ted Yorke was killed. We had 3 killed and 9 wounded. I fetched poor old Ted and carried him on my back. I had just returned when they shouted 'man wounded,' I ran out in the front of the trenches and it was a man of A Company, about 13 stone, they helped me get him on my back. We finished work at 5:30 a.m. Tuesday morning, properly tired out, so good morning and God bless you my loved ones. xxxxx

Monday 30 August 1915 Vermelles

I am too tired to sleep and it's a cold day, we are digging trenches again tonight. I had to bury our two men today, no Minister, so I used Edith's prayer book to read the burrial service. We went digging again and Lieutenant H S Mannsell was dangerously wounded and one other man. It took us two hours to get Lieutenant Mannsell out of the trenches, he was very heavy, I got back to reserve trench at 8:30 a.m. The heavy work of carrying the wounded had told on us, for we were all completely exhausted. On the way back we had to pass a main road and last night the Germans must have seen us, for tonight they put their machine-gun on us, we were soon lying down in the trench I can tell you. There is a communication trench that the Germans made when they occupied Vermelles and it runs along beside the road, of course it is quicker to walk along the road because you avoid the twisting and turning of the trench. As we were coming back this morning, the snipers had a few shots at us, they have their rifles fixed on the gap between the trees. As you pass the tree they fire, but they were just too late every time. Good morning and God bless you my loved ones. xxxxx

Tuesday 31 August 1915: Vermelles

Today I went into the ruins at Vermelles, just fancy a town without a solid house standing and occupied by troops. There is a hospital in the cellars of a building and I went to the Recovery Room that used to be, lo and behold it was turned into a club with a bar. I toured the Vermelles club, you can buy tea, cocoa, chocolate and such like so I sat down and wrote letters to Edith and Linda McKee. As I was writing to Edith the Germans started to shell us with 'Jack Johnsons,' they had their observation balloon up and they must have seen about 200 French civilians digging, they showed up very plain on the white chalk. This is one of the new places we have taken over

---

57   William never found the time to rewrite his diaries, so I feel honoured to be able to complete his wishes, albeit too late for him to see them.

from the French, we are going back to Sailly Labourse after digging. The Germans shelled again and a piece hit the Head Quarters of the South Staffordshire Regiment, wounding two men, we got to Labourse at 5:30 a.m. tired out. Good morning and God bless you my loved ones. xxxx

War Diary:
Battle of Loos September–October 1915

Wednesday 1 September 1915: Labourse

I feel very tired today and I have a cold so I expect that has a lot to do with it. We marched off at 4:00 p.m. to a position about 15 miles (24 kilometres) further back and on the way we stopped outside Bethune for tea. As we passed through Bethune we saw where the Germans had bombarded, they had missed the houses and the shells had fallen into a piece of waste ground. We also saw thousands of small ladders which shows we are going to make an attack, this is the proof. We got to Manqueville at 11:00 p.m. and found our billets, it rained all the way. Our battalion strength is 24 officers and 936 other ranks. Eric Bench went in to hospital with a knee injury, dislocated I think. I had a letter from Edith which I read and then turned in. Goodnight and God bless you my loved ones. xxxx

Thursday 2 September 1915: Busnes

Our battalion paraded at 5:30 p.m. and then we marched to billets in Busnes, we will be moving on tomorrow, it rained all the way. Goodnight and God bless you my loved ones.

Friday 3 September 1915: Busnes

We move again today, it is a very wet, cold day. I had a letter from Edith, she told me that my sister Adelaide is so ill that they have sent for her husband to come home from France. We marched off at 3:40 p.m. in torrential rain and on the way we passed the 2nd Division, who is also part of I Corps in the British First Army.[58] I saw Colonel

---

58 The composition of the First Army during the Battle of Loos was as follows: First Army commanded by General Sir Douglas Haig comprised the following: I Corps, IV Corps, XI Corps, and Indian Corps; I Corps (GOC Lieutenant-General Sir Hubert Gough) comprised the following: 2nd Division, 7th Division, 9th Scottish Division, and 28th Division; 7th Division commanded by Major-General T. Capper until 27 Sept 1915,

Sanderson who used to belong to my regiment and is now commanding the Royal North Lancashire Regiment. We arrived at Verquin, our destination, at 7:30 p.m. wet through, our billeting party got lost and they arrived two hours after us. We had new men drafted in to join us (1 officer and 39 other ranks) and we are billeted in a house with a severely wounded man. Goodnight and God bless you my loved ones. xxxxx

Saturday 4 September 1915: Verquin

We had a very quiet day today so I wrote to Edith, Mother and Linda McKee. I received a letter from home with all the news. Goodnight and God bless you my loved ones. xxxx

Sunday 5 September 1915: Verquin

The doctor woke me up last night to tell me to send stretcher bearers out with the digging party but I decided to go myself. We paraded at 8:00 a.m., then travelled a long way in motor-lorries before we reached the Vermelles trenches, two men were wounded while we were digging, an attack is coming off here shortly so we are sending another party out tomorrow. Goodnight and God bless you my loved ones. xxxx

Monday 6 September 1915: Verquin

We are busy preparing for the big attack and so I got all my washing done early today. Many guns have arrived here and I saw two 15 inch (380mm) guns go up tonight, we can hear the French guns bombarding the German lines on our right. We went out with the digging party same as yesterday. Goodnight and God bless you my loved ones. xxxx

Tuesday 7 September 1915: Verquin

It is a beautiful day, very quiet, I took the opportunity to rest and write some letters to my family. Goodnight and God bless you my loved ones. xxxx

followed by Major-General H. E. Watts comprised of: 20 Brigade, 21 Brigade, 22 Brigade, Divisional Artillery, Royal Engineers, and Medical Corps; 22 Brigade commanded by Brigadier-General J. Mc. C. Steele comprised the following regiments: 2nd Royal Warwickshire, 1st Royal Welch Fusiliers, 1st South Staffordshire, 2nd Queen's, and 7th King's.

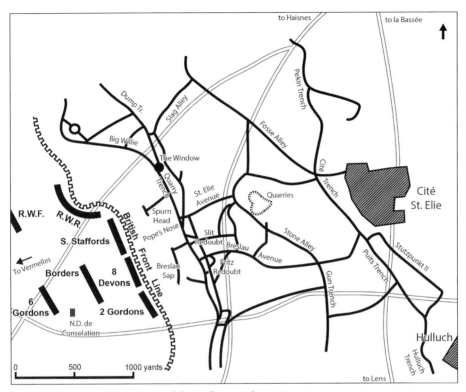

Map 8 Loos and vicinity.

Wednesday 8 September 1915: Vermelles trenches

We moved from Labourse to the trenches at 11:30 a.m. and had to go up in platoons at ten minute intervals. I called in the cemetery at Labourse to visit poor Ted Yorke's grave, he is the only English soldier buried there as it is a civilian cemetery. I sent a note to Fred Reeves to see if he could arrange to get it turfed and cleaned up by the Transport Group. We had a laugh as we came through Vermelles or rather what was left of it, we saw our men putting a 6 inch (152mm) Howitzer into a broken down house that was used by our miners (soldiers who do all the mining), on the door was chalked 'we work for a shilling a day and don't strike,' that is a good one for the Welsh miners. Our battalion with a paper strength of 20 officers and 736 other ranks arrived in the trenches at 4:00 p.m. to relieve the 8th Devonshire Regiment.[59] I inquired for

---

59   Atkinson, *The Seventh Division,* pp. 199–200: The 8th Battalion Devonshire Regiment
     held the front line and was active in patrolling and foiling the enemy's attempts to enquire
     into the preparations being made for the next attack. No man's land was much too wide,

Mrs Merton's brother, Tom Sheppard, found him and had a chat, he didn't know me and I didn't know him, but as soon as I told him who I was he said, "What Mrs Webb's husband." I was on the go until 9:30 p.m. running around the trenches. Goodnight and God bless you my loved ones. xxxxx

Thursday 9 September 1915: Vermelles trenches

I woke up to the tune of the German bombardment, a very misty morning, our big guns were very active also. It is a strange coincidence that every time we are in the trenches just before an attack I meet a Royal Flying Corps airman, the one I met today is a telegraphese to an observation officer. I had my coat open and my pendant with Marjorie's photograph was showing so he mentioned it and showed me a photograph of his little girl, she was Marjorie's double. We were working all day to strengthen our dug-out, so Goodnight and God bless you my loved ones. xxxx

Friday 10 September 1915: Vermelles trenches

I couldn't sleep for the cold and so I got up at 5:00 a.m., it is a beautiful day. A very heavy artillery duel started, the Germans got a direct hit on one of our field guns located in an old house and it killed 2 men and wounded 3 others. Harvey went to fetch some bread and was near the house so he dived into the house opposite. A draft of 2 officers and 18 other ranks arrived from Base for duty bringing our strength up to 22 officers and 756 men of other ranks. Our aeroplanes are very active flying over the enemy lines, the Germans shell them very badly but they still go over. I received a letter from Edith with a parcel filled with cake, bread, sweets, chocolate, salmon and writing paper, it was all very welcome and good of her to send it. Goodnight and God bless you my loved ones. xxxxxx

Saturday 11 September 1915: Vermelles trenches

About 8:30 p.m. a stretcher bearer of the Bedfordshire Regiment came to me to ask where he could take one of his men who had been hit, so I went with him to collect the injured man. However, he forgot where he left the man on account of the maize of trenches, we went about 2 miles (3.2 kilometres) around different trenches before we found the place where he was but he had already been taken to hospital. Alf Merton sent me a photograph of the 2nd Royal Warwickshire band (see photograph below), I

so to secure a satisfactory 'jumping-off line' for the attack the British front line had to be brought within 500 yards (461 metres) of the German trenches and two new support trenches dug between the new and the old fronts. This led to several sharp encounters, in one on 7 September 1915, a fighting patrol of the 8th Devonshire Regiment drove off an enemy covering party after a brisk "scrap".

11 Royal Warwickshire Regiment Band William Webb—middle row, second from left.

remember quite a few of the old faces. Goodnight and God bless you my loved ones.
xxxxxx

Sunday 12 September 1915: Vermelles trenches

We were relieved by the Queen's Regiment tonight at 5:00 p.m. and as we left
the trenches the Germans started shelling us, luckily we had no casualties. We
stopped at Sailly Labourse and had tea, then marched off at 9:00 p.m., people
were standing at their doors with lamps as we went by singing. When we marched
through Verquin we were told not to tell anyone what regiment or division we
were as they suspected spies were present. All the carts have had the brigade and
division painted out, we marched about 10 miles (16 kilometres) to a place called
Fouquereuil. We heard that the Medical Officer of the Queen's was killed just as
we left the trenches. Our doctor was upset as he was a great friend of the Queen's
doctor. I got into bed at 12:30 a.m. tired out. Goodnight and God bless you my
loved ones. xxxx

Monday 13 September 1915: Fouquereuil

At 8:40 a.m. we marched to a place called Le Harisoir, it is very hot and a lot of men
fell out with exhaustion, you can't expect anything else, we had our boots on all the
time we were in the trenches but did very little walking, marching is now very difficult for them. I heard that more men of the Queen's Regiment have been killed. Our
regiment broke a record the last time we were in the trenches, we had no casualties.
Goodnight and God bless you my loved ones. xxxx

Tuesday 14 September 1915: Le Harisoir

I had a good night's sleep last night and all is quiet today, we continue to prepare for the next attack but it is very cold so I wrote some letters to my family. Goodnight and God bless you my loved ones. xxxxx

Wednesday 15 September 1915: Le Harisoir

Today we had physical training then played B Company at football, we lost 4-0. It was here that a French woman gave birth to a child the other day and our doctor attended her, so they named the child Warwick George after our regiment. Goodnight and God bless you my loved ones. xxxxxx

Thursday 16 September 1915: Le Harisoir

We have been issued with new smoke helmets and they have got glass eye pieces and a tube to breathe through. We are still preparing for the next attack, getting bandages and all the other medical equipment packed, also we have been issued with various oils for use if they use burning liquid in their flame throwers. Cox came off furlough and he brought some tomatoes with him so we had a good feed. Goodnight and God bless you my loved ones. xxxxxx

Friday 17 September 1915: Le Harisoir

It's a beautiful day today so I did my washing and had a good bath, I feel about two stones (12 kg) lighter. All leave has been stopped. Goodnight and God bless you my loved ones. xxxxxx

Saturday 18 September 1915: Le Harisoir

Before breakfast I went out with the stretcher bearers, the regiment was practicing rapid loading, so I had to be there in case of an accident. After breakfast we practised the attack and every man was warned against talking amongst civilians just in case we are overheard and information about our attack reaches the spies. It's a beautiful day and I managed to buy some post cards with the various flags shown on them, I sent one to Edith and Marjorie, the other to mother. We heard that three new divisions were coming out and that the 2nd Battalion Royal Warwickshire Regiment will be the first regiment to go over the top. Goodnight and God bless you my loved ones. xxxxxx

Sunday 19 September 1915: Le Harisoir

It was a very cold night but a beautiful morning when we went on church parade. A fleet of our aeroplanes flew over this evening towards the German line, there were about twelve of them and I expect they are on a raid. Goodnight and God bless you my loved ones. xxxxx

Monday 20 September 1915: Le Harisoir

Eleven aeroplanes flew over again this evening, probably on another raid. I saw the baby that is named after our regiment, he is a fine child. Goodnight and God bless you my loved ones. xxxx

Tuesday 21 September 1915: Le Harisoir

I heard those aeroplanes come back at 1:00 a.m. and during the day we played B Company at football, the result was a draw. This is a suspense waiting for the attack, we move up nearer the front line tomorrow to a place called Noyelles.[60] We are expecting to go into the trench on Friday and over the top on Saturday. I am hoping and trusting in God to come through it safely. Goodnight and God bless you my loved ones. xxx

Wednesday 22 September 1915: Le Harisoir

I had a good night's sleep and awoke to a beautiful day. We moved off at 4:00 p.m. to Noyelles which is near Vermelles and as we passed through Bethune it was full of troops, we arrived at 9:00 p.m. Goodnight and God bless you my loved ones xxxx

Thursday 23 September 1915: Noyelles

Our batteries are positioned quite close to us and they have been shelling the German wire and trenches all day. In return, the Germans dropped a lot of 'Jack Johnsons'

---

60   The Loos battleground was situated immediately north of the mining town of Lens, in the heart of the industrial area of north-east France. The ground there was uniformly flat and dominated by slagheaps connected with the coal mining in the district. The combined Franco-British offensive attacked eastwards against the German Sixth Army and the plan was to attack on a twenty mile front between Arras and La Bassée, using the French Tenth Army and the British First Army. Experience at Neuve Chapelle and Festubert had shown that troops attacking on a narrow front would suffer from concentrated fire; the First Army therefore made their attack front as wide as possible. Air observations had revealed that the German defences had been massively strengthened in the area to be attacked. Not only had the front line been deepened, reinforced and equipped with many machine-guns and wide barbed wire belts, but an equally strong second and third line of defence had also been prepared behind it.

about 100 yards (92 metres) to our right. We moved up to the forward trenches at 11:00 p.m. tonight, it is raining and to make things worse my right boot has ripped across the sole and halfway across the front, so all the mud and water is getting in. We are standing in the trenches with mud up past our knees, I am tired out and wet through to my skin. It's 1:30 a.m. and our artillery is engaged in a heavy bombardment, I have got to lie down, I am so tired. I took my boots off and they are full with mud. Good morning and God bless you my loved ones. xxxxxx

Friday 24 September 1915: Trenches at Noyelles[61]

I was awaken at 2:30 a.m. by a tremendous roar of guns as our artillery continued the bombardment. We had one man wounded and I took him to our dressing station to dress his wounds, of course, I couldn't put my socks on, so I had to wear only boots which immediately filled with mud and water. The French on the right were also shelling very intensely making it a miserable day. I had to cut a sand bag up for socks but that did not help, I was up to my knees in mud and water. As before, during these bombardments I suffer with a terrible headache, I don't know darling if I shall be able to send you a post card today, I will if possible. I heard that the final bombardment starts at 5:50 a.m. tomorrow morning and we go over the top at 6:30 a.m., so I am going to try to get a sleep. Goodnight and please God protect me so that I can return home safely to my loved ones xxxx

Saturday 25 September 1915: Vermelles trenches (Battle of Loos)

Just after sunrise at 5:50 a.m. the British Artillery opened the intense stage of the final bombarded, trying to cut the barbed wire defences all along the German front lines; at the same time smoke candles were ignited and gas[62] poured out from the cylinders

---

61   Atkinson, *The Seventh Division*, pp. 201–204: The BEF deployed three Army Corps in their principal attack. The IV Corps was attacking on a frontage from just South-West of Loos to the Vermelles–Hulluch road, the I Corps on its left carried on to the Vermelles–Auchy lez La Bassée railway with two divisions and had a third attacking astride the La Bassée Canal; the newly formed XI Corps was held in reserve along with masses of cavalry, ready to exploit the advantage should the first attack succeed in breaking through the German defences. The I Corps would use the 7th Division on the right and the 9th Division on its left would attack in a North–Easterly direction whilst the 2nd Division would attack eastwards along the canal. The 7th Division was to use the 20 Brigade on the right of their divisional frontage with the 22 Brigade on the left and the 21 Brigade forming the divisional reserve. The assaulting battalions were the 2nd Gordons, 8th Devons, 1st South Staffords, 2nd Royal Warwickshires, with the Welch Fusiliers in support and the Queen's in reserve.
62   Ibid., pp. 205–208: What wind there was blew from the desired quarter, the south-west, but it was too light to carry the gas across to the German trenches, especially in front of the 22 Brigade front. On this part of the line the gas hung about the British trenches

that had previously been carefully positioned for the wind to blow the gas across to the German lines. At 6:30 a.m. our boys went over the top but when they reached the German barbed wire, they found that our artillery had failed to break holes in it,[63] so they were held up and suffered many casualties from the German machine-guns and rifle fire. The regiment made a fresh start and went in groups of five, this time they got through the wire but again the casualties were high. Captain Matear was killed, he was the first over the top and through the wire. Our poor old regiment has suffered terribly, our Commanding Officer Colonel B R Lefroy was killed, also the Adjutant Captain J P Duke, Captain J S Knyvett, Captain L R Swinhoe, Lieutenant R F Richardson, in fact we have only one or the most two officers left in the regiment. The casualties are extremely heavy, we went up to the barbed wire to help the wounded, what terrible sights to see the men laying there dead. I found Lieutenant H E Edwards, he had been killed so I took his personal things from him; the enemy fire was so intensive that we had to come back to the trenches. The Germans continued to bombard and machine-gun us but we went back up to the wire again; we couldn't get all the wounded back, we had no stretchers left to carry them. We took the first casualties down on the stretchers to the Royal Army Medical Corps but they didn't have any to give us in return. It is 12:00 midnight and we are still waiting for some stretchers, it has rained awful hard, I am drenched, cold, covered in blood and don't know when we shall be finished. Jock Baily and Blackwell, our stretcher bearers, were hit again, the Germans have started another heavy bombardment, our artillery is replying. We have had some small victories today taking about 60 German prisoners[64]

and many men, particularly in the Royal Warwickshires, were incapacitated by it. The barbed wire defences of the Germans had been hidden by long grass, and when the men of the South Staffordshire and Royal Warwickshire regiments reached it, they found long stretches uncut. Determined efforts were made to get through the obstacle and to cut the wire by hand, but from the trenches behind a deadly machine-gun fire poured down on them and casualties were numerous. The Royal Warwickshire Regiment had their Commanding Officer, Colonel Lefroy, killed, and several other officers fell with him. The Adjutant, Captain Duke, was wounded.

63   On 25 September 1915 during the attack by the 2nd Royal Warwickshire Regiment on the first line German trenches, Private Vickers on his own initiative, went forward in front of his company under very heavy shell, rifle and machine-gun fire and cut the wires which were holding up a great part of his battalion. Although it was broad daylight at the time, he carried out this work standing up and his gallant action contributed largely to the success of the assault. For this courageous act he was awarded the Victoria Cross.

64   The battalion war diary for this action runs as follows: "Our advance commenced at 6:30 a.m, we took the German front line trench, then the support trench and advanced into the Quarries as far as St. Elie. Captured about 60 prisoners; arrived at this position at 9:30 a.m. and kept to it till after dark when we had to retire owing to the 9th Division on our left retiring. Occupied the Quarries until midnight when we took up a position in the support trench 400 yards (365 metres) west of the Quarries." Total battalion losses for 25 September 1915: Officers killed: Lieutenant Colonel B R Lefroy DSO, Captain N H L Matear, Lieutenant F R Elderton, Lieutenant H E Edwards, Lieutenant Pennington,

12 Battle of Loos 25 September 1915, British soldiers lying dead near German barbed wire defences. (IWM Q28975)

but our casualties are very high, may God protect me and look after me for your sakes my loved ones. xxxxx

Sunday 26 September 1915: Vermelles trenches (Battle of Loos)

We continued to work throughout the night in terrible conditions, up to our knees in mud and it was pitiful to hear the wounded moaning as we moved amongst them to find our men. Other men from different regiments were saying "take me mate, I was hit at 6:30 a.m. yesterday," it makes one's heart bleed, but what can we do, we must find our own men first. Try and picture a moonlight night with men lying around dead and wounded, all shapes and sizes; we move and turn them over to find out who they are. The only light you get is from the star shells and the landing of artillery shells on the battle field. The Germans were firing gas shells, oh the stink of it, we had to put our gas helmets on; earlier our regiment was bombed out of the Quarries by gas

Lieutenant J S O Mansergh, Lieutenant K M Gaunt, and Lieutenant T E Newsome; officers wounded: Captain J P Duke, Captain L R Swinkie, Captain J S Knyvett, Lieutenant R F Richardson, Second Lieutenants – B G Hill, S W W Cannon, N Allen, E W Blenkiniop, P H Oremer; officers missing: Second Lieutenant P H Herbage; other ranks: Killed 64 men, wounded 171, missing 273. The 2nd Battalion Royal Warwickshire Regiment could only muster 140 men, Lieutenant H F William Freeman from the 3rd Battalion joined and took over the remains of the battalion in the trenches. See TNA WO 95/1664/3: 2nd Royal Warwickshire Regiment War Diary.

bombs. I am so tired, working all night, it is now 7:00 a.m. The Germans continued to shell us all day and we are still up to our knees in mud and water. We attacked again and took the Quarries, my poor old battalion is about wiped out again; we have worked all day on the wounded, dressing them and getting them away for the doctors to treat them. The Germans counter-attacked on our left, it is a coal pit, but they were driven off. I think we have done pretty well but I have not slept properly for four days and nights. I can't get a post card to you love and I know that you will be worried. I can't find out anything of my cousin Eric Bench, I don't know if he is alive or dead. I am going to go out and start searching for the wounded again in a few minutes, we are getting wounded in from all regiments. The shellfire has been terrific on both sides and plenty of rifle fire, strange how we always fight on Sundays. We have got all our wounded men in now and the dead is an awful sight. Captain Martin has seven bullet wounds, one through the heart, when he fell he must have turned round and got the other six. We do look a sketch, we are covered from head to foot with mud and my clothes are covered in blood. Water is an awful trouble to get here and we haven't any rations or mail for days, we shall have to fend for ourselves tomorrow. I have 21 years of service today, so Goodnight and God bless you my loved ones. xxxxx

Monday 27 September 1915: Vermelles trenches (Battle of Loos)

I managed to get some sleep last night and at 4:30 a.m. very heavy shelling started, the battle continues and it is a very hard fight, the Germans have brought up a lot more artillery and reserve troops. I can't find out anything about my cousin Eric Bench and I am getting worried that he may be injured or killed. Today we only muster 140 men but some may have got mixed up with other divisions, we are all very tired, worn out and hungry. I wonder if we will get relieved tonight; it doesn't look like it. The 2nd Division has moved up and they are fighting hard for the colliery, it is now 4:30 p.m. and our battle is raging, the fighting is very fierce and the artillery fire is terrific, oh how my head aches. I heard that poor old Ginger Aitken was killed today and very heavy fighting took place late this evening, it is awful, fight, fight, fight, no rest, I found out that Jack Shelly and Wocker were killed on Saturday. It is very cold and at last I managed to send post card to Edith and mother, so Goodnight and God bless you my loved ones. xxxx

Tuesday 28 September 1915: Vermelles trenches (Battle of Loos)

I laid down to rest at 2:00 a.m. tired out. We were asked if we would help out the Middlesex Regiment as they had only just arrived from England and were in an awful fix, the stretcher bearers must have lost their heads. We all went up to help them and got into the third line of the German Trenches, but we couldn't get the wounded out as they were fighting hard for the colliery and we couldn't get across no man's land. There is a terrific battle going on for the colliery, it is an awful hard position to take, one side gains control and then the other side counter attacks and retrieves it. I saw a

13 Battle Loos 25 September 1915, British soldiers lying dead in front of a captured German trench. (IWM Q28980)

fine sight, some men from the Scottish Regiment charging the colliery and overpower the Germans to take it. We found a wounded man of the Suffolk Regiment, he had been out in no man's land for three days, he was badly hit and I had to carry him on my back all the way back to the dressing station. The battle is still raging and there is no sign of getting relieved, it is a bit off, they have thousands of fresh troops, why don't they relieve us, we are only 140 strong and worn out, but still we must keep on fighting. I had a good laugh today, I was looking at different people and to see the muddy clothes, unshaven and unwashed faces, half without hats, myself included, we do look a disreputable lot, we will be so glad to get a wash, shave and brush up. It is an awful sight to see the dead lying in heaps, but what can we do, nothing, this operation has been a proper struggle today. Goodnight love, it is pouring with rain, so God bless you and keep my loved ones safe. xxxx

Wednesday 29 September 1915: Vermelles trenches (Battle of Loos)

A fierce artillery duel started about 6:00 a.m., the Germans have been dropping shells around us and it continued all day long, very fierce fighting in the trenches and bombing[65] all the time. General Capper[66] was wounded during the battle on the 26 September 1915 and he died the following morning. The weather is awful, raining in torrents, so we are up to our necks in mud, we can't get any water today and so we are feeding on bully beef and biscuits, nice, I haven't any teeth to bite with. I hear we are getting relieved tonight, I shall be so glad for we are properly worn out and I shall be able to write to Edith, I know she must be anxious, oh for a good sleep and a proper meal. The shelling continued all evening and the rain did not stop, we were relieved at 8:00 p.m. and just as we were leaving the trenches they fired their machine-guns on us, we had to lay down in all the mud and water until they ceased, then we moved on and just as we got on the road they fired four sweeping shrapnel shells at us. We dived into the communication trench on the side of the road, we had a narrow escape and afterwards we had a good laugh for our faces were covered in mud from the trenches. We moved up the trench a bit but it was too hard walking up to our knees in mud, so we got on the road again and eventually arrived at our billets at Sailly-Labourse utterly worn out. The Quarter Master had tea and soup waiting for us, it was God sent, I got to lie down at 1:45 a.m. Major A G Pritchard 2nd Bengal Lancers joined the battalion and took over command, Captain C Wasey 1st Royal Warwickshire Regiment took over duties of Acting Adjutant. God bless you my love. xxxx

Thursday 30 September 1915: Sailly Labourse

After a good night's sleep I spent the morning scraping the mud off my clothes, it was wonderful to have a good meal, then to wash and shave. I received three letters from Edith which I read and wrote replies to her, also all my family and friends had written to me showing their concern. I made my casualty list up today and cried when I saw

---

65   Atkinson, *The Seventh Division*, p. 218: At this time the Germans had a great advantage in the bomb they were using, their design being more reliable and easier to throw than any of those in use by the British, who constantly found themselves outranged and out-thrown. It was not until the more efficient Mills Bomb came into general use that the advantage was regained.

66   Ibid., pp. 222–223: Among those who had fallen on 26 September 1915 was Major-General T. Capper himself, who was the Commanding Officer of the 7th Division. He was right up in the front, actually directing an advance, and was seriously wounded by the side of a Platoon Commander of the Worcestershire, falling practically in the firing-line and close up to the enemy. He was taken back to a Casualty Clearing Station but from the first it was recognized that his condition was grave and his death, which followed next morning, was not unexpected. The Divisional Diary wrote: "All those who knew him will mourn the loss of a gallant soldier who, by his courage and devotion to duty, set a splendid example to every officer, NCO and man in the 7th Division. He was a fighting man who courted danger and was ready to face every risk himself that he asked his men to encounter. He had set his stamp on the Division." Major-General H E Watts superseded him as GOC.

the number of old comrades killed, we lost over 500 men[67] all told. I got new boots and Fred Reeves gave me a pair of socks which was a gift worth appreciating. I forgot to mention yesterday that I heard the Prince of Wales was visiting Vermelles and had just got out of his motor when a shell came over and blew his chauffeur and motor up. It is now 11:00 p.m. and I am off to bed, so Goodnight and God bless you my loved ones. xxxxxx

Friday 1 October 1915: Sailly Labourse

I was told today that I have been strongly recommended for good work in the last fight. I forgot to mention that poor old Cash was killed on 25 September 1915, I am thinking of his poor wife and must write to her. We had sudden orders to move to the trenches at Cambrin[68] to relieve the 2nd Battalion Royal Welch Fusiliers and we thought we were out for a good rest, heard that it is only for 48 hours. Arrived at the Cambrin trenches at 6:00 p.m., back to the same old thing, shells and bullets. Our regiment made one attack but we were repulsed, battalion strength in the trenches – 7 officers and 240 other ranks. Goodnight and God bless you my loved ones. xxxx

Saturday 2 October 1915: Cambrin trenches

It has been very quiet all day, Crisp and five others were sent to draw rations last night, they got lost and arrived back at 10:00 a.m. There is very heavy shellfire tonight but no attack planned. I heard that Aitken was not killed, but seriously wounded, also my name has been sent in for a recommendation. Goodnight and God bless you my loved ones. xxxxx

Sunday 3 October 1915: Cambrin trenches

The Germans bombarded us all night long, we thought they were going to attack. The troops on our right keep on taking and losing Hohenzollern Fort, we lost it again this afternoon and so it will mean another attack for them tomorrow. The shelling by our

---

67   Ibid., pp. 231–232: The Seventh Division losses were very severe, over 2,100 men in the 20 Brigade, nearly 1,500 men in the 21 Brigade, nearly 1,700 men in the 22 Brigade, with another 130 for the artillery, Royal Engineers and other divisional troops, not far short of 5,500 men in all. The 2nd Battalion Royal Warwickshire Regiment casualties were: killed 8 Officers and 56 men, wounded 10 officers and 143 men, missing 1 officer and 318 men, total 19 officers and 517 men.

68   Seventh Division had been in action for five days continuously, in miserably cold and wet weather, rations had been irregular in arrival, fighting heavy and casualties heavier, hardly a battalion had enough officers left to go round the companies and all ranks were absolutely worn out.

artillery has been heavy all day but we remained in our trenches. Goodnight and God bless you my love. xxxx

Monday 4 October 1915: Cambrin trenches

It is very cold and raining again but we get relieved tonight by the 1st Battalion Cameron Highlanders. My hand is poisoned and very painful, it is swollen and I can't use it. We moved out of the trenches at 5:00 p.m. and proceeded to billets at Essars. Goodnight and God bless you my loved ones. xxxxxx

Tuesday 5 October 1915: Essars

My hand is very painful and the doctor cut it open this morning to let the poison out. We had orders to move and I was just going to have a sleep, I am writing this with only one finger free, all the others are bound up. We had a draft of 50 men waiting for us when we got here, they are a welcome sight. It was raining hard as we marched to Beuvry and when we got there we had to wait four hours for our billets. We go back to the trenches on Thursday, so we are not going to get much rest, we are all very tired. We are billeted in a shop so Goodnight and God bless you my loved ones. xxxx

Wednesday 6 October 1915: Beuvry

The Germans sent a couple of shells into Beuvry, apart from that it is a nice day. My hand is still very painful, the doctor cut it open and cleaned it up. I received a letter from Edith and she told me her father had died, I wrote back left handed to Edith and her mother, it was very difficult. We had 10 officers join our battalion for duty today. Goodnight and God bless you my loved ones. xxxx

Thursday 7 October 1915: Beuvry

Had a good night's sleep, my hand is still very bad, we move today to reserve billets at Le Preol, only half an hour's walk. We had a draft of 4 officers and 109 men join the battalion for duty. Goodnight and God bless you my loved ones. xxxx

Friday 8 October 1915: Le Preol

The Germans attacked on our right this afternoon, so our artillery is bombarding them. At 6:30 p.m. we received orders to stand to,[69] ready to move off at a minutes notice, at 9:00 p.m. there is still a very heavy bombardment underway. This afternoon

---

69 This "Stand To!" alert was a result of the great German counter-attack of 8 October. See Atkinson, *The Seventh Division*, p. 233.

we had a parade to hear the last words of Colonel Lefroy read out to us. It affected us a lot, his last thoughts were with us. Goodnight and God bless you my loved ones. xxxx

Saturday 9 October 1915: Le Preol

The big guns were firing all night and we heard this morning that the Germans were repulsed all along our front line, we move to the trenches tomorrow. Today I heard that I have been recommended for the Distinguished Conduct Medal (DCM). Goodnight and God bless you my loved ones. xxxxx

Sunday 10 October 1915: Le Preol

The doctor had to treat my hand again today, afterwards we had a Church Parade and the Parson spoke to us about our Colonel's last words, it affected every one of us. We moved off to the Givenchy trenches at 12:15 p.m. to relieve the Royal Welch Fusiliers, when we arrived I went down to the front line, the trenches were all blown in from the bombardment the other night. Our battalion strength after recent drafts is 24 officers and 413 other ranks. The village of Givenchy is in between our front line and Cambrin, it is a beautiful village but unfortunately the church was blown to the ground by the Germans. I managed to obtain some coke and lit a fire in the dug-out, it is very cold. We are under bombardment night and day from the Germans and our artillery is returning fire at them, we heard tonight that our artillery caught the Germans nicely the other day during a counter-attack, they must have suffered very high casualties. I had a letter from home saying that my mother and sister Adelaide were very ill, I am very worried about them. Goodnight and God bless you my loved ones. xxxx

Monday 11 October 1915: Givenchy trenches

Our artillery was bombarding all the night but we saw a fine sight this morning, about six of our companies surrounded a German company and made them surrender. My hand is paining me awful but there is nothing I can do. We had 2 men wounded today. Goodnight and God bless you my loved ones. xxxxxx

Tuesday 12 October 1915: Givenchy trenches

Early this morning I went round the trenches to pick out dug-outs to put the wounded in, they are going to attack on our right and we are going to send gas over and use smoke candles, a kind of joint attack from here. Our artillery have cut the German barbed wire in front of our trenches, so I expect we shall come in for a bombardment. I expected a letter today from Edith but didn't get one, I did send her one. I have got an awful cold and my poison fingers don't seem to get much better. Goodnight and God bless you my loved ones. xxxxx

Wednesday 13 October 1915: Givenchy trenches

Had a very poor night's sleep my hand ached awful, the doctor cut right underneath the nail, one finger has turned into a whitlow, the other finger is healing a bit. I went round the trenches with the doctor and positioned the stretcher bearers at different points, the bombardment started at mid-day, we aren't doing anything here only a demonstration. We heard that we took Hohenzollern Redoubt quite easily and are now pushing on to Hulluch. A German trench mortar fell on one of our gas cylinders and gassed two of our men, we had four wounded today. The Germans fired phosphorous shells at us which burnt one of our men's eyes. Goodnight and God bless you my loved ones. xxxx

Thursday 14 October 1915: Givenchy trenches

We were relieved today by the 1st Battalion Royal Welch Fusiliers but we only go to the ruined village of Givenchy, it is pretty cold, so Goodnight and God bless you my loved ones. xxxx

14 Poison gas attack 13 October 1915 at Hohenzollern Redoubt. (IWM Q29003)

Friday 15 October 1915: Givenchy

We are billeted in an old school and the artillery guns are located behind us, when they fire the vibration is dreadful and they are firing night and day. It is a very foggy day, it seems strange that every time we make an attack the elements are always against us. We are being held in reserve and expect to go out for a welcomed rest. The Baptist Minister sent me a photograph of Corporal Rowley who escaped from Germany after being a prisoner of war for ten months. He photographed him in his clothes as he arrived at the depot and he looked a proper wreck. The billet we are in is fortified, in fact all the houses are. There is a strange view from our billet as we look toward the trenches, we can see the cemetery and Jesus hanging on the cross. I have often remarked how amazing it is that almost every crucifix stands untouched amongst the ruins. Goodnight and God bless you my loved ones. xxxx

Saturday 16 October 1915: Givenchy[70]

We were kept awake by the guns that were firing all night long, every time they fired the sound hit the wall and deafened us. Our guns have been firing continuously all day, it is a misty, cold day. We had another gag issued to us for the 'weeping shells,' these shells release a chlorine gas which is very irritating to the eyes. This gag looks similar to motor goggles and is used to protect our eyes. My hand is worse today, it became swollen again and full of matter. We move tomorrow, they say we are going to return to Le Cornet de Flandre for about five weeks. A draft of 80 men joined us for duty today that will help to rebuild our battalion. I hope so and I may be able to have a good rest and get my hand better. Goodnight and God bless you my loved ones. xxxxx

Sunday 17 October 1915: Givenchy

Our artillery bombarded the German lines all night long, the noise is unbearable and my head aches all the time. The doctor told me later that the Scots Guards had gone over the top and made some progress in Hohenzollern redoubt, fighting hard for all they are worth. It is a miserable misty morning and my hand is worse than yesterday. We moved out at 12:30 p.m. following a report that the Germans were shelling Beuvry and Bethune but we were all safe as we pass through. We saw where a German 280 mm mortar had fallen, it was at the corner of a street and it had blown two houses down killing 4 men and wounding 8 others, the base of the shell weighed over 210 pounds (95 kilograms). We are billeted on the side of a canal in Bethune and

70   There were more than 61,000 BEF casualties sustained during 25 September–16 October 1915 and 50,000 of them were in the main fighting area between Loos and Givenchy, the remainder in the subsidiary attacks. Of these, 7,766 men died. See *The Long, Long Trail* <http://www.1914–1918.net/bat13.htm/> (accessed 28 December 2014).

a draft of 80 men were waiting for us, Jack Turner, Corporal Lynch and I met with them. I received a letter and parcel from Edith containing salmon, sweets, cocoa, sugar, cakes and stationery. We move again tomorrow, so Goodnight and God bless you my oved ones. xxxxx

Monday 18 October 1915: Bethune

We marched off at 9:00 a.m. to Le Cornet Bourdois, it's a very cold day and when we arrived we were billeted in our old billet, the woman who owns it was pleased to see us. We had a blanket issued tonight so I hope for a good sleep, Goodnight and God bless you my loved ones. xxxxxx

Tuesday 19 October 1915: Le Cornet de Flandre

I was nice and warm last night but strangely I couldn't sleep. We had our recommendation cards from the Divisional Generals given to us today, I sent it to Edith with a letter. The doctor went on leave today and at 5:00 p.m. we had orders to stand to, maybe we aren't going to get a rest. We can hear a bombardment in the distance and later stand to was cancelled. Goodnight and God bless you my loved ones. xxxx

Wednesday 20 October 1915: Le Cornet de Flandre

Today is a beautiful day and we played two football matches. The Germans made an attack between Hulluch Road and the Quarries, they were repulsed with heavy losses. We heard that we go back to trenches but later orders for moving were cancelled. I am recording the last words that Colonel B R Lefroy left for our regiment and will keep them as a record. These are the words of one of the finest soldiers and gentlemen I have ever met. What could mean more to us, than to know he was thinking of his regiment as he laid dying; God bless him. Goodnight and God bless you my loved ones. xxxxxx

Last Words of Colonel B R Lefroy DSO 2nd Battalion, Royal Warwickshire Regiment Killed in action 25 September 1915

Sir,
I have to report to you that having been with the late Lieutenant Colonel B R Lefroy, DSO, at the time he was in the 22nd Field Ambulance fatally wounded, he charged me to send a message to the regiment. Tell them my last thoughts are with them, I pray that their bravery in the hour of severe testing may win them through to success. Wish to God I had been spared to serve and lead them a little longer, but as it is I trust that the men of the Warwickshires will pull together, work together, and uphold the credit, the good name, and the traditions that the Regiment has so nobly won. May God's blessing rest on them in their hour of

danger or peace, and may the heroic self-sacrifice of their officers, NCO's and men who have fallen inspire them to deeds of unfaltering and unfailing bravery.

L. Hamilton. Attached 22nd Field Ambulance

Thursday 21 October 1915: Le Cornet de Flandre

I refereed a football match today, then I saw the doctor, my hand is gradually improving. Following is a copy of a letter from Lieutenant Colonel East, the late Commanding Officer of the Royal Warwickshire Regiment, to Lieutenant Colonel A G Pritchard, the replacement Commanding Officer, dates 21 October 1915.

Letter to Lieutenant Colonel Pritchard from Lieutenant Colonel East

21 October 1915

Dear Colonel,
I write to you on hearing you have got command of my old battalion, to congratulate you, and if you get an opportunity, I shall be grateful if you will take it to let the survivors know how pleased I am of the splendid work they did in the great attack. How very sorry I am for the heavy losses again suffered by the battalion, and how splendidly the battalion held up the reputation it has already earned in the greatest war of all time. My thoughts are always with them and although I hear there are few left of those I spent such a happy time with, it is a great pleasure to know the grand old battalion refuses to be knocked out, and keeps rising up, filled with equally gallant men, no matter how they suffer. The battalion lost two of the most gallant and truly great hearted men I ever knew, in their Colonels Loring and Lefroy, and I hope it will be your good fortune to be spared to lead them to final victory, and to take heavy toll from the swine who have destroyed so many gallant men.

Signed
C.C. East
Late Colonel of Royal Warwickshire Regiment

What a grand message, I knew Colonel East so well, it was his only wish to lead us into action.

Friday 22 October 1915: Le Cornet de Flandre

Our regiment played football against the Royal Welch Fusiliers and lost 2-1. I received a letter from my mother, papers from Linda Mckee and cigarettes from the Sergeant of the 3rd Royal Warwickshire Regiment. Goodnight and God bless you my loved ones. xxxxx

Saturday 23 October 1915: Le Cornet de Flandre

One of my fingers is not healing but the other one is much better. We move tomorrow to Les Harisoir, I am sorry we are leaving here. Goodnight and God bless you my love. xxxx

Sunday 24 October 1915: Le Cornet de Flandre

We are all very angry about the execution of the British nurse Edith Cavell[71] by the Germans in Belgium, she will be avenged if we ever meet them again. We moved off at 2:00 p.m. and arrived at Les Harisoir at 4:30 p.m. I feel rather poorly today, I have been vomiting and the doctor took some more of my finger nail off to release the poison. It was twelve months today since we lost Colonel Loring in the big fight at Ypres. Goodnight and God bless you my loved ones xxxx

Monday 25–Thursday 28 October 1915: Les Harisoir

I did not feel well on Monday and so I laid down all day, I felt slightly better on Tuesday. I heard that King George V is coming on Thursday to visit the troops in our district. Mr Kirkland, our doctor, came off leave on Thursday and told me I was not to go up into the trenches until I was well again. King George V inspected the troops today but our regiment didn't see him. Goodnight and God bless you my loved ones. xxxx

Friday 29 October 1915: Les Harisoir to trenches

We marched off to Gorre at 9:50 a.m. today and the weather is wet and cold. Prior to leaving I saw the doctor; he cut the other piece of nail out and told me that I have to travel with the transport. We arrived at Gorre about 1:00 p.m. and the boys went straight into the trenches, I had to remain behind. The trenches are located just left of Givenchy and it is a very cold, wet night. I had a letter and a paper from Edith so I wrote back to her. I feel miserable being away from the boys, I would rather have gone up to the trenches. A draft came up this evening, Sergeant Mellins and Sergeant Cox with 21 men, Sergeant Mellins had lost seven of his men at Rouen. We are being issued with gum boots (waders) like the fishermen use, big mackintoshes and leather jackets, the men have refused to wear their fur coats again, they are very uncomfortable when wet. I am sleeping in an old barn with no door, it is awful cold and uncomfortable. Fred Reeves and Jack Pary have joined me. Goodnight and God bless you my loved ones. xxxxx

---

71   Edith Louisa Cavell (1865-1915). Her execution by German authorities in occupied Belgium received worldwide condemnation and extensive press coverage.

Saturday 30 October 1915: Gorre

I walked about 2 miles (3.2 kilometres) into Bethune to see the doctor, my finger seems a bit easier to use today. The seven men of Sergeant Mellins party that were left behind in Rouen arrived and I sent them on to the trenches. I received a letter from Jim Yorke thanking me for going to see his brother Ted's grave. Goodnight and God bless you my loved ones. xxxx

Sunday 31 October 1915: Gorre

Twelve months ago today the Germans tried to break through at Ypres and a lot of officers and men of our regiment were killed or captured. I read in the paper that King George V met with an accident whilst inspecting the troops, his horse reared and partially fell on top of him cracking his pelvis; that was the reason he didn't inspect our regiment. When Fred Reeves returned from the trenches tonight he said that two or our men had been hit by sniper fire. We have got to move tomorrow, I would rather be up in the trenches, our battalion strength is 19 officers and 528 other ranks. Goodnight and God bless you my loved ones xxxxx

15 The Loos Memorial to the Missing surrounds the graves of Dud Corner Cemetery in France. (The Long, Long Trail, http://www.1914–1918.net/bat13.htm/ (accessed 28 December 2014)

Numb. 29422.   1

SUPPLEMENT
TO

The London Gazette.

Of FRIDAY, the 31st of DECEMBER, 1915.

Published by Authority.

The Gazette is registered at the General Post Office for transmission by Inland Post as a newspaper. The postage rate to places within the United Kingdom, for each copy, is one halfpenny for the first 6 ozs., and an additional halfpenny for each subsequent 6 ozs. or part thereof. For places abroad the rate is a halfpenny for every 2 ounces, except in the case of Canada, to which the Canadian Magazine Postage rate applies.

SATURDAY, 1 JANUARY, 1916.

War Office,
1st January, 1916.

The following despatch has been received by the Secretary of State for War from the Field-Marshal Commanding-in-Chief the British Army in France:—

General Headquarters,
30th November, 1915.

SIR,

In accordance with the last paragraph of my Despatch of the 15th October, 1915, I have the honour to bring to notice the names of those whom I recommend for gallant and distinguished service in the field.

I have the honour to be,
Sir,
Your obedient servant,

J. D. P. FRENCH,

Field-Marshal, Commanding-in-Chief
The British Army in France.

ROYAL WARWICKSHIRE REGIMENT.

Davidson, Captain P. V. (Adjutant, Royal Warwickshire Regiment, Territorial Force).

Forster, Major (temporary Lieutenant-Colonel) G. N. B.
Richards, Captain C. E. M.
Strevens, Lieutenant (temporary Captain) H.
Bretherton, Lieutenant (temporary Captain) J. T.
Jackson, Lieutenant (temporary Captain) A. H. K.
Besant, Lieutenant T. L., Special Reserve.
Haskins, Second Lieutenant J. W. V.
Gilkes, No. 384 Corporal W. G.
Dark, No. 7187 Lance-Corporal J.

Brownfield, Captain R. J., Special Reserve (killed).
Brindley, Captain P. S., Special Reserve.
Maunsell, Lieutenant H. S. (died of wounds).
Pennington, Lieutenant J. (killed).
Richardson, Lieutenant R. F. (died of wounds).
Chavasse, Lieutenant C. C. H. (retired pay).
Dibben, Second Lieutenant W. L.
Elderton, Lieutenant F. R., Special Reserve (killed).
Forbes, Temporary Second Lieutenant A.
Hodgkinson, Lieutenant A., Special Reserve.
Stahn, Lieutenant A. E., Special Reserve.
Hyde, Quartermaster and Honorary Lieutenant W. N.
Webb, No. 4361 Serjeant W.
Crisp, No. 4811 Lance-Corporal F. W.
Hartley, No. 1283 Private A.
Tattem, No. 1253 Private A.
Twynham, No. 2416 Private J.
Underwood, No. 840 Bandsman F.

16 Lance Sergeant William Webb was 'Mentioned in Despatches' for gallant and distinguished service in the field at the Battle of Loos. It was published in *The London Gazette* on Saturday 1 Jan 1916.

War Diary:
Recovery after Loos November 1915–January 1916

Monday 1–Tuesday 2 November 1915: Gorre

We marched at 9:00 a.m. to a place east of Bethune called Gorre, it rained torrents all the way and it was very cold, we got wet through to the skin. Our battalion strength has increased to 28 officers and 691 other ranks and two more officers will join us tomorrow. On Tuesday morning the doctor inspected my chest, I had a touch of bronchitus, he asked me if I wanted to go to hospital, I said no. Just afterwards the Colonel sent for me and offered me a chance to go to our camp in Le Havre to replace Band Sergeant Cudly, so I accepted, I don't know when I shall go. It's an awful winter day, rain, rain, rain, and very cold. I saw the paper signed by our Commanding Officer promoting me to Band Sergeant, I wrote to tell Edith and also wrote letters to mother and my daughter Marjorie. Goodnight and God bless you my loved ones. xxxx

Wednesday 3 November 1915: Gorre

Our new doctor arrived this morning, Lieutenant J T Hurst, it was a fine morning but turned to rain in the afternoon. I received a parcel and letter from Lillie and Harold, the parcel contained two pairs of fine strong black socks, two packets of chocolate, fourteen packets of cigarettes, a very welcome parcel. I was disappointed to read Sir John French's despatch about the Battle of Loos and Vermelles and everyone I have spoken to agreed with me.[72] I had good news, my cousin Eric Bench was not killed, he was wounded and is now a prisoner of war. I am thinking of Edith, it is her Lodge night at 9:00 p.m. We heard today that the Germans are holding white flags up in front of the 1st, 3rd, and 7th Divisions, but their second lines are full of troops with fixed bayonets, ready to charge, we are too old and wise to be caught by that trick. I fancy another attack is coming off in this area shortly, so I need to recover. Goodnight and God bless you my loved ones. xxxx

---

72 The Battle of Loos called into question the leadership of Field Marshal Sir John French. He was superseded as BEF commander-in-chief by General Sir Douglas Haig in December 1915.

Thursday 4 November 1915: Gorre

I walked to the 22nd Field Ambulance base to see Billy Woolway and stopped to have dinner with him, heard we go into the trenches tomorrow. Goodnight and God bless you my loved ones. xxxx

Friday 5–Tuesday 9 November 1915: Gorre

Today is a very cold and wet day, our men moved into the Givenchy trenches but I was told to remain back at camp until my bronchitus cleared up. The Germans blew up a mine close by our trenches, it killed one man and wounded another. On Saturday we retaliated and blew up one of our mines, then the Bedford Regiment made an attack and occupied the crater made by the mine, they lost 6 men. On Sunday our regiment came out of the trenches and on Monday we moved off at 9:00 a.m. to Hinges near Essars, we stopped for a bath on the way and arrived at 11:30 a.m. Band Sergeant Cudly came up on Tuesday to see me and the Colonel stopped me and said he was sorry I was leaving but knew I needed a rest, he praised me for the work I had done for the regiment. I expect I shall go to Le Havre any day now. Goodnight and God bless you my loved ones. xxxx

Wednesday 10 November 1915: Hinges

I was promoted to Band Sergeant today, dated back to 26 September 1915, Cudly was promoted to Company Quartermaster Sergeant (CQMS) and Crisp to Band Corporal. Goodnight and God bless you my loved ones. xxxx

Thursday 11 November 1915: Bethune

We move to Bethune today and found a billet in a large school, we move back to the trenches tomorrow. It is an awful wet day, I wrote to Edith, had a letter from Eva and Flo, so I am off to bed early. Goodnight and God bless you my loved ones. xxxx

Friday 12 November 1915: Bethune

We moved into the trenches at Givenchy to relieve the 1st Battalion Cameron Highlanders, it is an awful wet day and the trenches are in very bad condition.[73]

---

73 The 7th Division including the Royal Warwickshire Regiment were in no state for further heavy fighting until the gaps in their ranks could be filled and officers and men could recover from the strain and exertions of the recent struggle at Loos. During the winter of 1915–1916, raiding had not become a regular policy due to shortage of ammunition; Loos had seen nearly all the carefully accumulated ammunition reserve expended and there was hardly any left to play with, so that the artillery found themselves handicapped

Private Morgan went on furlough tonight so I sent the German helmet I collected home to Edith. Our battalion strength is 16 officers and 502 other ranks. Goodnight and God bless you my loved ones. xxxx

Saturday 13 November 1915: Givenchy

Another very wet day, the trenches are in an awful state, mostly waist deep in mud, talk about the spirit of the British soldier, there they were in all that mud singing away like young men going to a picnic. I am expecting to move down to Le Havre camp on Monday 15 November 1915, I hope so. The mail came up today, I had a letters from Edith and Linda, papers from Edith with 'comic cuts' from Marjorie for daddy to have a laugh, a good laugh I had too. We move out of the trenches tomorrow to the reserve billets at Le Preole, so am off to bed, Goodnight and God bless you my loved ones. xxxxx

Sunday 14 November 1915: Givenchy Trenches

A very cold day but fine. Two German aeroplanes flew over our trenches today but they were chased away by our anti-aircraft guns and aeroplanes. One of our aeroplanes flew very low over the German trenches about 11:30 a.m., then it came straight back and all our artillery opened a terrific bombardment for a quarter of an hour, big guns, little guns, all sorts. We were relieved at 3:00 p.m. by the 1st Battalion Royal Welch Fusiliers and moved to Le Preol, I washed my clothes and had a bath. Goodnight and God bless you my loved ones. xxxx

Monday 15 November 1915: Le Preol

I left my old battalion this morning at 11:15 a.m., I felt so sad, just as I was leaving the Commanding Officer spoke to me again and wished me all the luck. We left Bethune station at 4:20 p.m. and made a fire in an old petroleum can, it is very cold in cattle trucks at night. Goodnight and God bless you my loved ones. xxxx

Tuesday 16 November 1915: Abbeville (France)

We arrived in Abbeville at 1:00 a.m. and went to the coffee bar to buy some tea, we don't leave until 10:30 p.m. tonight. It was snowing very hard so I went down to the

when retaliation was called for. Patrol activities were less restricted and November rains filled ditches to overflowing, reduced communication trenches to waterways and made it difficult for the men to keep their firing trenches even approximately dry. Apart from the rains the trenches needed constant repair, new trenches needed to be dug to strengthen their defences, parapets were falling in and some trenches were waist deep in mud. See Atkinson, *The Seventh Division*, pp. 233–235.

YMCA, a very comfortable place it is too. I felt lost so I spent most of my time in the YMCA and arrived back at the train around 9:30 p.m. We collected some coal from a railway truck and made another fire in our fire bucket, so we were pretty warm, we eventually left Abbeville at 11:50 p.m. Goodnight and God bless you my loved ones. xxxx

Wednesday 17 November 1915: Enroute to Havre

It is a fine day but our faces are as black as sweeps, so we opened a bully beef tin and had a shave; the train stopped at a station so we got out and had a wash under the spout they use to fill the engine with water, we felt quite fresh after that. We arrived at Le Havre about 12:00 noon and reached the camp about 1:30 p.m. where I reported my arrival. I understand there is a Sergeant's Mess on the camp just like in peace time. Travelling down in the train I ate the pastries and salmon Aunt Rebbeca sent to me, it was a wonderful treat. Goodnight and God bless you my loved ones. xxxx

Thursday 18 November 1915: Le Havre

I had a splendid night's sleep with six blankets, it was grand, then I was fitted with new clothes. Later I was talking to the Quarter Master, he said he was sorry, he didn't know I was coming and had filled Cudly's place with another Band Sergeant. I was disappointed and went to speak with the Sergeant Major, he said he wanted me to help him in the Ordnance Room, I start tomorrow. Goodnight and God bless you my loved ones. xxxx

Friday 19–Monday 29 November 1915: Le Havre

I started my new job, it is very easy and just what I wanted, writing and keeping clerical records, but I miss my old comrades who are still in the Givenchy trenches.[74] It is

---

74   Ibid., pp. 235–236: The mining activities led to several sharp encounters in the Givenchy trenches which reached their height towards the end of November, two large mines being exploded at the Duck's Bill (about 400 yards (366 metres) South East of Givenchy) on 25 November 1915, after a smaller mine had been exploded in the hope of inducing the Germans to man their trenches in anticipation of an attack. To increase this impression our men started throwing bombs and opened rapid fire for ten minutes before the big mines went up. The explosion was completely successful, though the Wiltshire Regiment had a company commander and several men killed by falling debris. This, however, did not prevent their dashing out and successfully consolidating the crater. Four days later another small mine was blown at the Warren, just north of the Duck's Bill, but it was too small to damage the German mine-galleries appreciably, so a new mine had to be prepared. In the middle of it two German deserters came over, announcing that the Germans were going to blow up big mines at the Warren and the Duck's Bill next day. To anticipate them, two mines were fired at 4:00 a.m. on the 30 November 1915 and the Yorkshire Regiment

good to be able to sleep every night and not to be disturbed or hear the big guns firing, I can hardly make it out, it seems so strange after so many months in the trenches. The next ten days were very quiet as I settled in to my new job. Goodnight and God bless you my loved ones. xxxx

Tuesday 30 November 1915: Le Havre

I went to a concert and found that they have got a nice little band here comprising of Band Sergeants and officers. The conductor is an officer and the son of Godfrey who I know very well. They have asked me to join the band but I told them I wanted a rest for a short time. I had letters from Edith, Jim, Linda and Mrs Slivey, Edith told me that Hope's husband was dangerously ill. Goodnight and God bless you my loved ones. xxxx

Wednesday 1–Tuesday 14 December 1915: Le Havre

The next two weeks were reasonably quiet except for a draft of fifty men who arrived at Le Havre on 1 December 1915 to join the Royal Warwickshire Regiment.[75] I had a letter from Crisp and he tells me that poor Dick Lloyd had been wounded, we have a saying that, "it is only a case of waiting, you are bound to get killed or wounded," I must write to Crisp to find out where he was wounded. Goodnight and God bless you my loved ones. xxxx

Wednesday 15 December 1915: Le Havre

I received bad news today from Edith who tells me that my mother[76] and youngest sister Adelaide are very ill and probably will not live much longer, I am very concerned for them and wish I could get home to see them. I have managed to escaped death at the front line and now to hear this bad news, I would rather be back in the trenches and hear good news. Goodnight and God bless you my loved ones. xxxx

---

hastened to occupy and consolidate the craters. They were hard at work at this when at 7:30 a.m. the German mines went off, doing much damage and burying over twenty men.

75   Ibid., pp. 237–238: On 2 December 1915, command of the line was handed over to the 33rd (New Army) Division and the 7th Division was withdrawn to a rest-area near Busnes. Three days later it started entraining for the South on transfer to the Third Army, which had been formed to take over the line east of Albert in the Somme Valley. The move was made on 7 December 1915 and the Warwickshires with 22 Brigade moved to a rest place near Molliens until February 1916. This was its first real rest and a chance to rebuild the nine battalions. Major General H.E. Watts was confirmed as Commanding Officer of the 7th Division, Major A.G. Pritchard, an Indian Cavalry officer, was in command of the Royal Warwickshire Regiment.

76   William's mother Millicent Webb (née Roe) 1853-1917 was born in County Limerick.

Thursday 16–Friday 24 December 1915: Le Havre

Mr Godfrey, the Bandmaster, was in the Ordnance Room this morning and they told him I could play the violin, so he asked me to play for the band, well I couldn't very well refuse. In the evening, we went to rehearsal at the Giana Theatre, Le Havre, I got back about 12:00 mid-night. On Friday 17 December 1915 I played in a concert in Le Havre, it went very well and I enjoyed the experience. We had rehearsal on Monday and the Royal Army Band from Woolwich played here on Tuesday 21 December 1915, I went to hear them play. Goodnight and God bless you my loved ones. xxxx

Saturday 25 December 1915: Le Havre

It is a fine morning on Christmas day, we enjoyed a good Christmas dinner of roast turkey and goose, then I spent the rest of the day writing letters and cards to my family and friends. Goodnight and God bless you my loved ones. xxxx

Sunday 26 December 1915–17 January1916: Le Havre

I put in for leave on 28 December 1915 to visit my mother and sister but I was told that it will not be granted until sometime in April 1916. I have to re-submit it when I have been back six months from the day I returned from my last leave. In the evening we put on a Pantomine for the troops in camp, it went better than I thought it would so we repeated it on Wednesday and Thursday, it was absolutely packed and we had to turn people away. I saw Corporal Whitehouse, he was a drummer with the band until he got wounded in the finger at Ypres on 24 October 1914. I received a letter from Edith and she told me that I was mentioned in Sir John French's despatch. On Monday 17 January 1916 I had to attend a court martial, the first one I have been on, a man from England was absent without leave. I have decided to discontinue the diary as nothing startling happens here.[77] Goodnight and God bless you my loved ones xxxx

---

77   From William's service record we know that he was granted leave from Le Havre from 5–12 April 1916 and he was employed as an Ordinary Room Clerk on 8 September 1916. On 5–12 October 1916 he again took leave from Le Havre and on 28 January 1919 he was demobilized from Le Havre. He retired from the British Army on 1 April 1919 after 25 years of service with the 2nd Battalion Royal Warwickshire Regiment. William Webb may have returned to his battalion after a period of rest in Le Havre but records have not been found to verify this. However, the remaining chapters of the book continues to describe the actions of the 2nd Battalion, Royal Warwickshire Regiment through to the end of the war.

17 & 18 Le Havre camp pantomime December 1915 William Webb –
seated front row far right.

Part II

The 2nd Royal Warwickshire Regiment 1916-1918

Royal Warwickshire Regiment:
The Somme July–October 1916[1]

The "Big Push"

The 7th Division experienced major changes during its rebuilding after the Battle of Loos and by late December 1915 the 91 Brigade, composed of the 20th, 21st, 22nd, and 24th battalions of the Manchester Regiment, had replaced the 21 Brigade which was transferred to the 30th Division. To further mix the experienced infantry with the lesser experienced, the 20th and 24th Manchesters were posted to the 22 Brigade, the Queen's and South Staffordshire Regiments replacing them in the 91 Brigade.

The formation of the 7th Division in early 1916 was as shown below:

- 7th Division commanded by Major General H. E. Watts comprised mainly of: 20 Brigade, 22 Brigade, 91 Brigade, Divisional Artillery, Royal Engineers, and Medical Corps.
- 22 Brigade commanded by Brigadier General J. Mc. C. Steele comprised the following regiments: 2nd Royal Warwickshire, 1st Royal Welch Fusiliers, 20th and 24th Manchesters, 22nd Machine-Gun Company, 2nd Royal Irish joined 24 May 1916.
- 2nd Battalion Royal Warwickshire Regiment was commanded by Major A G Pritchard (Indian Army) until 14 April 1917.
- On 29 April 1916 the 7th Division was transferred to the XV Corps (Lieutenant-General Sir H S Horne), in which were also the 17th, 21st, 33rd, 38th (Welsh) Division. They formed a part of the Fourth Army under General Sir H Rawlinson.

---

1   The next three sections are primarily based on TNA WO 95/1664/3: 2nd Battalion Royal Warwickshire Regiment War Diary and Atkinson, *The Seventh Division 1914–1918*.

1 February–30 June 1916: Preparing for the Battle of the Somme

The 2nd Battalion Royal Warwickshire Regiment[2] together with many other battalions of the 7th Division had lost almost all their regular soldiers that landed in Belgium in October 1914; they had bravely fought in the First Battle of Ypres, Neuve Chapelle, Festubert and Loos. William Webb was one of the few survivors of the Royal Warwickshire Regiment but now remained at the Base Camp in Le Havre recovering from injuries while, in early February 1916, the 7th Division returned to the trenches. Their three brigades were positioned opposite Mametz and Fricourt, the 91 Brigade on the right opposite Mametz, the 22 Brigade (including the Royal Warwickshires) holding the middle section with the 20 Brigade on the left facing Fricourt.

The German line was considerably higher than the British line giving them a tactical advantages and much better facilities for observation. They had developed several lines of new trenches with redoubts and strongpoints and an equally strong second line a mile or so to the rear and higher up the slope. For any British attack to take place, a greater weight of artillery and supply of shells would be needed and so there was no prospect of any major operation in the near future for the division. However, that did not preclude doing all that was possible to harass the enemy. The chalky ground allowed more activity in mining and the Tunnelling Companies, using infantry working parties from the reserve battalions, were extremely busy creating new mines in strategic positions. The Germans frequently bombarded the British trenches and often followed the violent shelling with raids that were generally repulsed but caused many casualties. Fighting patrols comprising of an officer and about thirty men were sent out to attack German working-parties and bomb dug-outs, taking prisoners whenever the opportunity presented itself. By June 1916 all units were confident and ready for action but the British Army had insufficient quantities of artillery and ammunition for a sustained attack of any magnitude. Preparations for the coming offensive were made by digging new assembly and communication trenches, improving roads, developing water supplies, preparing ammunition storage dumps, constructing dug-out for use as dressing-stations, battle headquarters and other purposes. This work was generally done by working parties from the reserve battalions, later the Labour Corps was developed recruiting efficient labour from China and South Africa.

The Battle of the Somme

Many battles took place at the Somme during the period 1 July 1915 to 19 November 1916 and the map shows the placement of the British, French and German forces during that time. British and French Armies are shown on the left of the Front Line

---

2   TNA WO 95/1664/3: 2nd Battalion Royal Warwickshire Regiment War Diary. The battalion strength had increased to 34 officers and 846 other ranks.

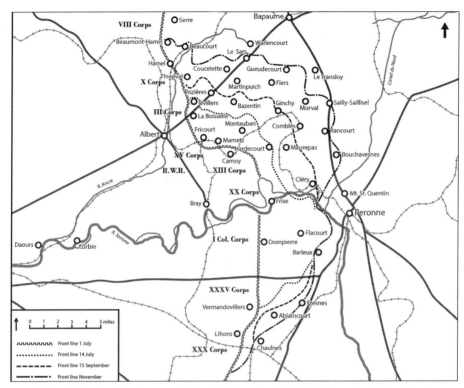

Map 9 Battle of the Somme 1 July–19 November 1916 XV Corps including Royal
Warwickshire Regiment.

and denoted as 'XV' meaning XV Corps, of which the 7th Division, 22 Brigade, 2nd
Battalion Royal Warwickshire Regiment were a part. The German Corps are shown
on the right of the front line.

1 July 1916: Capture of Mametz

The village of Mametz lay in and behind the first German defensive position on
the Somme, which in this area consisted of three principal fighting trench systems
connected by many communication trenches. It was an exceptionally strong position
to have to attack. The German front line ran approximately in parallel with the British,
and was called Bulgar Trench, Mametz Trench, Danube Trench and Kiel Trench;
behind it and in front of Mametz was a second line that incorporated Cemetery Trench
and a key machine-gun post ('the Shrine') at the village cemetery. Well behind the
village on higher ground ran the third line incorporating Fritz Trench and Railway
Alley. The area fell within the boundary of the British XV Corps under Lieutenant
General Henry Horne, his infantry force consisted of the 7th and 21st Divisions in the

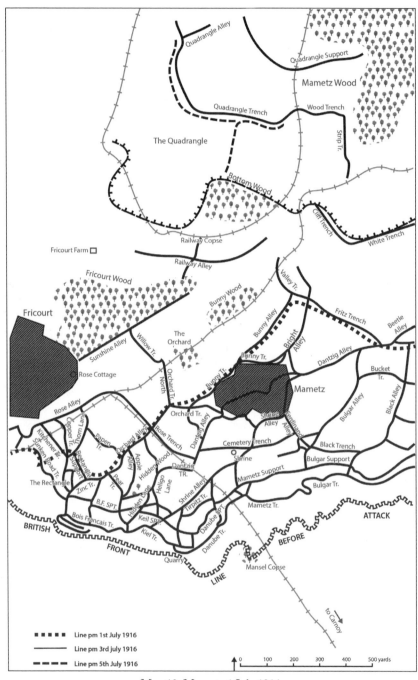

Map 10 Mametz 1 July 1916.

front lines, with the 17th (Northern) Division in reserve some 2 miles (3.2 kilometres) behind. Facing them were just six battalions of the *German 28th Reserve Division.*

The British bombardment started on 24 June 1916 and for one week they pounded the barbed wire defenses and trenches of the German line hoping to catch the enemy manning their front trenches. Ammunition had been systematically stored around the British gun positions using motor-trucks to transport it from the rail-head. At night, patrols were pushed out to investigate the state of the enemy barbed wire defenses and machine-gun positions. The German artillery had vigorously replied to the bombard-ment and had destroyed the British jumping-off places, although special assembly trenches were dug further back and could be used by the assaulting battalions.

The XV Corps objective on 1 July 1916 was the line running south and south-west of Mametz Wood, the 7th Division on its right was attacking Mametz village, advancing due north, while the 21st Division was to strike eastward on the other side of Fricourt. The 22 Brigade was entrusting its attack to the 20th Manchesters with the Welch Fusiliers in support, the Royal Warwickshires[3] and Royal Irish forming the Divisional Reserve along with platoons from the 24th Manchesters and 54th Field Company.

On the evening of 30 June 1916, all battalions had taken up their positions and a steady artillery fire was maintained all night. At 6:25 a.m. on 1 July 1916, the final intense bombardment began and at 7:22 a.m., batteries of Stokes mortars opened fire and local commanders ordered the release of gas on the centre of the front facing Fricourt that was not initially being attacked. Four minutes later a discharge of smoke was launched on the flanks of both the 7th and 21st Divisions. At 7:28 a.m. a number of mines were blown under enemy positions: the 178th Tunnelling Company RE blew three large mines near Fricourt and one at Bulgar Point, a strong point facing the 91 Brigade, the latter position was completely destroyed. At zero hour (7:30 a.m.) the leading lines of infantry moved forward across no man's land under heavy enemy machine-gun fire and some rifle fire.

The 91 Brigade, though sadly diminished and greatly exhausted, advanced across the German front line (Bulgar Trench), past the second line (Cemetery Trench), then captured the strongpoints in Mametz itself. It then pushed on past the deep Danzig Alley communication trench and took the third enemy line, Fritz Trench. The 22nd Manchesters were assembled astride the Mametz – Montauban track and the 1st South Staffords opposite the Bulgar Point strongpoint, which was destroyed in the mine explosion just before zero. The 2nd Queen's and 21st Manchesters were in close support behind the attacking battalions. The 22nd Manchesters and 1st South Staffords quickly crossed the narrow no man's land but came under fire from German machine-guns in Danzig Alley communication trench as they approached Cemetery Trench and the edge of the village. By 8:00 a.m., the Staffords were well

---

3   TNA WO 95/1664/3: 2nd Battalion Royal Warwickshire Regiment War Diary. The battalion strength on 1 July 1916 was restored to 38 officers and 1,049 other ranks.

into the village ruins and the Manchesters were pressing on to Bucket Trench, having almost gained their objectives. However, German resistance began to stiffen and the leading men were forced back to Cemetery Trench. At 9:30 a.m. the support battalions were ordered up to reinforce, with little effect. Divisional Commanding Officer Major General Herbert Watts ordered the artillery to re-bombard the area of Danzig Alley and Fritz Trench but it was not effective and did not even stop some German counter-attacks from Mametz itself. The effort was repeated at 12:25 p.m., the Corps having heard that Pommiers Redoubt had fallen in the attack on Montauban, and the 91 Brigade having reported sight of enemy troops massing to counter-attack from Danzig Alley. This time the bombardment did the trick, although one enemy field gun firing at close range continued to cause trouble until its detachment was killed. Parties bombed along Danzig Alley and Bright Alley by 1:40 p.m.

Two companies of the Royal Warwickshires from reserve were placed under Colonel Gordon's disposal and ordered up to Mametz. About 4:30 p.m. detachments of the Royal Warwickshires and 21st Manchesters were organized to advance to Bunny Trench and Bunny Alley under covering fire from the Queen's, they reached this objective about 7:40 p.m. A renewed attack on the western portion of Mametz by the Gordons, supported by the Royal Warwickshires and some of the Devonshire Regiment, had succeeded completely, some 600 defenders surrendering. Orders were issued to consolidate the line and two companies of the Royal Warwickshires connected up the 22 Brigade with the 91 Brigade at the north-west corner of Mametz. The job of 20 Brigade was to advance across the German front line (Mametz, Danube and Kiel Trench) and form a defensive flank facing Fricourt. The latter village itself was not being attacked; the 21st Division was on the far side of it. The 2nd Gordon Highlanders were to advance alongside the South Staffords of 91 Brigade and through the western half of Mametz. The 9th Devons, across the Albert to Péronne road, were to advance in parallel with the road towards and through Hidden Wood. The 2nd Gordons moved off towards the enemy front line but their left company ran into uncut barbed wire, hidden in a dip. Surrounded by unexploded British shells, many men fell to German machine-gun fire from 'The Shrine,' a machine-gun post at Mametz cemetery, as the wire was negotiated. Even so, the Gordons got as far as the second enemy position at Shrine Alley by 7:55 a.m. and maintained touch with the Staffords further along in Cemetery Trench. They were unable to progress from there and spent much effort in clearing dug-outs of the enemy. Across the road the 9th Devons advanced from a line some 250 yards (229 metres) behind their own front trench, so badly had this been damaged by shellfire. They were hit by heavy machine-gun fire from Fricourt Wood, the German support trenches and Mametz. At least half of their casualties for the day were incurred before they had even reached Mansel Copse, just ahead of the front line. The survivors pressed on into the German front and support trenches but by now all the battalion's officers had become casualties. As early as 7:40 a.m. the final company was ordered to advance but lost all its officers in crossing no man's land. The same thing happened to two companies of the 8th Devons when they were ordered to reinforce.

Capture of Mametz

At 2:30 p.m., an attack was made by the 21st Division on Fricourt and the 7th Division organised a fresh attack to take advantage of it and assist the battalions now held up in Cemetery Trench, Shrine Alley and in the outskirts of Mametz. Two companies of the 2nd Royal Warwickshires and two of the 8th Devons attacked at 3:30 p.m., after thirty minutes artillery support. It was enough for the German garrison of Mametz, 200 men emerged with hands up before the new attack had even reached the old German front line. Just after 4:00 p.m., the whole of Mametz had fallen and within another hour the situation was quiet. The 2nd Queens were consolidating Fritz Trench and South Staffords were in Bunny Alley by 7:30 p.m. The 91 Brigade had succeeded in all its objectives. By that time, the roads up to the old German front line had been put in a reasonable state and communication trenches were also being worked on. The 7th Division reported that things were very quiet and that further advances towards Mametz Wood could be made if fresh troops could come up. But none did and the moment, tragically, was lost. The whole of the new 7th Divisional front was wired that night, by parties from all three Royal Engineer Companies and the pioneers of the 24th Manchesters. The casualties for the 7th Division on the day were very heavy, the vast majority from machine-gun fire.

2–5 July 1916: Capture of Fricourt

The 7th Division pushed forward in the enemy trench complex and materially assisted in the eventually successful attack of the 17th (Northern) Division that captured Fricourt on 2 July 1916. Two batteries of XIV Brigade RHA under command of the 7th Division moved up into Queen's Nullah and began firing to cut the barbed wire defences in front of Mametz Wood.[4] At 3:00 p.m. on 3 July 1916, patrols reported that Mametz Wood was empty of German troops; this was not entirely true. The 2nd Royal Irish Regiment and 1st Royal Welch Fusiliers were ordered up to occupy a line on the southern edge of the wood but it was not until dawn on 4 July 1916[5] that they were fully in position. During the night, a detachment of the *55th Landwehr* was discovered in the wood by a patrol of the 2nd Royal Irish Regiment and driven off. That evening units of the 38th Division arrived to relieve the 22 Brigade, who returned to Heilly for a well-deserved rest.

---

4   TNA WO 95/1664/3: 2nd Battalion Royal Warwickshire Regiment War Diary. Two companies of the Royal Warwickshire Regiment together with the remainder of the Gordons held a line from Mametz to the craters along Orchard Alley facing Fricourt Wood. On 3 July 1916 two companies moved to Danzig Alley and two companies remained in Danzig Trench.

5   TNA WO 95/1664/3: 2nd Battalion Royal Warwickshire Regiment War Diary. The battalion came under the orders of the 91 Brigade's Brigadier and took up position along White Trench and north of Bottom Wood, covering the whole of the 7th Division's front.

19 Royal Warwickshire Regiment Advancing up a communication trench 1 July 1916.
(IWM Q65405)

A rain-delayed attack to capture Mametz Wood, Wood Trench and Quadrangle Trench took place at 12:45 a.m. on 5 July 1916. The 2nd Royal Irish Regiment and 1st Royal Welch Fusiliers of 22 Brigade together with the 9th Northumberland Fusiliers and 10th Lancashire Fusiliers of 52 Brigade, formed the assaulting force. The Royal Warwickshires had already relieved the 91 Brigade and the 20th Manchesters were too weak to be used. Quadrangle Trench and Shelter Alley were gained but the Irish were held up by uncut wire and enemy counter-attack. Mametz Wood and Wood Trench remained in German hands. Meanwhile, ground conditions were deteriorating due to heavy rain and the British right was waiting for the French, who could not be ready for the next phase until 8 July 1916. The capture of Mametz is one of the outstanding successes to the 7th Division's credit. The defences which faced it were most formidable and were held by a well-trained, well equipped enemy so that only by great determination, devotion and daring was success achieved. The cost had been heavy; 65 Officers and 814 men killed, 1 Officer and 471 men missing, 85 Officers and 2,388 men wounded, a total of 151 Officers and 3,673 men.[6]

6   TNA WO 95/1664/3: 2nd Battalion Royal Warwickshire Regiment War Diary.
      Casualties for the 2nd battalion Royal Warwickshire Regiment from 1–5 July 1916 were:

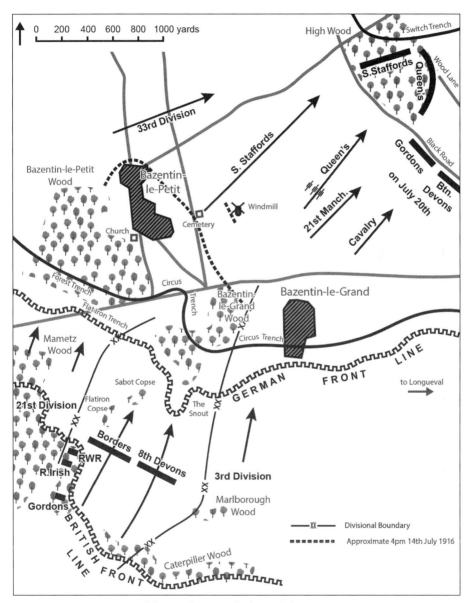

Map 11 Bazentin Ridge 14 July 1916.

14–17 July 1916: The Battle of Bazentin Ridge

The 7th Division had a brief period of rest after Mametz to incorporate the large draft of reinforcements, most of them from other regiments. The Divisional Artillery had little or no rest, guns and men were both worked to the verge of exhaustion and by the evening of 11 July 1916 Mametz Wood[7] had been cleared. The Germans had been pushed back to their second line of defense which ran from the Albert–Bapaume road on the west to Longueval and Delville Wood on the right. Divisional orders for the attack were issued on 12 July 1916, the 7th Division was to be on the right of the XV Corps, the 3rd Division on its right and the 21st Division on its left. On the night of 13–14 July 1916 the troops assembled silently by crossing no man's land, which was up to 1,200 yards (1,097 metres) wide, then crawling to within 100 yards (91 metres) of the German front line.

The Divisional Artillery, still without having had a day off since the preliminary bombardment had begun, maintained a steady bombardment, which proved to have been most effective, especially in cutting the wire. After a hurricane bombardment from 3:20 a.m. to 3:25 a.m. the assaulting battalions, 8th Devonshire and Border Regiments of 20 Brigade, moved forward. The night was cloudy and they crawled steadily forward with an incredible silence, getting near to the German line without being detected. As soon as the bombardment lifted they sprang to their feet and rushed forward into the German trenches, catching them by surprise and killing many with their bayonets. By 5:00 a.m. 20 Brigade had secured its objectives and the way was clear for 22 Brigade to go through. The Royal Warwickshire Regiment who led were detailed to secure the western end of Circus Trench, and cover the advance of the Royal Irish. They had started forward at 4:30 a.m., passed through the Border Regiment and made good Circus Trench practically unopposed.[8] The Royal Irish

---

Officers killed – Lieutenant A Hodgkinson, Lieutenant E J Martin, Lieutenant M N Haseler, and Lieutenant A J Vardy; officers wounded – Lieutenant Chepmell, Lieutenant A J Adams; other ranks – killed 3, wounded 98, missing 14. The battalion moved to camp at Heilly on 5 July 1916.

7   TNA WO 95/1664/3: 2nd Battalion Royal Warwickshire Regiment War Diary. Two companies of the Royal Warwickshire Regiment proceeded to Mametz Wood on 11 July 1916, their casualties were; officers – Lieutenant T A K Gildea; other ranks – killed 2, wounded 13, missing 4. The remainder of the battalion bivouacked in Citadel Line.

8   TNA WO 95/1664/3: 2nd Battalion Royal Warwickshire Regiment War Diary, 13–20 July 1916: The battalion left the eastern corner of Mametz Wood at 4:30 a.m. and passed over the German front line trench and reformed south of Bazentin le Grand Wood. From this point the objective was Circus Trench which C Company took under very heavy fire. D Company followed up in support and after consolidating, went on to assist the Royal Irish Regiment in Bazentin le Petit Wood who had severe fighting at close quarters driving the Germans out of the southern portion of the wood and village. The company did splendidly losing about 80 men and at 2:30 p.m. reformed in Circus Trench with C Company. Half of B company pushed on to the Bazentin le Petit and Bazentin le Grand Road, several casualties occurred from machine-gun fire but they pushed on

Regiment then moved upon Bazentin le Petit successfully securing the cemetery and the village, many prisoners were taken including a German officer.

Meanwhile on the other flank the men of the Royal Warwickshire Regiment were busy consolidating their position and had sent a party of men along a narrow ravine leading east to investigate the defenses of Bazentin le Grand. This party came in contact with Germans on the north and north–east edges of the village and engaged them, together with some Northumberland Fusiliers of the 3rd Division they soon cleared the village. The German artillery fire had increased and a strong German counter-attack on the Royal Irish Regiment forced them to retire from the village.

Appeals for reinforcements and ammunition had already been made and attachments of the 20th Manchester Regiment arrived with ammunition. A company of the Royal Warwickshire Regiment together with the Gordons and Welch Fusiliers counter-attacked to clear Bazentin le Petit Wood and retake the ground between the cemetery and the windmill. Farther to the right the German counter-attack made no ground whatsoever against the Royal Warwickshires or the 8th Devons in Bazentin le Grand Wood. The arrival of reinforcements soon enabled the Royal Irish to restore the position at Bazentin le Petit, while the Royal Warwickshires pressed forward up the village, pushing the Germans back. The fighting was severe, but luckily the Germans had run out of bombs; by 2:00 p.m. they had been driven out of the village and had lost heavily by Lewis-gun fire as they fled. Several attempts were made to capture High Wood and at 7:00 p.m. the Queen's Regiment backed up by the South Staffordshire Regiment pushed forward to the eastern edge of the wood, which they managed to secure and maintain throughout the night.

Further attempts to take High Wood were made by the 33rd Division on 15 July 1916 but by this time the Germans had reoccupied the wood in numbers, backed up by strategically positioned machine-guns and artillery. At 11:15 p.m. orders were given to evacuate High Wood and consolidate their other positions. A further attack was planned for 3:35 a.m. on 20 July 1916, the 33rd Division was to attack High

to Bazentin le Grand village, the company kept up a running fight but were not strong enough to dislodge the enemy. Sergeant Roultney captured four machine guns, then the Germans counter-attacked but were driven back by B Company assisted by A Company. At about 8:00 p.m. the whole battalion took up a position covering the north–east of the village Bazentin le Petit, A and B Companies in the vicinity of the cemetery. B and C Company were north–east of the village with patrols on the west side of the village. All four companies were shelled constantly but dug-in and saved a great many casualties by their prompt action in consolidating. This position was kept all through 15 July and the battalion was relieved at 2:00 a.m. on 16 July. They bivouacked in Fritz Trench and remained there until 19 July when two companies occupied the trench to the east of Bazentin le Petit Wood and two companies remained in support.

Battalion casualties during these operations 13–20 July 1916 were: Officers killed – Lieutenant A J Purcell, officers wounded – Lieutenant R Corywright, Lieutenant G V Biden, Second Lieutenant A C Coldicott, Second Lieutenant F Devis, and Second Lieutenant P H Hollick.other ranks – killed 219, wounded 142, missing 62.

20 Royal Warwickshire Regiment Lying exhausted in the grass after battle.
(IWM QCO204)

Wood itself and the 7th Division was to advance clear of the eastern edge. The two
lead battalions were the Gordons and the 8th Devonshires,[9] both struggled gallantly
forward but the suffered severely from the enfilade fire from High Wood. Eventually,
after hanging on for an hour, the survivors of the leading companies had to crawl
back to Black Road which the supports were consolidating. Reinforcements came up
to assist but a German counter-attack forced them to retreat with high casualties. The
total casualties suffered in the fighting for the Bazentins and High Wood amounted
to within a few hundred of those incurred round Mametz, coming to 125 officers and
3,343 men, with the grand total since 1 July 1916 of over 7,500 of all ranks.

9   On 20 July 1916 east of High Wood, France, Private Theodore William Henry Veale
     of the 8th Battalion Devonshire Regiment, hearing that a wounded officer (Lieutenant
     Eric H Savill) was lying in the open within 50 yards (46 metres) of the enemy, went out
     and dragged him into a shell hole and then took him water. As he could not carry the
     officer, he fetched volunteers, one of whom was killed. Heavy fire necessitated leaving
     the wounded man in the shell hole until dusk when Private Veale went out again with
     volunteers. When an enemy patrol approached, he went back for a Lewis gun with which
     he covered the party while the officer was carried to safety. For this gallantry in the face of
     the enemy he was awarded the Victoria Cross.

Sergeant Bill Hay of the 1/9th Battalion Royal Scots, described the attack thus:

> That was a stupid action, because we had to make a frontal attack on bristling German guns and there was no shelter at all. There were dead bodies all over the place where previous battalions and regiments had taken part in previous attacks. What a bashing we got. There were heaps of men everywhere – not one or two men, but heaps of men, all dead. Even before we went over, we knew this was death. We just couldn't take High Wood against machine-guns. It was ridiculous. There was no need for it. It was just absolute slaughter.

The British field guns had difficulty supporting attacks on High Wood because they had to fire over Bazenin Ridge. The low elevation of the guns meant the shells were just skimming over the British trenches and the margin for error was small with numerous casualties from friendly fire. On 18 August the 33rd Division was once again called on to attack High Wood but again it ended in failure. The 7th Division tried to attack on 24 August between High Wood and Delville Wood and, as preparation for this assault, a machine-gun barrage was fired by the 100th Machine-Gun Company which in twelve hours fired over one million bullets from ten machine-guns. This attack was also unsuccessful.

26 August 1916: Ginchy

After a few weeks of rest 22 Brigade returned to the front to relieve the 14th Division on the eastern edge of Delville Wood and the 20th Division facing Ginchy. The Royal Welch Fusiliers took over the left of the line, the 20th Manchester Regiment being on the right, the Royal Warwickshire Regiment in support and the Royal Irish in reserve. The Germans held a small corner of Delville Wood and several trenches which ran across the top of the ridge leading from Delville Wood eastward and flanked the approaches to Ginchy from the west. It was essential for the 22 Brigade to capture these trenches and on 27 August 1916 bombers of the Royal Welch Fusiliers began fighting for the possession of Ale Alley, which entered Delville Wood at its north–east corner. A bitter struggle followed against German machine-gun fire and although 50 prisoners were taken, they were not successful and Ale Alley remained in German hands. On the night of 28–29 August 1916, working parties of the Royal Warwickshire Regiment did fine work in pushing forward over 100 yards (91 metres) from Stout Trench and beginning a new trench to which the name Porter Trench was given. For three more days the 22 Brigade stuck to its line, despite constant shelling and sniping; the Welch Fusiliers gained some ground in Ale Alley by bombing. The Welch Fusiliers casualties of 200 men in four days testified to the severity of the fighting, while the Manchesters had about 150 men, almost all due to bombardment. The Royal Warwickshire Regiment casualties were; killed 1 man, wounded 14 men. They were relieved on the night of 29–30 August 1916 by the South Staffordshire and 21st Manchester Regiments with the Queens as the support battalion.

About 10:00 a.m. on the 31 August 1916 the Germans started a heavy bombardment using a large proportion of gas shells; this was followed by several attacks but
the South Staffordshire Regiment put up a good fight. At 8:30 p.m. on 2 September
the 22 Brigade relieved the 91 Brigade, their position had somewhat improved and
they were ready for the attack on 3 September. The Welch Fusiliers went into Edge
Trench and along Devil's Trench, the 20th Manchesters took over Stout and Porter
Trenches, the Royal Warwickshires[10] were in Folly Trench and the Royal Irish back
in Pommiers Trench. At midday on 3 September, the 22 Brigade went 'over the
top,' the bombers of 91 Brigade and a party of the Queen's simultaneously making a
bombing attack on the east corner of Delville Wood. Initial reports indicated that all
was going well, however, before long the Welch Fusiliers reported that the bombing
attack on the east corner had failed. The companies on their left which had attacked
Hop Alley and Beer Trench had lost heavily from machine-gun fire, and were held
up short of Hop Alley where the survivors had dug-in amongst the shell-holes. The

---

10   TNA WO 95/1664/3: 2nd Battalion Royal Warwickshire Regiment War Diary, 3–4
September 1916:
At 7:00 a.m. on 3 September 1916 two companies (A and B) of the Royal Warwickshire
Regiment moved up from Montauban Alley and took their assembly position with C
and D Company in Folly Trench. Battalion Headquarters moved to a position west of
Waterlot Farm where they remained for the rest of the operation. While in the assembly
position they suffered casualties from enemy shell fire, one man killed and eight wounded.
At zero hour (12:00 noon) the companies advanced very steadily in artillery formation
toward their objective. The order of the companies was A Company on the right, B and
C Companies in the centre and D Company on the left facing north along Ale Alley. At
1:40 p.m. a runner from D Company reported that they were held up by machine-gun
fire in Hop and Ale Alleys and was digging in. At 1:43 p.m. a runner from B Company
reported that they had reached their objective and was digging in. The objective of A, B
and C companies was the Blue Line which they had to consolidate, it was an imaginary
line running through the west end of Ginchy. The 20th Manchester Regiment were
reported to be through the village but at 4:21 p.m. a verbal message was received that
the troops were leaving the village. When this was found to be true and the heavy
casualties we had suffered were known, it was decided to relieve the brigade. At 11:00
p.m. headquarters moved to Folly Trench and later back to Pommiers Redoubt. Few men
came in but the majority of them were holding their original objective in Ginchy, one
detached group of C and D Company under Captain H P Williams Freeman and Second
Lieutenant B Willis (Royal Engineers) hung on for 36 hours after the brigade had been
relieved. Another detached group of A Company under Lieutenant J S Harrowing and
Second Lieutenant H Sulman, hung on in the south end of Ginchy for three days after
the brigade had been relieved being unable to get any communication from headquarters.
This was of great value to the position of the troops in Guillemont. The casualties for the
brigade were rather heavy for this operation; Officers killed – Captain W S de C Stretton,
Lieutenant G R Haves Sadler, Second Lieutenant C M Loring. Officers wounded
– Captain C Wasey, Second Liutenants; E R Bottrill, J J McKinnell, F W Walton,
M K Twycross, F H Simms. Officers missing believed wounded – Captain A Forbes,
Lieutenant D W Arnott. Other ranks – killed 30, wounded 197, missing 90, a combined
total of 320 men.

right company managed to fight their way into Ginchy but came under heavy fire and all their officers became casualties, they held on until they were joined by some men of the Royal Warwickshire Regiment. Three companies of the Royal Warwickshires had moved forward in support of the attack but came under heavy fire, casualties were numerous but they reached their objectives and dug-in.

On their right, the 20th Manchesters reached Ginchy and pushed into the village, overcoming the resistance offered but came under machine-gun fire when they reached the orchard, most of their officers being hit. To secure Ginchy and make good the ground gained it was clear that another effort must be made on the left, where the Germans were reported to be in force. The Welch Fusiliers had very few men in hand and were short of bombs while the situation with the Royal Warwickshires was not satisfactory. General Steele decided to send the Royal Irish to attack Hop Alley from the south and four sections of bombers to renew the attack against the eastern corner. Before these plans could be carried out the 20th Manchesters were forced to move out of Ginchy by a vigorous German counter-attack carrying with them some of the Royal Warwickshires and Royal Irish. However, the remaining Royal Warwickshires fought back and held on to their line, using effective Lewis gun fire to check the counter-attack, they held on for two nights before retiring, Ginchy had been lost and about one hundred Royal Warwickshire men were reported missing.

21 British soldiers digging a communication trench in Delville Wood. (IWM Q4417)

At 8:00 a.m. on 4 September 1916 the attack on Ginchy was renewed by the 9th Devonshire Regiment supported by covering fire from the survivors of the 22 Brigade who were still in Stout Trench. They pressed on gallantly and at first made good progress, but enemy machine-guns mowed them down in scores and a mere handful penetrated into the village, only to be overpowered. That night (4–5 September) General Green took over from General Steele and another attack was launched by two companies of the Queens at 5:30 p.m. to consolidate Hop Alley. On 6 September at 5:00 a.m. another attack on Ginchy was launched by the Gordons, backed up by the 9th Devons now barely 400 strong; they swept into Ginchy but once again it proved easier to take than to retain. By 8 September 1916, all the infantry of the 7th Division were on their way back to a rest area near Hallencourt, sadly depleted and exhausted by hard work and the struggle against disadvantages of ground and position. The slippery ground alone had handicapped the attacks enormously and the unending digging needed in the middle of the fighting and shelling had added to the strain. The failure to retain the ground gained had been largely due to the lack of training of the recent drafts who formed a high proportion of its battalion and to the inexperience of most of its officers and NCO's. The men had too often not known what to do and the heavy casualties amongst the officers had left them with no one to show them. The 7th Division casualties came to 53 Officers and 1,090 men all told; the Royal Warwickshires with 11 Officers and 331 men were the hardest hit but the 20th Manchesters lost 11 Officers and 264 men, the Royal Irish 13 Officers and 210 men and the Welch Fusiliers 13 Officers and 255 men.

17 September 1916: Return to the Somme

After ten days of rest round Hallencourt, the 7th Division received orders to move north on 17 September to Flêtre, Bailleul and Godewaersvelde as its destinations. The infantry went first, being concentrated in the new area in time for the 20 and 91 Brigades to take over the Le Touquet and Ploegsteert sectors on 19 September, the 22 Brigade coming into line three days later. Relaxation was not practicable and after taking over the new line much was done to worry the enemy by harassing their wiring and working parties, as well as improving the British line. Nearly a dozen raids were attempted during the six weeks that the 7th Division spent in the trenches, none on a large scale. The Welch Fusiliers made a successful raid on 30 September–1 October 1916, in which the German trenches were entered, several of the enemy were shot and their dug-outs bombed. 30 casualties were inflicted on the enemy at a cost of 2 killed and 2 wounded. The Royal Warwickshires made a raid the same night inflicting many casualties on the enemy in a bombing fight, getting away with nine wounded all of whom were brought in. A further raid a fortnight later with one battalion from each brigade was less successful, one party being caught and dispersed by machine-gun fire in no man's land, the other two being turned back. On 14 October, the 2nd Battalion Royal Irish Regiment left the 22 Brigade and was replaced by the 2nd Battalion Honourable Artillery Company.

Royal Warwickshire Regiment:
The Hindenburg Line November 1916–July 1917

In August 1916 the German leadership along the Western Front had changed as General von Falkenhayn resigned and was replaced by Generals Paul von Hindenburg and Erich Ludendorff. The new leaders soon recognized that the battles of Verdun and the Somme had depleted the offensive capabilities of the German Army. They decided that the German Army in the west would go over to the strategic defensive for most of 1917, while the Central Powers would attack elsewhere. During the Somme Battle and throughout the winter months, the Germans created a prepared defensive position behind a section of their front that would be called the Hindenburg Line, using the defensive principles elaborated since the defensive battles of 1915. This was intended to shorten the German front, freeing ten divisions for other duties. This line of fortifications ran south from Arras to St Quentin and shortened the front by about 30 miles (48 kilometres). British long-range reconnaissance aircraft first spotted the construction of the Hindenburg Line in November 1916.

Withdrawal to the Hindenburg Line:

On 15 November 1916, the Seventh Division left Flanders and marched southward back to the Somme, the weather was not too bad for the season but turned to snow and rain later. They marched until they reached Doullens on 21 November 1916 and the next day the 22 Brigade (including the Royal Warwickshires) reached Raincheval and Marieux. They had marched 82 miles (132 kilometres) in seven days and the area they had now reached lay just behind the part of the line which had witnessed the last 'push' of the Somme offensive, that begun on 13 November 1916. Beaumont Hamel had been captured and other important gains made astride the Ancre, which here cut quite a deep valley through the ridge running north–west from Péronne, with steeply rising ground on either side. The offensive had carried the line to the north and north–east of Beaumont Hamel and though by 22 November 1916 the heavy fighting had died down, the position was far from stabilized. The area was a network of trenches, some disused and some incomplete. Some trenches collapsed as quickly as they were dug and the Ancre mud made life very difficult for the troops, the bad weather, which had been the main cause for the breaking-off of active operations, had left the ground in a fearful state. Men often had to be dug-out of the mud and the communication trenches were mostly impassable, to reach the front lines was practically impossible. Despite all precautions, such as rubbing their feet with whale-oil, many men had to go to hospital with 'trench feet,' the result of exposure and wet conditions. Ration parties brought up dry socks along with their rations and there was a regular competition in the brigades to see which unit would have the fewest cases of 'trench foot' per week. The men fought the conditions with remarkable resolve often leaving the trenches wet through and chilled to the bone.

December 1916 saw little improvement in the weather, there were some colder spells in which the ground began to dry, but the rain soon returned. There were many patrol encounters, a good deal of shelling from the British side and continuous sniping which increased the number of casualties. The New Year brought no improvement in the conditions or the weather but preparations for the attack on the German held Munich Trench was planned and the operation fixed for 11 January 1917. The 22 Brigade relieved the 20 Brigade on the night of 5 January 1917 and continued the good work, collecting another fifty prisoners in less than a week. The attack had been carefully rehearsed and for forty-eight hours before the attack the positions to be assaulted had been heavily bombarded. It was moonlight when the attack started, but so effective was the barrage that the assailants reached their objectives almost without casualties and speedily overcame the German garrison.

The attack was a complete success, all three battalions reaching their objectives as quickly as the ground would allow and speedily overcoming the survivors of the trench garrison, who had been completely surprised. Before the end of January, the 7th Division was enjoying a well-deserved rest. It had remained in line for ten days after the capture of Munich Trench, the 22 Brigade relieving the 91 Brigade on the night of 12/13 January and being itself relieved by the 20 Brigade three days later. Battle casualties for January 1917 came to 30 Officers and 600 men. The rest to which the 7th Division was withdrawn on 20 January was about the longest it had yet experienced, Divisional Headquarters were established at Marieux and the troops rested here until 23 February when they moved to Bertrancourt. General Watts, the Divisional Commander, was promoted to command a corps and he was replaced by Major-General G de S Barrow who had been commanding an Indian Cavalry Brigade since January 1915. He had only just taken over this new front (23 February 1917), with the 91 Brigade in the line, the 22 Brigade (Royal Warwickshire) at Beaumont and the 20 Brigade at Bertrancourt, when things began to happen. Starting at 6:00 a.m. on 25 February the advance, though somewhat delayed by fog, made good progress. Pendant Copse was soon passed and the South Staffordshire Regiment secured Pendant Trench soon after. They then bore to the left and lost direction in the fog, coming under machine-gun fire from an orchard north–east of Serre. This, however, they captured and soon after 9:00 a.m. were established in Wing Trench. That evening the 22 Brigade came up and relieved the 91 Brigade, who went back into reserve.

It was the 22 Brigade who were selected to attack Puisieux for which the V Corps now issued orders. The Welch Fusiliers were to lead the attack with two companies of the Borders on their left, but as they moved forward they encountered stubborn opposition. Despite this the Welch Fusiliers pushed on and by 7:30 p.m. had reported back to the brigade that they had secured their first objective, Kaiser Lane, after hard fighting. From here their right company worked forward on to Sunset Trench, while the left company worked forward into Soap Alley. During the night the Germans launched one quite serious counter-attack, however, the Welch Fusiliers with their Lewis Guns repulsed it without much difficulty. The fight continued all day, the Borders pushing the enemy back down Knife and Fork Trenches towards Bucquoy.

That evening the Royal Warwickshires relieved the Borders but when they prepared to renew the attack next morning (27 February 1917) they found the enemy vanished and Puisieux clear. The 20th Manchesters were ordered up to relieve the Welch Fusiliers who had suffered severely, having over 150 casualties including six Officers. Meanwhile the Royal Warwickshires' patrols reached the high ground over-looking the valley which runs up between Puisieux and Bucquoy. They got within rifle range of Bucquoy but it was evident that the Germans were not intending to quit the village without a fight and they could be seen digging in vigorously a little further south of the village. After dark, patrols attempted to cut the wire by hand but machine-gun fire prevented their accomplishing anything. For the next three days the position remained unchanged; the 22 Brigade pushed patrols forward, only to find Bucquoy strongly held and the hostile sniping and machine-gun fire, if anything, increased. Before a properly prepared attack could be delivered news came in, on the morning of 17 March 1917, that Bapaume and Achiet le Petit had been evacuated and that the 7th Division was to push on at once. The Welch Fusiliers thrust patrols forward into and through Bucquoy, finding the village clear. The Germans continued to retreat leaving enormous damage as they retired, obstructing roads, cutting down trees, setting skillfully prepared booby traps and delayed-action mines. There were no good billets and, in a late and cold spring, marked by blizzards and snowstorms in mid-April, the sick list increased significantly and pursuit was slower than expected. Nightfall on 17 March 1917 had left the leading troops of the 7th Division on a line stretching from Logeast Wood (East of Ablainzeville) to the Bucquoy–Ayette road. During the night orders were received for an advance at daybreak to Courcelles le Comte and the dismantled railway south–east of that village. The Welch Fusiliers and Royal Warwickshires were to lead with a section of the 104th Battery accompanying the advance guard.

The 22 Brigade started its task at 6:00 a.m. and met little opposition, but they were delayed by the numerous obstacles that the Germans had left in their path. By 7:30 a.m. they had secured their objective, a few German cavalry clearing off to the east as the leading line reached the railway. During the morning the Corps cavalry reported both Ervillers and Hamelincourt clear and the Royal Warwickshires sent a patrol into Moyenneville which was also found unoccupied. The Corps ordered the 7th Division to occupy an outpost line stretching from Ervillers to Moyenneville and Hamelincourt and the main body was to consolidate behind as the contingency of a German counter-attack could not be ruled out.

Early next morning the cavalry pushed forward to reconnoiter the Hindenburg Line between Lagnicourt and Henin sur Cojeul, the 7th Division's advanced guard (the Royal Warwickshires and Welch Fusiliers) moving in support of it. It soon appeared that the enemy was holding a line from St. Leger to Boyelles but he did not offer much resistance and was soon cleared out of the village. The day of 19 March 1917 closed with the 20th Manchesters holding an outpost line, the Welch Fusiliers at Courcelles and the Royal Warwickshires at Ablainzeville, little progress having been made. This was largely due to the difficulties of getting guns and transport forward over ruined roads and 20 March saw little change. The 7th Division was up against the outworks of the Hindenburg Line and until more artillery could be brought forward there was little chance of a further advance. Orders were issued for an attack to be made by the 22 Brigade; these were countermanded and the brigade retired to Bucquoy and Puisieux for a week out of the line, though not of rest.

The approaches to the German defenses were open with little cover and both villages were strongly protected by broad belts of barbed wire, so their capture did not promise to be easy. The objective was to take any ground close to the German line that could be gained without heavy fighting so as to secure a good jumping-off place for the next attack, but the Germans repeatedly counter-attacked these positions. On 28 March at 5:15 a.m. the troops began advancing to attack Croisilles but came under heavy machine-gun fire, being checked just short of the wire. Further attempts were

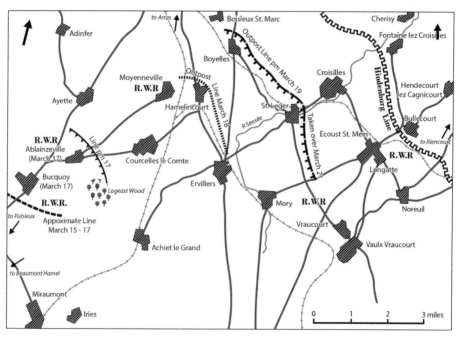

Map 12 Positions of the Royal Warwickshire Regiment during the German withdrawal to the Hindenburg Line.

made by the 22nd Manchesters, South Staffordshires and the reserve company, but they all came under enfilade fire and being isolated could only hold their ground until nightfall. Casualties were heavy for both battalions; the South Staffordshire Regiment lost over 130 men, nearly 60 of them missing, and the 22nd Manchesters lost over 90 men. In the meantime the 22 Brigade had relieved the 92 Brigade and renewed efforts to take Croisilles. Before the next attack could be delivered the command of the 7th Division had again changed hands, General Barrow being replaced by General T H Shoubridge who had recently been commanding a brigade in the 18th Division. He was an energetic and vigorous officer who was to command the 7th Division until the Armistice 1918. The 7th Division had taken its full share of work in pursuing the Germans to the Hindenburg Line. The 22 Brigade had taken over Croisilles and Ecoust on the evening of their capture, having the Borders attached to it as a reserve, whilst the 22nd Manchesters were still completing the clearing up of Croisilles. Orders for the 7th Division were to consolidate its position and to push forward nearer to the Hindenburg Line so as to reduce the distance to be crossed when the main attack was launched. It was intended that the Hindenburg Line would be attacked at Bullecourt and so their guns were busy weakening defenses. The Germans shelled crossroads and other likely targets fairly severely and were on alert to prevent patrols investigating their lines too closely, so the 22 Brigade had quite a lively time. The casualties for the 7th Division for the period 29 March–5 April 1917 amounted to 36 officers and 727 men but the line was pushed well forward, as much as 800 yards, and a good jumping-off position had been secured.

On 11 April 1917 the 7th Division stood by all day in readiness to support the Fifth Army's attack. The 62nd Division was attacking Bullecourt itself with an Australian Division on its right. Unfortunately, the ground gained could not be held. A new attack was to be delivered on 3 May with the 62nd Division attacking Bullecourt, the Australians attacking the Hindenburg Line to the east of that village and the Third Army attacking Fontaine lez Croisilles with the hope of joining hands with the 62nd Division on the right of the Sensée. The 22 Brigade had come up to Mory on 2 May in readiness to support the attack, the 20th Manchesters and the Royal Warwickshires being at L'Homme Mort, south of Ecoust and Mory Copse respectively. The attack on 3 May started at 3:45 a.m. and the 20th Manchesters and the Royal Warwickshires were ordered up to the railway embankment south of Bullecourt. At 11:45 a.m. General Shoubridge also arrived on the embankment to take over the frontage held by the 185 Brigade and was very concerned at the situation. The 62nd Division had withdrawn to the embankment while the Australians were clinging stubbornly to about 1000 yards (914 metres) of Hindenburg Line and, unless Bullecourt could be secured, it was doubtful if they could maintain their hold. Orders were issued for the 22 Brigade to attack Bullecourt and take the village as its first objective, and the Hindenburg Line north of the village as its final goal. The Welch Fusiliers were to attack at 10:30 p.m. on the right and left of the Longatte – Bullecourt road and join up with the 20th Manchesters and the Royal Warwickshires to push forward and take the final objective. It was still daylight when the Honorable Artillery Company

22 Royal Warwickshire Regiment 20 April 1917 Front line trench near St Quentin.
(IWM Q2086)

and the Welch Fusiliers reached the embankment. Their advance had been detected
by the Germans and heavy machine-gun fire held them up but they pressed forward
nevertheless, only to find the wire presented a troublesome obstacle. Both battalions
succeeded in forcing their way into Tower Trench (in front of the southern edge of
Bullecourt) and cleared it after a stubborn hand-to-hand tussle, capturing about fifty
prisoners. Casualties had been heavy and Germans emerged in numbers from dug-
outs in the village, so Bullecourt could not be held and by 2:30 a.m. on 4 May both
battalions had been thrust out of the village.[1]

Accordingly instead of the Royal Warwickshires and 20th Manchesters starting
the second stage of the attack at 2:00 a.m., they had to be put in at 3:00 a.m. to
repeat the first phase. As they were forming up they were caught by the German
barrage and lost heavily, the 20th Manchesters being scattered and disorganized

---

1   When 20 Brigade entered Bullecourt four days later an NCO and 9 men of the
     Honourable Artillery Company were found holding out there: they had established
     themselves in a dug-out and, utilising a Lewis Gun effectively, had beaten off all efforts to
     overwhelm them.

and the attack held up until 4:00 a.m. The Royal Warwickshires started quite well like the Welch Fusiliers; they got into the front trench and even penetrated into the village, only to be dislodged by counter-attack. The majority of the survivors fell back to the embankment but about fifty men with three officers managed to hold on in Tower Trench. A report showed that eighty Welch Fusiliers were inside the German wire near the Crucifix but had not reached the front trench, while the party of the Royal Warwickshires astride Longatte road was still holding on but that was all. The front trench (though full of dead, both British and German) appeared to be unoccupied. Losses were heavy and the 22 Brigade was in no condition to repeat the attack. In the evening the Royal Warwickshires and Welch Fusiliers pushed forward strong patrols to investigate the situation and, if possible, occupy the road running through Bullecourt from south–east to north–west and contact any detachment still holding out in the village. The Germans held their fire long enough to let the patrols get close up to them but when they did let fly the volume of their fire showed conclusively that they still held Bullecourt in strength. A few men managed to dash into Tower Trench and start bombing down it but were soon overpowered, all efforts to reinforce them being prevented by machine-gun fire. During the night of 4–5 May the Welch Fusiliers went back to Ecoust, the 20th Manchesters and Royal Warwickshires being still behind the embankment. In the evening of 5 May the 20 Brigade relieved the shattered 22 Brigade, which withdrew to Courcelles and Gomiecourt having lost 16 Officers and 375 men killed and missing, nearly 800 men in all. The Royal Warwickshire Regiment[2] was the chief sufferer with nearly 260 casualties, amongst those killed being Lieut. Harrowing who had done so well at

---

2   TNA WO 95/1664/3: 2nd Battalion Royal Warwickshire Regiment War Diary, 3–4 May 1917:
The strength of the battalion going into battle was 20 officers and 609 other ranks. After the two day action the battalion strength was 8 officers and 362 other ranks. Explanations as to cause of attack failure were:
1. Concentration of troops prior to attack probably observed by enemy as he put down a heavy barrage at 3:30 a.m. which had to be passed through.
2. Sudden alteration of plans which only allowed hurried consultation with officers commanding the companies at 3:40 a.m. on place of deployment.
3. Positions held heavily by machine-guns and second belt of wire uncut on fronts attacked by battalion.
4. It appears that the village was honeycombed with dug-outs and under-ground passages which allowed the enemy to get behind our men. One sergeant described it like being in a maze.
5. The fact that the enemy outranged us with his egg bombs.
6. The difficulty of obtaining information was very great owing to the nature of the ground and to the large number of machine-guns and snipers. Fifty percent of runners became casualties.
7. The extremely heavy enemy shelling on the whole front in addition to three heavy barrages which he put down along the line of track.
8. The smoke and dust caused by shelling made it difficult to see any distance.

Ginchy. It was now decided to renew the attack from the south and to combine it with a fresh advance from the line reached by the South Staffordshires. This was to be made by two comparatively fresh companies of the 22nd Manchesters, while for the new attack from the south the Royal Warwickshires were called upon. This battalion had been placed at the 91 Brigade's disposal on 11 May 1917 and had spent the next days in cellars at Ecoust, the usual quarters for a battalion in reserve which were both fairly comfortable and provided good cover. However, after the losses the Royal Warwickshires had suffered on 3 May, to put them in again so soon was trying them pretty highly. Nevertheless, they lined up on a tape from the Longatte road to the Crucifix and went forward at 3:40 a.m. on 13 May to clear the so-called "Red Patch" which the 22nd Manchesters were attacking from the east. It was a complicated operation and very difficult for the gunners to support; if the barrage which was to help the Royal Warwickshires was too far forward, it was bound to hamper the advance of the 22nd Manchesters. From information gleaned by patrols it was believed that the front trench would be found empty but, as before, it proved to be held in strength and the Royal Warwickshires were received with a hot fire from rifles and machine-guns as well as being vigorously shelled. On the right a few men somehow worked through the wire and reached the center of the village but the bulk of the battalion got held up outside the wire and ultimately had to be withdrawn after losing four officers and nearly sixty men.[3]

At 5:30 p.m. on 4 May 1917 it was agreed that the battalion in conjunction with 1st Royal Welch Fusiliers should push forward strong patrols into Bullecourt, about 200 men were collected and Captain V Sharkey was placed in command. They pushed forward to the Sunken Road at the west end of the village and at 11:00 p.m. commenced the attack. The enemy held his fire until they reached the second belt of wire, which was uncut, and then opened strong rifle and machine-gun fire which caused heavy casualties. Communication was impossible as the signalling lamp was broken by shell fire and both pigeons had died of shell shock. The attack was a failure and casualties for the day were as follows:Officers killed – Lieutenant J S Harrowing Medical Corps), Second Lieutenant A G Fawdry. Officers wounded – Second Lieutenants; H Toft, W E Frost, R G Hudson, N Miller, W E Ward, J E W Rance (Medical Corps). Officers missing – Lieutenant N A M Ring, Second Lieutenants E Heatherington, F G Burrell, H H H Lister; other ranks – Killed 13, wounded 146, missing 82, a combined total of 241 men.

3   TNA WO 95/1664/3: 2nd Battalion Royal Warwickshire Regiment War Diary. At 12:30 a.m. on 13 May 1917 the battalion formed up on a tape in front of the railway track between Ecoust and Bullecourt, and were in position by 3:10 a.m. At 3:40 a.m. our barrage opened and the battalion went forward. We penetrated the village on the right but were unable to remain there. At 10:00 a.m. orders were received to withdraw all men possible to the camp near Mory, this was done without casualties and the remainder of the men returned at night and the next day. Casualties for this attack were: Officers wounded – Captain H Langman (Medical Corps), Captain R Raphael, Second Lieutenant E C Lawledge, P A M Edlin; other ranks – killed 3, wounded 36, missing 17, a combined total of 56 men.

Various other attacks were made between 13 May and 16 May 1917, without success, and the 7th Division was sadly reduced when, on 16 May, General Shoubridge handed over the line to 58th Division. Bullecourt had cost the 7th Division 128 officers and 2,554 men, 40 officers and 879 men, being killed or missing. The task set for the 7th Division at Bullecourt had been of no mean difficulty and the Commander-in-Chief paid the 7th Division the special compliment of calling in person on General Shoubridge to congratulate him on the grit and determination they had displayed.[4] To have to make a series of small attacks, starting from trenches full of unburied dead, was as hard a trial as the division had ever been put to. To be put in again, as the battalions of the 22 Brigade (Royal Warwickshires, Welch Fusiliers) were, without any real rest and without reinforcements, asked much of both officers and men.[5]

Aftermath

The last fortnight of May and the first few weeks of June saw the capture of a considerable stretch of the Hindenburg Line. The bitter fighting around Bullecourt had ceased and the 7th Division was being rested, as losses had depleted its ranks considerably and drafts were not plentiful. However, they remained in this quarter with General Shoubridge who found himself in charge of a front some 4,500 yards (4115 metres) long, extending from north–east of Croisilles to east of Bullecourt. The end of July saw the great offensive opened at Ypres and it soon became apparent that the 7th Division would be moving back to the main scene of offensive activity in Flanders. The infantry and the Royal Engineers of the 7th Division moved to the Adinfer area for refitting and intensive training on 10 August. Around 3 September, Major C S Burt was promoted to command the 2nd Battalion Royal Warwickshire Regiment.

4   TNA WO 95/1664/3: 2nd Battalion Royal Warwickshire Regiment War Diary. Second Lieutenant N Miller was awarded the Military Cross and Corporal Brindley S/N 4417 was awarded the DCM.
5   TNA WO 95/1664/3: 2nd Battalion Royal Warwickshire Regiment War Diary. Private S Cunnington S/N 1529 was shot at 6:00 a.m. for desertion.

Royal Warwickshire Regiment:
Third Battle of Ypres September–November 1917

Polygon Wood (26 September – 3 October 1917):

The 22 Brigade relieved the Australians at the end of September 1917 and took over the northern portion of the eastern edge of what had been called Polygon Wood in 1914 but, by 1917, it was only a few stumps sticking out from a swampy and muddy surface and hardly a building between Ypres and Gheluvelt could be recognised as having once been a house. The bombardments had torn the country apart, blocking up streams and ditches with debris, causing obstruction and impeding such natural drainage as existed. In many places to quit the duck-board tracks was to invite death by suffocation, yet to keep to these tracks was to risk being caught in the barrages which from time to time crashed down on the only routes available for troops movement. The 22 Brigade occupied the front line with the Welch Fusiliers on the right in Jetty Trench, the 20th Manchesters continuing the line northward in front of Jubilee Trench and the Royal Warwickshires were in support at Hooge. There had been little opportunity to consolidate and the 22 Brigade had no time to improve their line before, about 5:00 a.m. on 1 October, a tremendous barrage was put down and maintained for over an hour. Then about 6:15 a.m. waves of infantry began swarming forward, pressing hardest against the Welch Fusiliers. The attack was so vigorous that, despite the Fusiliers' heavy rifle fire, some of the leading enemy troops reached the British line, only to be wiped out immediately. Succeeding waves were crushed by the accurate British barrage, machine-gun fire, rifle fire and a counter-attack by the Fusiliers that captured some German prisoners. But the repulse did not finish the Germans who repeatedly tried to advance. Between 9:00 a.m. and 10:00 a.m. an urgent request went out for ammunition and a company of the Royal Warwickshires moved forward with eighty boxes. This company had to face the barrage which the Germans were maintaining for some depth behind the front and support lines, but going through it unflinchingly though with many casualties. Its arrival was very welcome, for the Welch Fusiliers were beginning to run short and had lost so heavily that Colonel Holmes used this company to fill the gaps in his line. All day the struggle continued, the German guns pounding away and their infantry repeatedly trying to advance. Communication between the front line and the authorities in the rear was interrupted, all telephone lines were cut and most runners became casualties. Another company of the Royal Warwickshires brought ammunition about 4:00 p.m. and was retained until about midnight, when things went quieter. There had been two or three calls for help after dark but, as before, directly the barrage came down the German attacks faded away and the 22 Brigade triumphantly retained its line intact.

The Welch Fusiliers, who had borne the brunt of the fight and whose stubborn defence was very specially praised by the Divisional Commander, had 131 casualties in total, 2 officers and 41 men killed and missing, 6 officers and 82 men wounded. Largely owing to the 22 Brigade's fine defence on 1 October 1917, the British attack on 4 October found the Germans shaken and demoralized and they put up little resistance and surrendered freely. Sir Douglas Haig's aim in this attack was to secure the main line of the ridge east of Zonnebeke on a 7 mile (11.2 kilometres) front, from the Menin road to the Ypres–Staden railway. The 7th Division was fourth from the right of the twelve divisions employed in the attack and had as its objective the ruined hamlet of Noordemdhoek on the Broodseinde – Becelaere road. At 6:00 a.m. on 4 October, the British barrage started and the 8th Devons and South Staffordshires moved forward together, both battalions having prepared to tackle several pillboxes each, but they were prepared for that, and while Lewis gunners engaged the pill-boxes in front, bombers and riflemen worked around to the rear and rushed them. The Germans were in unusual strength but proved ready to surrender, the 8th Devons taking over 200 prisoners and the South Staffordshires, who found a lot of the enemy in small pits, disposed of them with the bayonet. Practically everywhere the objectives had been reached, over 5,000 prisoners had been taken and the Germans had suffered very high casualties. The situation on the division's right was, however, far from satisfactory and the 7th Division was ordered to take over from the 21st Division the frontage opposite Reutel, and that on 9 October 1917 when the British left was tackling Poelcapelle and Houthulst Forest, the 22 Brigade should try its luck against Reutel.

8 October 1917 passed quietly but very heavy rain seriously interfered with artillery preparation for the next attack. The Royal Warwickshires and the Honourable Artillery Company (H.A.C.) were in reserve along with the 9th Devons. On the evening of 8 October, General Steele issued his orders for the attack on 9 October, the H.A.C. and Royal Warwickshires were to attack on the right and the left respectively, each having two companies in front and a third in support. The objective was the Blue Line of 4 October, which if attained would give good observation down the valleys of the Reutel and Polygon Becks. Troops were in position in time for "Zero" at 5:20 a.m. on 9 October and started on time. Within half an hour green lights along the line of the objective indicated that it had been taken. Then the H.A.C. reported that they had driven the enemy from Reutel, shooting many down as they made off, and had secured part of the cemetery east of Reutel, However, they were being held up short of Juniper Cottage by heavy fire from machine-guns resulting in heavy casualties, especially officers. Next it became clear that there was a gap in the Royal Warwickshires' line near Judge Copse, from which a considerable fire was being maintained. Support was sent in and the position was finally made good, thereby completing the capture of the

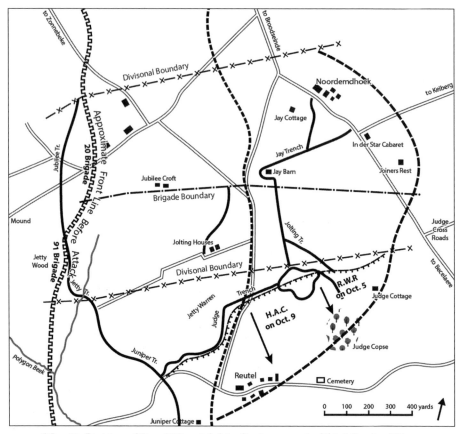

Map 13 Position of Royal Warwickshire Regiment at the Third Battle of Ypres
9 October 1917.

Blue Line. All through 10 October the German bombardment persisted, causing many casualties, though again no counter-attack attempted to recover their lost ground.

At 4:30 p.m. on 10 October, troops of the 23rd Division began to appear to relieve the 22 Brigade who had been hardest hit, losing 57 officers and 1,256 men since 1 October. The Royal Warwickshire Regiment's casualties[1] were 6 officers and 63 men killed, 84 men missing, 7 officers and 230 men wounded.

1   TNA WO 95/1664/3: 2nd Battalion Royal Warwickshire Regiment War Diary. Battalion casualties for the actions 8–11 October 1917 were: Officers killed – Captain C L N Roberts, Captain G C Blandy, Captain D Augutt, Second Lieutenants – J S Firth, R C Stable, J H Davies; officers wounded – Lieutenant P A M Eblin, Second Lieutenants – J A Dorey. J M Green, S J Hollyoak, S Cattell, H J B Woodfield; other ranks – Killed 59; wounded 188; missing 70; shell shock 2. These figures vary slightly from those mentioned

Third Battle of Ypres: Gheluvelt

The infantry of the 7th Division entered into ten days of rest and were far enough back to be fairly comfortable. The 22 Brigade stayed in Meteren at first, and then at Reninghelst, and it rained most of the time. The billets were good, blankets were issued and football was played when the weather permitted. New men were drafted in to fill the gaps left by recent fighting but the numbers were insufficient and the troops understood that further attacks were going to take place to ensure the Germans did not regain the initiative. On the evening of 24 October, the 20 and 91 Brigades relieved portions of the 14th and 37th Divisions astride the Menin road West of Gheluvelt. Conditions had been bad enough in Polygon Wood, here they defied description. The ground was even wetter and muddier, to leave the duckboard tracks was even more likely to mean being swallowed up in some bottomless pit of a mud-filled shell-hole and rapid movement was out of the question. Orders were for the 7th Division to attack on 26 October to capture Gheluvelt, or where it once stood, and with it secure the Tower Hamlets ridge east of the Basseville Brook. Success would considerably improve the tactical position on the British right and the attack would, it was hoped, act as an effective diversion while the main Allied attack was being delivered away to the left in a more northerly direction. The main attack on 26 October was entrusted to the 20 and 91 Brigades, the 22 Brigade providing the brigade reserve, the Welch Fusiliers supporting the 20 Brigade and the 20th Manchesters being at the disposal of the 91 Brigade. The attack started with the first faint glimmer of light. Promptly the German barrage came down, though it mostly fell behind the attacking battalions. The South Staffordshires reached their objective and a savage fight followed. The company's two officers were killed and all the senior NCOs but the men stuck to their task and in the end the survivors, commanded by a corporal, found themselves in possession of the mound. They had taken a machine-gun and had inflicted heavy casualties on the Germans but they were rather isolated. The company on their left had been mown down by a crossfire of machine-guns and the other attacking battalions of the 91 Brigade fared even worse. All the troops were fighting against machine-gun pillboxes and the impossible mud and conditions prevailed.

Although they entered Gheluvelt, they could not hold it against German counterattacks, sustaining losses of 110 officers and 2,614 men, while the 7th Division claimed that the elements and not the enemy had beaten them. Many had suspected before the start that what they were asked to do was impossible and the Divisional Commander in his letter to the troops after the battle admitted as much.

above as they were recorded in the field on 11 October 1917. Figures mentioned above were recorded at a later date.

23 Third Battle of Ypres 22 August 1917, British soldier stands over the grave of a comrade.
(IWM Q2756)

General Shoubridge later observed:

> They went forward under the worst conditions of mud and fire and would not
> give in until they died or stuck in the mud, no soldier can do more.

With that tribute the 7th Division may be content; it had failed but the causes of
its failure lay outside its control. Its men had gone into the attack knowing that the
chances were all against success and they had attacked as if they had believed the
prospects to be all in their favour. Gheluvelt stands out in the Division's story as a day
of loss and disaster but of honourable defeat. It was to be the division's last fight in
France. Meanwhile the offensive continued with the First Battle of Passchendaele (12
October) and Second Battle of Passchendaele (26 October–10 November).

With two of its infantry brigades shattered and reduced in their struggle against
insuperable disadvantages at Gheluvelt, the 7th Division was in no condition for a
prolonged spell in the front line and, on 29 October, was relieved by the 39th Division.
The 7th Division was withdrawn to Blaringhem for refitting as many gaps in the ranks
had to be filled. On 8 November, when the division was inspected by the King of the
Belgians, the parade state showed clearly how heavily it had suffered at Gheluvelt. The

22 Brigade barely reached 600 men and it was of special note that there were present on parade a mere 15 Officers and 948 other ranks who had landed in Belgium with the Division in 1914. Of these 181 men belonged to the RAMC and the Divisional Train contributed 240 men. The Royal Warwickshire Regiment[2] contributed only 78 men still present with the 7th Division. The casualties for the 7th Division's infantry came to three times the original establishment of a division and some battalions were reconstructed six or seven times. Total battle casualties for the infantry were 2,327 officers and 53,161 men since 1914.

2   TNA WO 95/1664/3: 2nd Battalion Royal Warwickshire Regiment War Diary. On the evening of 27 October 1917 the battalion relieved the 22nd Manchester Regiment at Canada Street and Hedge Street. Their B Company furnished a party of one officer and thirty other ranks to act as Tunnel Major and Guard at Brigade Headquarters at Hedge Street, also a party of one officer and 50 other ranks for detonating bombs at Bardenbrug Dump. The battalion was relieved on 28 October 1917 by the 1/1 Cambridge Regiment. Casualties for 27–28 October 1917 were: Killed 3; Wounded; Missing 6.
    Under the authority granted by His Majesty the King, the Corps Commander has awarded the Military Medal to the undermentioned NCO's and men for gallantry in the field: Service Number (S/N) 1825 Acting CSM H Ward, S/N 1441 Sergeant F Moon (killed), S/N 260577 Private A Lucas (wounded), S/N 266918 Private R Birch (wounded), S/N 1222 Private H Taylor, S/N 12487 G Curtis, S/N 27244 Private C Southgate, S/N 1713 Lance Corporal H Halliday, S/N 10431 Sergeant W Evans, S/N 846 Sergeant W Chatterly (wounded), S/N 12614 Sergeant J Johnson (Bar to Military Medal). S/N 1131 Sergeant W H Harris.

The Royal Warwickshire Regiment: Move to Italy November 1917–December 1918

The Asiago Plateau

On 14 November 1917, the 7th Division received orders to move to Italy[1] to stem the Austro-German offensive. The Italians were particularly amazed at the cheeriness of the British troops, at their laughing and singing on the march, and the mere arrival of the British and French troops in the country improved the situation for the Italians. When General Plummer assumed command of the British forces in Italy, on 10 November, the Italian retreat had been arrested at the River Piave and there seemed hope that this line might be maintained. At the end of November, the British took over a section of the Piave Line with the French on their left, and the Italian Third Army lower down the river on their right. The next few months were reasonably quiet and the front now entrusted to the 7th Division was the rocky plateau on the right of the Brenta, north–west of Bassano. This plateau, which forms the southern edge of the mountain chain, rises sharply up from the plains to about 4,000 feet (1220 metres) above sea level. It was a stiff climb up, the weather was bitterly cold, the ground was covered in snow and the sentries had to be relieved every hour. The plateau was fairly thickly wooded so, although fuel was available, transport of ammunition, rations and other stores was difficult. Many of the tracks up the slopes were one-way tracks, so passing was difficult and had to be planned carefully. Drinking water was another problem, having to be pumped up from the plains; the pools on the plateau were fit only for washing and for the horses to drink. Accommodation was bad and the rocky ground made defences hard to construct, so life was strenuous and uncomfortable for the men.

The troops had marched from the Montegalda area to Thiene, from which place motorised trucks took them up to the mountains where the reserve battalions were accommodated in huts. The 7th Division had Italians on its left and the 23rd Division

---

1   TNA WO 95/1664/3: 2nd Battalion Royal Warwickshire Regiment War Diary, 18 November 1917: The battalion marched to Hedin Station to entrain for Italy. The train travelled via Marseilles, Toulon, Cannes, Nice, Genoa to Cerea, the battalion then marched 56 miles (91 Km) over four days to billets in S. Giorgio.

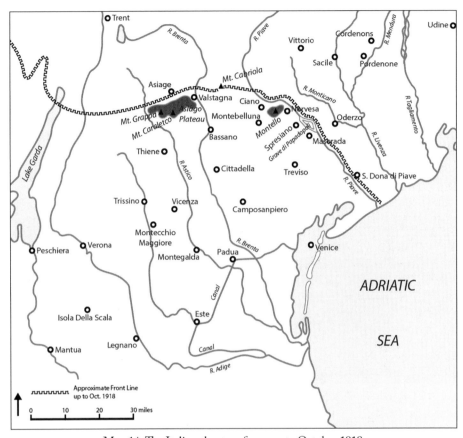

Map 14 The Italian theatre of war up to October 1918.

on its right. Two brigades were in line, the 91 Brigade occupied the right sector and the 22 Brigade the left sector. Patrols reconnoitred the enemy's line to find out spots which might be raided and the Divisional Artillery was much more active than the Austrian gunners. On 7 April 1918, the Welch Fusiliers started the raids with which the 7th Division was to worry the Austrian enemy and establish over him a distinct moral ascendancy. The Austrian trenches at Casa Ambrosini were rushed, seventeen enemy killed in a sharp encounter and a prisoner brought back for questioning. An attempted raid on Vaister by the 22 Brigade a week later was aborted when a large covering party was encountered in no man's land and the garrison thereby put on alert. On 16 April the Royal Warwickshires raided Casa Ambrosini with considerable success, the Austrians hardly waiting to receive them but fleeing into our barrage and suffering heavily, besides leaving several dead in the trenches.

24 Royal Warwickshire Regiment Italian Front 1918 Purchasing hot chestnuts.

On the night of 17–18 April 1918 both the South Staffordshires and the 20th Manchesters visited the enemy's lines at Vaister. After crawling to within 150 yards (137 metres) of their objective they attacked under cover of rifle grenades and a barrage from twelve howitzers, quickly forcing their way in, surrounding a house and bombing two large dug-outs. These proved to be full of Austrians, of whom over twenty were killed with the bayonet. Meanwhile, the flanking platoons were now far enough round to intercept the enemy's retreat and they collected twenty prisoners, at a loss of only six wounded. These successful raids continued until the end of May, when relief came with the 48th Division and the troops of the 7th Division proceeded to an area round Trissino for rest and training.

Early in June 1918, the 22 Brigade had the honour of being inspected by the King of Italy. However, the much-needed rest was to be rudely interrupted when, in the small hours of 15 June, sounds of tremendous firing from the direction of the plateau disturbed the sleep of the division and orders were soon received for the troops to stand to. The 48th Division's front had been penetrated and the Austrians had pushed on to the position of the 35th Battery, which was in close support 100 yards (91

25 7th Division troops during Battle of Piave River June 1918 King Victor Emmanuel III inspecting the troops. (IWM Q26692)

metres) behind the front line. Major Hartley, its C.O., emerged from a dug-out to find an Austrian planting a yellow flag at its entrance. He promptly shot him and, assisted by a few men armed with rifles, kept the Austrians at bay, preventing their getting into the gun pits and allowing the breech-blocks to be removed from the guns. Early in the afternoon the position was completely re-established by a counter-attack.

July 1918 saw the harassing of the enemy vigorously pursued and the Austrians remained remarkably quiet, they rarely venturing into no man's land in any force. With August came still more Austrian deserters and with them rumours that the enemy were going to withdraw to a new position some way in the rear, near Gallio. To test the truth of this story it was decided to raid at four different points simultaneously, each attack being carried out by not less than two companies. The 7th Division's gunners had fired plenty of barrages and all were extremely accurate and, despite stout resistance, all the raids were successful. On 19 August General Shoubridge handed over command and proceeded to Trissino, where 7th Division was now concentrated in "General Headquarters Reserve" after two hard months on the Asiago.

The Grave Di Papadopoli

The Trissino country in which the 7th Division now found itself established was a pleasant change from the Asiago Plateau. By 7 October 1918 the 7th Division had shifted eastward to an area north–west of Vicenza and had been told to prepare for an attack in the near future at a spot which was not divulged. The division did not stay long in its new area and on 13 October the troops began moving by rail to Treviso, a move carried out with every precaution to secure secrecy. The 22 Brigade was actually out on a route march when it received its order to entrain but despite the rush, the move was completed without any serious hitch. Orders were received on the 17 October for the relief of an Italian Division along the right bank of the Piave, north-east of Treviso. The 7th Division was taking the right of the new British Line, having the Italians downstream and the 23rd Division on the left. The main difficulty was the passage of the River Piave which was a formidable obstacle for the division to cross. At Salettuol, in the middle of the Division Line, it was nearly 2,500 yards (2286 metres) wide though a large island, the Grave di Papadopoli, occupied part of the intervening space. This island was about 3 miles (4.8 kilometres) long and over a mile wide at its broadest, the largest of the many shoals and islands in the river bed. What doubled the hazard of crossing was that incessant rain had swollen the river into a high flood, so bridges and pontoons were not practical as a means for the troops to cross.

Finally a battalion from the 22 Brigade successfully landed on the island and surprised several Austrian outposts, disposing of them with the bayonet. However, the Austrians could not be prevented from giving the alarm; their barrage came down within a few minutes but, by 11:00 p.m., all three companies were ferried across and began their advance down the island. Fierce fighting continued as the 7th Division advanced, but by 5:00 a.m. all resistance was over and the British consolidated a position in the centre of the island facing south-east, with the Welch Fusiliers thrown back as a defensive flank to the north-east. Later on 25 October 1918, the Royal Warwickshires crossed and took over the portion of the island already captured by the Welch Fusiliers, thus setting all that battalion free to support the Honourable Artillery Company. Just before dawn the next day, the Austrians suddenly attacked in great strength but the attack was repelled and the Honourable Artillery Company pushed on to the far end of the island, clearing it completely and taking many prisoners. By the evening of 26 October 1918, the 22 Brigade had built a bridge across the Piave from Salettuol and the 20 and 91 Brigades were able to cross over without a hitch.

Battle of Vittorio Veneto

With only one bridge, crossing the River Piave after dark on 26 October 1918 in readiness for the attack on Vittorio Veneto the next day took some time. The chief village on their front was Cimadolmo and before 8:00 a.m. its capture had been reported at Brigade Headquarters, while twenty minutes later over one-hundred prisoners of the Austrian 7th Division were brought in. At 9:30 a.m. the advance to the next objective began, the "Blue Line" a few hundred yards beyond the Tezze–S. Polo di Piave road. The country in between was cultivated land, dotted with farms which had been turned into fortresses and manned with machine-guns. One by one these strongpoints were mastered and their objectives taken, while hundreds of prisoners had been brought in, many of whom seemed to have no regret at being out of the war. The night passed quietly and at 7:00 a.m. on 28 October, orders were received from the division to secure the final objective, the advance to start at 12:30 p.m. Fighting had not been heavy although some Austrians had been taken prisoners, others fleeing before they could be captured. The next important obstacle ahead of the division was the Monticano River which, though shallow and only about 15 yards (13.7 metres) across, flowed in a deep bed between high banks which had been protected by barbed wire and turned into a formidable position. Soon after midday patrols had reached the Monticano River to find it strongly held, with many machine-guns in action. The Manchesters, under cover of the vineyards, reached the near bank and had a hard fight for fire supremacy. Whilst the enemy was distracted the Queen's rushed the bridge which was left intact by the failure of the demolition party to fire the fuses. Advancing towards Cimetta the Queen's encountered considerable opposition but made ground steadily and took several prisoners. With the help of the South Staffordshires, the village of Cimetta was secured with a good haul of prisoners.

The Queen's alone had 100 casualties, including 23 killed and missing, and the troops were much exhausted; they had been marching and fighting without any rest for three days on end. The 22 Brigade, which had spent the day of the attack digging in as far as possible on the Grave de Papadopoli to shelter from the Austrian guns and bombing aeroplanes, had now reached the front. Early on 30 October 1918, the 22 Brigade began the advance towards the River Livenza, 12 miles (19 kilometres) away, beyond which the Austrians were going to make a stand. The Welch Fusiliers and the Royal Warwickshires were in front, in touch with the 23rd Division on the left and with the Honourable Artillery Company following. Progress was not rapid, the troops being far from fresh and many of them footsore; their boots had been thoroughly saturated in wading the River Piave and had dried hard, there having been no chance to change their socks or even remove their boots. As opposition was expected, the leading battalions were extended in attack formation but they met hardly any enemy. The few Austrians encountered were mostly trying to escape and surrendered promptly. The advance continued through Codogne and Roverbasso to within 1 mile (1.6 kilometres) of the Livenza. Here the Royal Warwickshires met some rifle and machine-gun fire from beyond the river. All the bridges had been destroyed and the river was too wide and too deep for tired troops to attempt to cross at night. During 31 October and 1 November, the work of repairing bridges went on steadily while the infantry enjoyed a welcome rest and change of socks. On the evening of 1 November, the 22 Brigade crossed the river and established an outpost line from north of Brugnera to Sacile. Early on 2 November the advance was resumed, the 20 Brigade crossing at Sacile while the 22 Brigade used the pontoons near Cavolano. Evening found the 20 Brigade at Cordenons and the 22 Brigade at the bridge over the Meduna, east of Pordenone. The troops had been warmly welcomed by the population whose delight at their liberation from the hated Austrians was unbounded. For 3 November, the orders were to push on to the Tagliamento, beyond which the Austrians were standing. This involved crossing the Meduna but the road and railway bridges had been destroyed and the Austrians occupied the far bank, backed by long rows of guns. To have attacked with two weak and exhausted brigades, only a few field guns and very little ammunition would have been farcical. However, there was no need to attempt anything as desperate as an attack. General Green had been advised that the Austrians had reported to him that an armistice had been signed, making the Tagliamento the line of demarcation, and it was already in force. Actually the armistice had been signed that afternoon to come into force at 3:00 p.m. next day, until which hour the advance might continue and any Austrians taken would become prisoners of war. The next day the Royal Warwickshires and the Welch Fusiliers crossed the Tagliamento in attack formation. Some of the Austrian officers protested to General Shoubridge that they ought not to be expected to surrender, pending the armistice coming into force, but nearly a whole division laid down its arms cheerfully and submitted to being marched back in columns under escort.

The 7th Division's final success had been the least costly of all its major operations, a total of 14 officers and 575 men wounded and 3 men missing, 748 in all. The collapse of the Austrians in this last great battle of the Italian campaign must not obscure the special importance of the 7th Division's work. The success of the whole attack depended largely on the 22 Brigade's capture of the Grave di Papadopoli. This served as jumping-off ground, not only for the division but for the units on its flank, and the bridge-head which the British X1V Corps thus established enabled the Italians to neutralize the failure of their own attempts to cross the Piave. The collapse of Austria, followed a week later by the armistice with the German Empire, meant that for the 7th Division, the demobilization of so many men eager to return home was soon to become the priority. On 14 November 1918 the Divisional Headquarters was established at Sossano where they remained for almost a month and then, in December 1918, demobilization finally began.

Epilogue

Lance Sergeant William Webb Service Number 4361 2nd Battalion Royal Warwickshire Regiment

---

Lance Sergeant William Webb was demobilized and returned safely to England on 28 January 1919. He retired from the British Army on 1 April 1919 following twenty-five years of service with the 2nd Battalion Royal Warwickshire Regiment (1894–1919). For his service during the First World War, he was awarded the Victory Medal, British War Medal, 1914 Star with Clasp and Rosette, Long Service and Good Conduct Medal, and was 'Mentioned in Despatches' (*London Gazette No 29422 dated 31 December 1915*). He was also awarded the Queen's South Africa Medal with six battle clasps for service during the Boer War. We have searched battalion and British Army records to determine where William was deployed from January 1916 to January 1919, to the best of our knowledge, we believe he worked at Base Camp

in Le Havre and joined the Divisional Band, although he may have returned to his regiment prior to or after the Battle of the Somme.

After retiring from the army, William, Edith and their daughter Marjorie, lived in Plymouth, Devon. On 3 February 1920 Edith gave birth to twins, Eric Hugh Webb and Joyce Edith Webb, shown in the photograph below. Her first born twins, Ethyl Lillie and Frances Harold, died in 1913, age two months, whilst they were living in Malta.

26 The Webb twins: Eric and Joyce.

181

William and Edith's three children (shown in photograph below) eventually married and produced seven grandchildren between them, Victor Woodfield (Marjorie's son), Diana Webb (Eric's daughter), and Deirdre, Sandra, Clive, Cheryl and Tania Horsnell (Joyce's family).

William worked at the Royal Naval Armaments Depot at Bull Point, Plymouth, and continued his interest in Freemasonry by achieving the title of Lodge Master. He died in Plymouth on 9 March 1953 at the age of 72; Edith died eight months later at the age of 71.

The 2nd Battalion Royal Warwickshire Regiment, as with many other infantry units of the British Army, were blessed with brave men like William. Some were lucky to return home after the armistice; sadly, many did not return. These brave men asked nothing for themselves, but gave all they could so that we could live in freedom, as we do today. This book, *Time to Remember*, is dedicated to William Webb and his gallant comrades of the 2nd Battalion Royal Warwickshire Regiment. Finally, William's family would like to share a poem specially written as a lasting remembrance of his life:

27 William Webb with his wife Edith, Daughters Marjorie (left), Joyce (right), and son Eric (rear).

28 Grandma and Grandad Webb with three of their grandchildren Victor (rear right) Deirdre (Lower right) Sandra (centre).

William Webb (1880–1953)
Memories of war

Imagine, you awake one day
To find your loved one far away,
Fighting a war that can't be won
Takes the toll on old and young.

Your son has gone the Boers to fight
For Queen and Country, is it right?
Imagine the fear in a soldier boy
Nineteen years old and full of joy.

He lands in a country far away
Not knowing how long he's going to
    stay.
Imagine his thoughts as the bullets fly
He's wet and cold, and must not die,

He misses his home, his Mum, his Dad,
He never thought it could get this bad.
At home tears flow, then Mum feels
    better
Today the postman brought a letter,

It feels so good to know he's well
Though far away and going through hell.
Dad is silent and deep in thought
He knows the dangers that soldiers
    fought,

He prays that soon war will be done
And, once again, he'll hug his son.
Two years later, home he came
Medals of honour in his name.

World War One started yesterday,
I've packed my case and on my way
Again to fight for what is right
The enemy being the German might.

Imagine my wife being left alone
With terrible thoughts and empty home,
Will I ever see her again?
That's my thought as I board the train,

We are off to fight in the trenches of France
Trying to prevent a German advance.
This war is deadly we may not survive
The dead lie around me, few are alive.

Imagine a trench and you're knee-deep in
    mud,
You're cold, you're wet and covered in blood,
Bombs drop close by and the bullets whizz past
We're going to attack, my time's come at last.

Imagine the feeling at the end of the day
As you lie in the trench and here you must stay.
You have lost all your friends, but you're still
    alive
Thank God once again, He helped me survive.

The guns have gone silent, "It's time," someone
    said
To bring in the wounded, to bury the dead.
Can you imagine, how you would feel
If you had to experience something so real?

We fought for a cause, some might say,
"For their tomorrow we gave our today"
I feel so sad for those who have died
But also relieved, for I have survived.

I'm writing a letter to my dearest wife
But must not reveal the terrible strife
Words are a comfort as if from above
So from me it's
"Goodnight and God bless you my love".

Gerald W. Buxton
April 2014

Bibliography

Atkinson C T, *The Seventh Division 1914–1918*, (Uckfield: Naval & Military Press reprint of 1927 edition).

The Long, Long Trail, <http://www.1914–1918.net/bat9.htm/>

TNA WO 95/1664/3: 2nd Royal Warwickshire Regiment War Diary.